The South of the Mind

The South of the Mind

AMERICAN IMAGININGS OF
WHITE SOUTHERNNESS, 1960–1980

Zachary J. Lechner

The University of Georgia Press

ATHENS

© 2018 by the University of Georgia Press
Athens, Georgia 30602
www.ugapress.org
All rights reserved
Set in Minion Pro and Proxima Nova by
Graphic Composition, Inc., Bogart, Georgia

Most University of Georgia Press titles are
available from popular e-book vendors.

Printed digitally

Library of Congress Cataloging-in-Publication Data

Names: Lechner, Zachary J., 1979– author.
Title: The South of the mind : American imaginings of white southernness, 1960–1980 /
    Zachary J. Lechner.
Other titles: Politics and culture in the twentieth-century South.
Description: Athens : The University of Georgia Press, [2018] | Series: Politics and culture in
    the twentieth-century South | Includes bibliographical references and index.
Identifiers: LCCN 2018008667| ISBN 9780820353715 (hardcover : alk. paper) | ISBN
    9780820353906 (pbk. : alk. paper) | ISBN 9780820353708 (ebook)
Subjects: ISBN: Southern States—Civilization. | Southern States—History—1951–
Classification: LCC F209 .L43 2018 | DDC 975—dc23 LC record available at https://lccn.loc
    .gov/2018008667

For Sarah

CONTENTS

The South of the Mind

Raising the White South

Richard N. Goodwin seemed like an unlikely booster of the South. A Jewish Bostonian, he had served as an advisor and speechwriter for two U.S. presidents, John F. Kennedy and Lyndon B. Johnson. He was perhaps best known for his participation in the federal government's painful efforts to force the Deep South to desegregate in the early to mid-1960s. Nonetheless, in 1972, he was an enthusiastic—and the sole nonsouthern—contributor to a collection of essays on the present-day South titled *You Can't Eat Magnolias*. The book was a product of the L. Q. C. Lamar Society, an organization composed of southern politicians, writers, journalists, and business leaders dedicated to creating a positive postsegregation future for their region in the midst of a continued economic boom.

Goodwin's piece, "The End of Reconstruction," sought to recover a usable southern past, one that rejected racist practices and looked to southern rural traditions as a model for the rest of the nation. In doing so, Goodwin designated his imagined South as the antithesis to modern American society. Depicting a United States that was "confused, divided, and in turmoil," the Bostonian asserted that "what America hungers for is not more goods or greater power, but a manner of life, restoration of the bonds between people that we call community, a philosophy which values the individual rather than his possessions, and a sense of belonging, of shared purpose and enterprise."[1] Goodwin painted a depressing portrait of American society as a place of coldness and dislocation: "Modern man is confined and often crippled by the world he lives in. A city dweller, he is cut off from sustaining contact with nature. It is almost impossible for the individual to escape the vast and frenzied throng of strangers, stripping him at once of isolation and a place in the community."[2]

Goodwin sharply contrasted the South with his dystopian view of the nation, arguing that southerners (i.e., white southerners) had retained their bonds of community. In setting the South against the foil of an urbanized United States, he further implied that southerners still drew strength from their rural roots. Such roots made the region perfectly suited to combat the dilemmas of "modern man." Indeed, he wrote, in the South "there is a sense that life is more than the accumulation of material goods; a belief in the individual, not as a solitary wanderer, but as a person whose place among his fellows is to be secured and respected; and, above all, a fierce desire that people be able to shape their own destiny in their own way." The history of southern racial strife "has blurred these virtues," Goodwin concluded. "But I believe they are there, and I know the country needs them."[3]

Goodwin's sentiments about the "liberating" disposition of southern culture may have appeared surprising coming in the aftermath of the tumultuous southern civil rights movement. During this period, news coverage had often cast white southerners as villains. Yet a diverse group of other Americans, ranging from novelist Harper Lee to rock critic Lester Bangs, echoed Goodwin's views during the 1960s and 1970s, celebrating the white South as a purported repository of discarded values. A variety of individuals during and after the civil rights era, including writers, journalists, filmmakers, musicians, and politicians, imagined the white South as a tradition-loving, communal, authentic—and often, but not always, rural or small-town—region that both represented a refuge from modern ills and contained the tools for contesting them. These perceived problems consisted of anomie, spiritual decline, flagging masculinity, racial disturbance, governmental deceptions, division over the Vietnam War, and technocratic overreach. In such fantasies, white southerners emerged as antithetical to "modern man": close to the land, exhibiting a manly toughness, driven by commonsense thinking rather than the demands of technology and the dictates of outside experts. This fantasied South also inevitably included "familism," in the word of Earl Hamner Jr., the creator of the hugely popular drama *The Waltons* (1972–1981), a CBS television series about a close-knit white family in rural Virginia during the Great Depression and World War II.[4] While commentators bemoaned the "decline" of the American family in the late 1960s and 1970s, they calculated the white southern family unit as exceptionally strong.

Such imaginings typically used the white South, couched in largely male or masculine terms, as a critique of mainstream American culture. The source of that corrupt culture, it seemed, could be either urban or suburban. Obviously, urban and suburban life differ vastly, but in the popular media of the 1960s and 1970s, observers frequently presented the increasing violence of inner cities and the cultural homogenization of the suburbs as intermingled poisons, both withering the bonds of the "traditional" or "natural" American existence. In the end, the urban-suburban distinctions lacked a difference; the South of the Mind could serve as an antidote for both sets of ills. To be sure, conceptions of the white South were unusual and powerful tools for expressing discontent in the 1960s and 1970s.

Such fantasies about the South occurred in a specific historical moment, as Americans encountered a society hemmed in on all sides by political and cultural unrest. In a book that attempted to assess the South's role within the nation in the early 1970s, southern journalist John Egerton repeated this common refrain of an uncertain America, its people confused, searching for misplaced values, and desperate for relief. "We are too shellshocked to be outraged anymore," he claimed. "Assassinations and riots and Vietnam and the campus revolts and the drug scene and crime in the streets and crime in the corporations and crime in the government are just too much to grasp. It takes no nostalgic longing for 'the good old days,' no disdain for 'progress,' no pessimistic nature, to see a tragedy of historic proportions gathering on the horizon. The America of righteousness and certitude and invincibility is up against some problems that don't have ready solutions and questions that don't have easy answers."[5]

In the midst of these disorienting changes and America's self-questioning, Egerton was not as hopeful (or deluded) as Richard Goodwin about the South's capacity to save the nation, because he was convinced that the region was increasingly becoming like the rest of the homogenized and commercialized nation. Egerton applauded what he considered the waning of the South's overt racism, but he feared the loss of "the moonlight and magnolias, the courtesy and kinship, the friendliness and hospitality, the importance of things personal and concrete, the sense of pace and place and space and grace and soul" that he and others ascribed to the region.[6] While Egerton rejected a timeless, unchanging South, such a perception did appeal to other cultural producers and analysts who thought of the region not as a victim of U.S. consumer culture but rather as an asylum from it.

The anxiety over the consumer culture from which the imagined white South promised an escape was hardly an invention of the 1960s or 1970s. Indeed, this anxiety dated to early post–World War II handwringing over the increasing shift to a consumption-based U.S. economy. This development spurred both excitement and uncertainty, for it represented a conflict between "traditional" values and the emerging notion of individual "lifestyle." As scholar Roland Marchand maintained, "The word *style* suggested free choice, the uninhibited search for what looked and felt right."[7] Historian

David Farber contends that this development, although titillating, nagged at people concerned about losing a way of life based on self-sacrifice and delayed gratification: "Many Americans worried about the moral quality of this 'uninhibited search' for self-expression." They, in fact, posed the question, Farber continues, "Did the consumer frenzy promoted by the 'buy now, pay later; be whomever you want to be' ethos compromise older values of family, religion, and community?"[8]

By the late 1960s, consumerism's offspring, ranging from suburbanization to the sometimes shoddy and faceless features of American life, continued to preoccupy cultural producers and anticonformist politicos. Folk singer-songwriter Malvina Reynolds had written of the suburbs as incubators of Cold War orthodoxy in her 1962 composition "Little Boxes" (later made into a minor hit by fellow folkie Pete Seeger). The song's narrator posits that, like their parents before them, when suburban children grew up, they attended college "where they are put in boxes / And they come out all the same."[9] As what? Boring professionals ready to replicate the soul-sucking process awaiting them in the suburbs. Five years later, in the midst of the hippie counterculture's rejection of cultural blandness, the Monkees, an extraordinarily lucrative pop act, reinforced the cliché of suburban conformity in their hit single "Pleasant Valley Sunday." Written by the songwriting team of Gerry Goffin and Carole King about their community in West Orange, New Jersey, the song lampoons this "status symbol land" with its "rows of houses that are all the same" and its "creature comfort goals [that] only numb my soul."[10]

These invectives against the nation's supposedly cheap and deadening commercialized suburban culture also formed a key component of the New Left's social critique in the 1960s. Searching for "a meaning in life that is personally authentic," as Students for a Democratic Society's (SDS) Port Huron Statement articulated, political radicals complained of the effects of consumerism on the postwar generation.[11] In his book *Armies of the Night* (1968), a firsthand account of the 1967 March on the Pentagon, author Norman Mailer described leftist radicals as driven by a hatred of authority and the ways in which this authority evidently created an inauthentic version of reality. Cultural arbiters, furthermore, from network television producers to advertising executives, hyped a vapid suburban lifestyle and kept people's brains doped with and jumbled by television. When viewing this medium, Mailer wrote, rebellious youth "had had their minds jabbed and poked and twitched and probed and finally galvanized into surrealistic modes of response by commercials cutting into dramatic narratives, and parents flipping from network to network."[12] For the New Left, the author concluded, the "shoddiness" of modern life, its disposability and distance from anything meaningful, was especially troubling.[13]

The wide variety of apprehensions that made the white South a beguiling alternative could be reduced to a more singular concern: "rootlessness." In 1972, popular sociologist Vance Packard characterized the United States as "a society torn of roots."[14] Packard believed that Americans had become socially disconnected from each other, but anxieties about rootlessness also conceived a broader dislocation of Americans from some ill-defined traditional center based in producerism and delayed wish fulfillment.

Liberals were not the only Americans bothered about the effects of "rootlessness" and cultural insipidness and laxity on U.S. society in the 1960s and 1970s. Numerous conservative-leaning Americans honed in on how these issues might be undermining the family. Historian Dominic Sandbrook writes, "At the heart of the new culture wars was a growing sense that the institution at the center of the national moral order—the American family—was under unprecedented threat."[15] Sandbrook sees that tension at the heart of such diverse events as the violent Kanawha County textbook controversy of 1974, in which parents voiced their fears that liberal elites were infusing their children's education with moral depravity and unsettling countercultural values, and Francis Ford Coppola's prestige gangster film *The Godfather* (1972). Coppola's movie struck chords by "offer[ing] a taste of Old World 'authenticity' in a suburban, rootless world" while "look[ing] back to the unchanging virtues of family and faith."[16] It should come as no surprise, then, that by the early 1970s, according to historian Rick Perlstein, "nostalgia was becoming a national cult."[17] The *Saturday Evening Post* reemerged, pulling at Americans' yearnings to escape to the "good old days" by reusing old Norman Rockwell covers. In his film *American Graffiti*, director George Lucas focused on small-town teenagers who got their kicks through the simple pleasures of cruising and blasting rock 'n' roll. The film's tagline was "Where were you in '62?"; it was released in 1973.[18] Nostalgia was now nearly instantaneous. Such was the rapid loss of innocence wrought by Vietnam, Watergate, and the cultural conflicts of the previous decade.

Conservative leaders from Jerry Falwell to Richard Nixon played to the nation's nostalgic tendencies, too. And they spoke in the language of "traditional values" as they excoriated the cultural upheavals of the era. Falwell, an evangelical Southern Baptist pastor from Lynchburg, Virginia, railed against cultural permissiveness, and cofounded the Moral Majority in 1979. The political lobbying organization "was created," according to its first brochure, "to give voice to the millions of decent law abiding, God-fearing Americans who want to do something about the moral decline of our country."[19]

While he did not couch his candidacy as a religious crusade, Nixon rose to the presidency with similar assertions that under 1960s liberalism the nation had become a cesspool of moral corruption. He stressed that street crime, race riots, anti–Vietnam War protesters, and out-of-control youth were dragging down the country. The president petitioned what he called the "great silent majority of Americans" to join him not only in acceding to his war policies but also in pushing back against the loud voices on the Left who were shouting for political and cultural change. Historian Jim Cullen has argued, "For Nixon, the white South was a key component of the 'silent majority' that formed his political base and was a symbol for the resistance to the reform movements of the 1960s."[20] More than that, Nixon envisioned the South as quintessentially "American" for its disproportionately high and steadfast support for the Vietnam War and its symbolism as a bastion of traditional values. The president exploited that construct when he ventured to Nashville in March 1974 for the opening of the new Grand Ole Opry House, one of the few places in America where he could still receive a warm reception as Watergate unraveled his presidency. Although by the 1970s country music had become increasingly nationalized, with country radio and record sales thriving outside the South, the genre retained a strong association with southernness as well as whiteness. So when Nixon told fiddling star Roy Acuff on stage that night that "country music speaks of family, our faith in God, and . . . patriotism" and that "those combinations . . . are essential to America's character at a time when America needs character," his words reflected his own imaginings of the white South as a safeguard against the forces of moral laxity and liberalism.[21]

For various music fans, counterculturists, film and television power brokers, and culturally conservative voters, white southernness was a highly malleable and useful narrative concept for both southerners and nonsoutherners that addressed the overarching dilemma of rootlessness from no single political position. The idea's usage in popular discourses highlighted the national desire to avoid anomie in a technocratic society and to recover a feeling of stability in the modern age. This imagined South's "ruralness," in the form of either agricultural living or a small-town existence linked to a surrounding countryside, often formed the core of its perceived authenticity or its embodiment of an idealized way of life. White southerners, the Band's Robbie Robertson once stated, were different because they "lived this world from the standpoint of a rocking chair."[22] In his and other observers' minds, they were a people directly tied to or with an indelible memory of the land, a trait that kept them grounded and faithful to timeless values, in contrast to their spiritually rudderless fellow Americans.

These cultural imaginings of the South as white, working-class, rural, masculine, and anachronistic were largely constructed by and for white Americans. Such fantasies of the southland were nothing new. As Jim Cullen writes, white Americans have often taken comfort in these images: "For some, it could be seen as a place apart, relatively free of the corruptions that had corroded modern life—sterile suburbs, mindless consumption, scarred landscapes at home as well as abroad. This is a very old trope in life in the United States, one that runs from the plantation novel of the 1830s through the Agrarian essay collection *I'll Take My Stand* (1930) and into [Bob Dylan's] *Nashville Skyline*, three very different cultural manifestations of a similar underlying regional nostalgia."[23] This earlier history of thinking about white southern culture as a safeguard against the encroachment of modern consumer society is worth dwelling upon, for it created a language that commentators in the 1960s and 1970s would draw from for their own assessments of the utility of white southern life for the nation. Importantly, each of these efforts was also driven in part by fears of change and modernity and of the presumed erosion of tradition. Traditions are social constructs; they are actually "invented," as Marxist historian Eric Hobsbawm has explained, and the "invention of tradition" has corresponded historically with disquietude about the aggravations of modern life. Hobsbawm identifies the association "between the constant change and innovation of the modern world and the attempt to structure at least some parts of social life within it as unchanging and invariant."[24] It was this discomfort with the dislocating effects of modernity and the eagerness to locate an alternative past or an alternate present that drove many imaginings of the South earlier in the twentieth century.

Imagining the South in the Twentieth Century

One of Cullen's examples, the Nashville Agrarians, so named in part because many of them were connected with Vanderbilt University, were among the most outspoken defenders of the South—namely, the rural South—in the first third of the twentieth century. Written by "Twelve Southerners," the essays in the Agrarians' 1930 work *I'll Take My Stand: The South and the Agrarian Tradition* ranged in content, but all were united by their authors' belief that modernism in the form of "industrialism" threatened to wreck the southern lifestyle. This modification was not merely an economic emergency, the writers insisted; more importantly, to them, the turn away from agrarianism—one that would only escalate in the following decades—represented a hazard to the South's distinctive identity and culture. Criticizing the American faith in "progress," the authors collectively professed in the book's introduction that industrialism was a soulless system that had already conquered most of the nation and was now menacing the *soulful* society of the South. Under a traditional agrarian system like in the South, "the responsibility of men is for their own welfare and that of their neighbors; not for the hypothetical welfare of some fabulous creature called society."[25] *I'll Take My Stand*'s contributors presented southern rural life, now besieged from without, as a superior form of social organization. It allowed people to put *down* roots that the industrial order conspired to *up*root. Simply put, "the culture of the soil is the best and most sensitive of vocations."[26] The book had amazing staying power. As the South continued to pivot away from its reliance on agrarianism and embrace industrialization, the Twelve (white) Southerners' predictions seemed all the more relevant. Historian Louis D. Rubin, writing in a 1962 edition of *I'll Take My Stand*, conceded that while the Agrarians' image of southern life may have been idealized, "it was a society that *should* have existed—one in which men could live as individuals and not as automatons, aware of their finiteness and their dependence upon God and nature, devoted to the enhancement of the moral life in its aesthetic and spiritual dimensions, possessed of a sense of the deep inscrutability of the natural world."[27] Richard Goodwin could not say it any better ten years later. The Agrarians' vision of the South as a bulwark (crumbling as it was) against consumerist and industrialized American society, where families took care of their members, lay at the center of fantasies of the region even decades later.

The search for the authentic South continued unimpeded in the second third of the twentieth century. Shortly after the publication of *I'll Take My Stand*, seventeen-year-old Texan Alan Lomax accompanied his folklorist father John on his journeys through the South in search of the undiscovered music of rural southerners. Over the next several decades, Alan, often with assistance from others, would crisscross the region, interviewing and recording thousands of songs. Lomax's interest in the blues led him to the tumble-down shacks of countless black sharecroppers and tenant farmers. The songcatcher saw the blues as the authentic expression of a people struggling against the interrelated oppressions of racism and economic inequality. He later remembered the seductiveness of this culture for Americans trying to maintain tradition in a confusing contemporary world. Reflecting in his 1993 book *The Land Where the Blues Began*, Lomax wrote, "feelings of anomie and alienation, of orphaning and rootlessness—the sense of being a commodity rather than a person; the loss of love and of family and of place—this modern syndrome was the norm for the cotton farmers and the transient laborers of the Deep South a hundred years ago."[28] Lomax's conception of the black people who conjured up the blues as "rootless" clashed with imaginings of southern culture as intimately bound together and familial; however, he inferred that through the blues, these individuals forged connections that Jim Crow could not permanently sever.

Lomax, it should be remembered, recorded many rural white southerners, too. It was these members of farm families, similarly seeking to maintain close ties despite crushing economic hardship, who formed the basis of writer James Agee and photographer Walker Evans's Dust Bowl–era classic *Let Us Now Praise Famous Men* (1941). The book recorded the lives of three hard-scrabble white southern sharecropping families. Both the text (written by Agee) and the accompanying pictures (snapped by Evans) chronicled their daily afflictions, but also their spirit of perseverance, while capturing them as profoundly antimodern. Like Lomax, Agee and Evans crafted visual and literary images of noble southerners as authentic folk who bravely fought to hold onto their humanity outside of the debasement of modern life. It was a problematic—and captivating—delineation.

Equally driven by an appetite for understanding the place of the South and its white people in a changing world, North Carolina journalist W. J. Cash released the twentieth century's most influential book about the region, *The Mind of the South*, to widespread critical acclaim in 1941. Absorbing much of the acerbic style of his mentor H. L. Mencken, who penned some of the most damning—and hilarious—treatments of the South ever written, Cash set out to dismantle the romanticized Old South myth. He set up the antebellum South, instead, as a place characterized by fierce individualism and violence, where a "naïve capacity for unreality" thrived.[29] The Old South, in Cash's assessment, lacked culture and refinement. It seemed in truth to have, as later critics noted, no mind at all. "Being static and unchanging," Cash wrote, "the South was, of course, an inherently conservative society—one which, under any circumstances, would have naturally been cold to new ideas as something for which it had no need or use."[30] The death of the Old South did not sweep away these attitudes; it actually hardened them into a form of defiance against the twentieth century's snowballing modernization and progress. Summing up his thesis, Cash invoked what he considered the two halves of the (white) southern mind:

> Proud, brave, honorable by its lights, courteous, personally generous, loyal, swift to act, often too swift, but signally effective, sometimes terrible, in its action— such was the South at its best. And such at its best it remains today, despite the great falling away in some of its virtues. Violence, intolerance, aversion and suspicion toward new ideas, an incapacity for analysis, an inclination to act from feeling rather than from thought, an exaggerated individualism and a too narrow concept of social responsibility, attachment to fictions and false values, above all too great attachment to racial values and a tendency to justify cruelty and injustice in the name of those values, sentimentality and a lack of realism—these

have been its characteristic vices in the past. And, despite changes for the better, they remain its characteristic vices today.[31]

The Mind of the South would serve as a bible for outsiders looking to fathom the region for the next few decades. Critics initially showered it with nearly universal praise. *Time* proposed that "anything written about the South henceforth must start where [Cash] leaves off."[32] Even as it faced growing criticism in the late 1960s and 1970s, the work remained an important touchstone, read as a volume of serious ideas worthy of analysis.[33] Cash's book, which has never been out of print, remained the most widely read treatise about southern identity during the civil rights movement, and its images of violent, pathological, immovable, and intellectually deficient white southerners were reflected in breathless civil rights reportage. Cash hardly placed the South in a good light, and certainly most commentators then and since have seen his work as a largely negative interpretation of the region and its white inhabitants. Still, one could easily appreciate the white southerners of Cash's imagination as the keepers of tradition, bravely—and fruitlessly—pressing their shoulders against the crushing wheel of modernity. In short, the book was somewhat open to interpretation, allowing one to frame white southerners as violent deviants outside of the American narratives of democracy and progress and, alternately, as admirable rustics, unbending defenders of the old ways empowered by their historical closeness to the land.

As Cash, Lomax, and the Agrarians illustrated, various incarnations of the imagined South were alive and well in the early to mid-twentieth century. Two factors served to make such imaginings of the South in the 1960s and 1970s different from these and even earlier manifestations. First was the shifting complexion of southern and national race relations. The 1960s civil rights movement challenged the Jim Crow racial order in the South. While news coverage and popular culture often amplified the characterization of the white South as peculiarly and deeply racist, other popular discourses competed with this negative image, suggesting that the white South might escape its racist heritage. In a broad sense, we must ponder the imagined Souths of the era as part of Americans' efforts to make sense of their fluctuating, and often conflicted, thinking about race. Popular discourses constantly had to contend with the question of southern racism and did so in multiple ways, alternately downplaying it, arguing that the region's bigotry was part and parcel with larger national prejudices, presenting it as a desirable trait for combating increased demands by minorities, or, like the L. Q. C. Lamar Society, affirming that white southerners were in the process of repairing the racial schism and had lessons to teach the rest of the nation. With the national racial order in flux, the perception that the South was peculiarly racist lost ground, reducing the strength of this iconography as applied to the region and its white inhabitants. This change in attitudes about southern bigotry was groundbreaking. Now white southernness could function equally as a solution and as a pariah in the national consciousness, without racial concerns *necessarily* getting in the way.

The second factor that differentiated imaginings of the South in the 1960s and 1970s from those that had come before was the pervasive power of the rural South in the American mind in the midst of the region's changing economy and demographics. As the South became increasingly integrated politically and economically with the rest of the nation, many Americans still perceived it as a culturally distinctive rural bastion. No doubt influenced by the popular literature of William Faulkner and Erskine Caldwell, films like *Gone with the Wind* that promulgated a "moonlight and magnolias" mythology, and the Nashville Agrarian movement's propagandizing of rural settings as the southland's essence, the rural southern imaginary treated the region as existing out of time in an antimodern past in which most white southerners still lived away from cities and worked with their hands. This was ironic in light of recent southern history. After World War II, federal government investment, local municipal incentives, and right-to-work laws enticed northern businesses to move south. The resulting southern portion of the Sunbelt boom pushed the region further into the political and economic mainstream of U.S. society.[34] Thus, as the South shed its status as a backwater, many Americans found utility in a version of southernness that was culturally distinctive and out of step with the rest of the nation. Yet they saw in white southern culture not backwardness, but the deep roots of tradition. This led scores of filmmakers, novelists, journalists, musicians, and other cultural producers, beginning in the early 1960s, to frame the white South, frequently but not exclusively in rural incarnations, as the antithesis of modern society. While focusing on specific, contemporary anxieties about consumerism and suburbanization and an unstable racial landscape, these Americans linked imaginings of white southernness in the 1960s and 1970s with the earlier out-of-time fantasies of the region's whites. In this endeavor, they tended to ignore the increasing distance between their visions of and the actual lived experience of the region's people.

These fantasies of the 1960s and 1970s can be best unmasked and analyzed by turning to cultural discourses, often in the realm of popular culture. The "uses" of the South were largely cultural; in addition, discourses most often encountered, responded to, and invoked southernness as a cultural creation. Analyzing culture does not, however, mean overlooking politics. Indeed, the

South as both a place and an idea loomed over U.S. politics in the 1960s and 1970s. This methodology underlines the importance of southernness, for instance, in the nonsouthern embrace of contrasting figures like southern governors Jimmy Carter and George Wallace.

Importantly, for those who wished to exercise it, the South of the Mind morphed easily to meet different needs. Similar sociocultural anxieties, for example, drove both the era's hippie counterculture and conservative backlash, as typified in Wallace's politics and Lynyrd Skynyrd's music. Just as counterculturists frequently exploited a rural or small-town, family-oriented, and communal imagined South in their critique of mainstream, urban, technocratic society (chapter 2), many working- and middle-class white Americans simultaneously utilized these traditional values as antidotes to the feminized and antiestablishment cultural politics that they assigned to the counterculture. Wallace supporters invoked the white South and "southern" principles in their endorsement of his masculine, reactionary politics (chapter 3). The embrace of ostensibly timeless white southernness, then, often possessed similar origins but divergent uses.

Probing the South (of the Mind)

Because it analyzes the role of ideas about the South, this book is not a work of southern history, per se, but an investigation of constructions of the white South that illuminates the larger story of postwar American culture and its discontents. Numerous scholars of U.S. culture, largely in the field of "new southern studies," have drawn on theoretical insights to delve into Americans' past constructions of imagined Souths. They differentiate their work from the "old southern studies," which, according to "new" proponent Jon Smith, is overly nostalgic and obsessed with the "loss" of memory, "the sense of place, and the sense of community."[35] Influenced by Benedict Anderson's concept of "imagined communities," the new guard avers, without necessarily addressing the cultural attractiveness of white southernness in the civil rights and post–civil rights era, that the reality of the region often had little to do with how Americans conceived it.[36] The new school also upholds the nation's enduring claims of southern distinctiveness while contending that nonsoutherners have consistently defined themselves against the South. These scholars often touch on what academic Tara McPherson terms "our cultural schizophrenia about the South," that is, the tendency at certain times in U.S. history for people to define the region as the keeper of idealized national values or, alternately, as an archive of un-American qualities.[37] It is a viewpoint shared by journalist Peter Applebome, who contends, "Over the years, the rest of the nation has

Ping-Ponged between views of the South as a hellhole of poverty, torment, and depravity and as an American Eden of tradition, strength, and grace."[38]

The ability of Americans to hold multiple, sometimes conflicting, ideas about the South in their minds calls forth psychologist Leon Festinger's theory of cognitive dissonance.[39] According to this concept, people who are presented with conflicting, or dissonant, ideas will work to resolve them to achieve consonance. And, yet, the opposite has been true for people's views of the South historically. While certainly some Americans have had overwhelmingly positive or negative ideas about the region, many others have been able to accept contrasting explications of the region and its people, like those that Applebome describes, without being overwhelmed by the dissonance. That is because these individuals likely felt no discord. The ideas that circulated about the imagined white South in the 1960s and 1970s (e.g., familial and communal versus hypermasculine and violently racist) could speak to the varying concerns of a single person, one who was agitated about the alleged breakdown of the family *and* the rising crime rate in the country's cities. It is also quite possible that this lack of dissonance stems from Americans' comfort with their conflicted thinking about the South, a phenomenon that is so historically ingrained that they are not even aware of the incongruity, and therefore feel no need to resolve it.

Nevertheless, the South of the Mind in the 1960s and 1970s was mythological in the way that it helped to resolve anxieties related to modernity through the power of a bygone, often rural, South. In this sense, Mike Chopra-Gant relays, in a reference to Claude Lévi-Strauss's theoretical work, that myths "symbolically resolv[e] real, irreconcilable social contradictions by displacing them from lived experience to the realm of narrative, where it becomes possible to symbolically resolve problems that are, in reality, insoluble."[40] Similarly, for Americans the challenges of modernity (and its accompanying issues of urbanization, suburbanization, and consumerism) seemed so intractable—if not incomprehensible—that it was natural for the white South, as an antimodern refuge, to stand as a helpful alternative, one based on the easily called upon and deployed battery of connotations that Americans had already assigned to the region by the mid-twentieth century. Understanding the mythical underpinning of imaginings of white southernness—as good or bad—is central to appreciating the nation's conflicted relationship with the South. Furthermore, by understanding the prevailing ideas about the region bouncing around Americans' brains at any point in time, we can learn much about national politics and culture.

Scholars working largely in the historical discipline have been slower to broach the subject of the imagined South. An early exception is Howard Zinn, author of the 1964 book *The Southern Mystique*. Its lengthy final chapter, titled "The South as Mirror," was trailblazing in its bold claim that the popular belief that the South was aberrational, or America's Other, was misguided. Admittedly, Zinn claimed, "it is racist, violent, hypocritically pious, xenophobic, false in its elevation of women, nationalistic, conservative, and it harbors extreme poverty in the midst of ostentatious wealth."[41] But in his estimation, the South was essentially the nation on steroids. The entire United States "embodies all of those same qualities. That the South possesses them with more intensity simply makes it easier for the nation to pass off its characteristics to the South, leaving itself innocent and righteous."[42] Zinn's thesis was provocative, clear eyed, ahead of its time—and little read.

Following the lead of the "dean of southern historians" C. Vann Woodward, much scholarship during and since the 1950s has focused on analyzing what, if anything, remained distinctive about southern identity. In the midst of the "Bulldozer Revolution" and the gradual decline of racial prejudice in the post–World War II era, Woodward sought to locate the remains of "southern identity."[43] He discovered them in a shared southern heritage that broke sharply with the national story of exalted innocence that Zinn resented. Sharing Woodward's contention that despite modernizing influences a distinctive southern identity remained, sociologist John Shelton Reed would later write of an "enduring South" that persisted into the early 1970s: "White Southerners continue to display surprisingly strong feelings of attachment to 'their people' . . . [and] some degree of sectional feeling is still to be found."[44] By the end of the sixties, with the rest of the nation at pains to sustain a narrative of American triumphalism, with military stalemate plaguing U.S. forces in Vietnam and racial uprisings sweeping through northern and western cities, Woodward expected that the United States might gain insights from the southern past to work through its present foreign and domestic difficulties.[45] More recently, scholars like James C. Cobb have continued this investigation of southern identity, one that frequently urges southerners to arrive at a more inclusive definition of what it is to be southern. Maintaining that a sense of southern distinctiveness and "the obsession of Southerners with their Southernness" persists, Cobb argued at the end of the twentieth century that in order to escape the homogenization of modern America, southerners "will have to move past stereotype and caricature and face up to the monumental challenge of transforming the divisive burden of Southern history into the common bedrock of a new regional identity on which all Southerners, regardless of race, are free to build."[46]

During the 1990s and early 2000s, historians working outside of the field of southern history focused extensively on the South's political and cultural influences, with limited or no references to its fantasied qualities in 1960s and 1970s America. Dan T. Carter and other researchers have frequently emphasized the so-called "southernization of American politics" in this period.[47] This argument is undergirded by its emphasis on the Southern Strategy thesis, the idea that the Republican Party gained the support of southern whites by promising to slow the pace of civil rights gains and that the rise of the national conservative movement in the 1970s can be explained by its adherence to race-baiting southern-style politics.[48]

Peter Applebome and Bruce J. Schulman have added a cultural dimension to "southernization." Applebome singles out his contribution to the southernization thesis in his book's title, *Dixie Rising: How the South Is Shaping American Values, Politics, and Culture*. Writing of the contemporary (mid-1990s) South, he discloses that it is "a place that had managed to maintain its identity while also putting its fingerprints on almost every aspect of the nation's soul, from race, to politics, to culture, to values."[49] Focusing on the "long 1970s" (1969–1984), Schulman reinforces Applebome's treatment of cultural southernization in his book, *The Seventies: The Great Shift in American Culture, Society, and Politics* (2001). Schulman dubs the transition as the "reddening of America." He explains the spread of southern culture like the rise of "southern" or "redneck chic," for instance, as simply a reflection of the antiliberal backlash of the 1970s.[50] This perspective parallels Applebome's vision, which conflates southernization with the dominant spread of conservative attitudes. The situation was much more complicated. The charms of the white South lay beyond a simplistic liberal-conservative, Democratic-Republican divide. Moreover, Schulman's and Applebome's studies leave readers with the inaccurate impression that Americans wholeheartedly and uncritically adopted "southern" attitudes.

James N. Gregory further explores the cultural dimension of southernization in his book *The Southern Diaspora: How the Great Migrations of Black and White Southerners Transformed America*.[51] He addresses, though, how transplanted southerners changed American society after World War II rather than how Americans wielded *ideas* about the South. Predating Gregory's work by twenty years, James C. Cobb's 1982 essay "From Muskogee to Luckenbach: Country Music and the 'Southernization' of America" has come closest to explaining why at least one aspect of southern culture garnered renewed curiosity in the 1970s. Examining the South's cultural rise through the lens of country and western music, Cobb stresses the influence of national humiliations: "At the end of the 1970s, the resonance of country music for a nation reeling from the disappointments of Vietnam and Watergate and the shocking discovery of the racial divisions and economic woes confronting communities outside the South should have been obvious enough."[52] Cobb is not necessarily wrong in his conclusion, but his periodization ignores the fact that Americans were already worried about the blanding of the country and other cultural dilemmas even before they began to read rundowns of governmental deceit, nonsouthern racism, and perplexing economic problems in national publications in the late sixties and early seventies. In reality, these issues only exacerbated existing and deeper concerns about the confining structure of modern society.

More recent historiography has veered away from the above works' focus on the supposed southernization of national political and cultural attitudes. Instead of equating southernness with conservatism, they draw more heavily on cultural studies insights to find that Americans have frequently treated "the South" as a patchwork of ideas and values on which they have drawn selectively based on their needs and desires. This focus has resulted in a better comprehension of the detailed and contextualized uses of fantasied, antimodern Souths.

An important precursor to such scholarship and one invested in many of the questions that drive *The South of the Mind* is Jack Temple Kirby's *Media-Made Dixie: The South in the American Imagination* (1978; revised 1986). The book focuses singularly on popular culture representations (e.g., films, books, and television programs) of the South during the twentieth century. Kirby directs his attention to such topics as D. W. Griffith's *The Birth of a Nation*, Claude Bowers's popular and Dunning School–influenced Reconstruction scholarship, Erskine Caldwell's novels about uncultured rural white southerners, and the rehabilitation of the South in the national consciousness during the 1970s. Kirby's book is helpful in outlining different versions of the South that populated the public mind, including what the author titles "The Grand Old South," "The Visceral South," and "The Devilish South." But in communicating these trends, Kirby provides neither a clear thesis about the nature of these imaginings nor adequate historical context to explain why such images predominated during certain times. In addition, he showcases popular culture, even when adequately contextualized and even in the case of *The Birth of a Nation*, as merely a reflection of society rather than as a more complicated and fluid form, capable of *creating* meaning.[53] My work builds on Kirby's scholarship by attempting to understand not only how popular culture (and political) imaginings of the South shaped the region's image but also how such fantasies proved culturally and politically expedient for southerners and nonsoutherners alike.

Scholars following in Kirby's footsteps have detailed the South as a historical and cultural construct central to the process of identity formation in the United States, with Americans often latching onto the white South as a haven from rapid and alarming socioeconomic changes. Although addressing an earlier period, from approximately 1880 to 1945, Karen L. Cox's *Dreaming of Dixie: How the South Was Created in American Popular Culture* (2011) explores the popularization of the "moonlight and magnolias" myth of the South and relates its national embrace to apprehensions about modernity.[54] Anthony Harkins makes a similar argument about the nation's love-hate relationship with white southern mountain people in *Hillbilly: A Cultural History of an American Icon* (2004). Despite recognizing that hillbillies have served as a source of pity and derision, Harkins contends that in literature, cartoons, television, and film "the term and idea have also been used to challenge the generally unquestioned acceptance and legitimacy of 'modernity' and 'progress.'"[55] Hillbillies form a part of the "white trash" that gives title to Nancy Isenberg's 2016 book about the place of poor whites in the American consciousness since colonial times. Various white southerners, from Andrew Jackson to Honey Boo Boo, figure prominently in her work, which contemplates how the troubling "class" of white trash has informed American identity.[56] My work takes on some of these historians' subjects, as well as their attention to the cultural work performed by imagined white southernness. It extends beyond hillbilly and white trash iconography and Old South representations, though, to assert that a broader vision of the white South addressed a variety of cultural needs during and after the civil rights movement.

In addition to building on the scholarship of imaginings of the South, *The South of the Mind* also expands on the work of Matthew D. Lassiter and Joseph Crespino's groundbreaking *The Myth of Southern Exceptionalism* (2010). These historians and their fellow contributors offer two major revisions to the historiography. First, they strike at the idea of southern distinctiveness: that southerners have experienced a unique history that contrasts with the rest of the nation's past. Second, they question the usefulness of southern history as an academic subfield, providing many examples of how scholars can better incorporate the study of the region into the larger tapestry of American history. Despite their attack on the parochialism of the field of southern history, Crespino, Lassiter, and their volume's contributors consider it vitally important to investigate how post–World War II Americans have imagined the South and continued to cling to the idea of southern distinctiveness.[57] By holding fast to fables of a unique South, they figure, Americans have unfailingly exploited the locale to address both regional and national concerns. I accept Crespino and Lassiter's conclusions while following their advice to seek new angles for integrating southern history into the national narrative.

The following chapters detail imaginings of the white South during the 1960s southern civil rights movement; country-rock music and the South in the countercultural mind; the Masculine South(s) of George Wallace, *Deliverance*, and *Walking Tall*; the contrasting southernness of Lynyrd Skynyrd and the Allman Brothers Band; and the enticement of Jimmy Carter's "healing" southernness during the 1976 presidential campaign. In each of these examples, popular discourses positioned the white South as capable of restoring an American culture beset by minority challenges to white male authority, presumed technological overreach, racial and political rancor, and/or feelings of social disconnectedness.

Chapter 1 discusses the multiple ways in which commentators in the North and South dealt with the ever-present issue of race in their views of the white South during the 1960s civil rights movement. These imaginings were manifested in a set of archetypes: the Vicious South, the Changing South, and the Down-Home South. These representations permeated journalistic, literary, filmic, and televised accounts of the region for years to come. The Vicious South presented white southerners as un-American, angry, backward racists, while the Changing South suggested that although they suffered from the stain of bigotry, their efforts to mend the region's strained race relations might hold the solution for the nation's ever more visible racial problems. Even in the midst of southern racial unrest and the ubiquity of these race-centric Vicious South and Changing South discourses, the Down-Home South cast aside the race issue and celebrated an honorable, anachronistic white South, addressing anxieties about consumerism and modernity. Each narrative, including the Vicious South's presentation of rough-and-tumble, manly white southerners, would provide the raw materials for future versions of a fantasied white South in the 1960s and 1970s.

This constructed white South found many allies among the antimaterialistic and antimodern hippie counterculture (chapter 2). Frequently encountering pastoral images of the rural South through country-rock music, counterculturists writing in the underground press typically envisioned the region as both a retreat from modern U.S. society and a possessor of lost values with which to combat the racist, undemocratic, technological nightmare they rechristened "Amerika." Indeed, hippies often extolled country-rock artists like the Byrds, Bob Dylan, and the Band, who sang of an idyllic South, one untouched by the ravages of time and "progress." Many counterculturists acknowledged the intensity of white southern racism, yet they often treated this deficiency as a symptom of a larger national sickness and decried nonsoutherners' easy scapegoating of white southerners.

As they wrestled with racial conundrums and exemplified a vague traditionalism, post–civil rights imaginings of white southernness frequently rested on the notion that the South was imbued with manly qualities absent in the non-South (chapter 3). This Masculine South discourse flowed into the content of and commentary about assorted elements of late 1960s and 1970s political and popular culture, including the presidential bids of segregationist Alabama governor George Wallace, the novel and film versions of *Deliverance* (1970 and 1972, respectively), and the motion picture *Walking Tall* (1973). Wallace's physicality and combative views on the campaign trail underscored his attacks on a purportedly weakened and feminized American society run by nitwitted "experts," college professors, and other cultural elites. The governor positioned himself as the representative of a manly white South that promised the use of violent repression to restore domestic control over racial minorities and youthful dissenters. For many Wallace supporters, the candidate's racism lent credence to his promise for a return to traditional values. *Walking Tall* similarly blasted so-called cultural permissiveness and promoted "southern-style" violence while underlining the racial enlightenment of its hulking white protagonist, Tennessee Sheriff Buford T. Pusser. The film's use of a bucolic pastoral South as a restorative foil for urban iniquity and facelessness paralleled *Deliverance*, where a frightening rural southern landscape offered both life-threatening tribulations and liberation from the seeming softness of suburban life. In these examples, the Masculine South endorsed the use of "southern" violence as a regenerative force capable of restoring America's flagging vitality.

Hard-driving manhood also pervaded the white southernness contained in the music and public personas of the Allman Brothers Band and Lynyrd Skynyrd, the most popular purveyors of 1970s southern rock (chapter 4). Despite that similarity, the two groups offered divergent commentaries on the white South. The Allman Brothers Band exhibited a countercultural ethos. It featured an integrated lineup, and its fans embraced the group's racial egalitarianism. Lynyrd Skynyrd's members, in contrast, situated themselves as defenders of white southernness and reflected much of the masculine resentment of George Wallace's South. In their responses to the two bands, fans and music writers demonstrated the often overlapping allure of the groups' differing takes on the white South, in both reactionary and progressive forms.

The winning 1976 presidential run of Jimmy Carter, governor of Georgia and dedicated southern rock fan, further underscored the complicated magnetism of the white South in the 1970s (chapter 5). Drawing on both elements of working-class, good ole boy rural southern culture and a racial enlightenment born of the civil rights movement, Carter positioned his healing southernness as central to his persona as a leader capable of ameliorating the country's post-Vietnam and post-Watergate political and cultural malaise. The candidate trumpeted his small hometown of Plains in rural southern Georgia as a beacon of tradition, where he claimed to have learned to rise above the local racist culture while honoring southern values of family, land, and religious faith. Carter's southernness thus managed to invoke the alluring qualities of the white South while eschewing its stereotypical provincialism and racism.

Rather than try to complete the impossible task of exploring every popular imagining of the white South between 1960 and 1980, I have chosen subjects of analysis for their popularity as well as their ability to draw attention to the flexibility of discourses about white southernness. The South of the Mind stretched to meet the needs of seemingly divergent groups of people, spanning from supporters of the traditionalist George Wallace to adherents of the counterculturist Abbie Hoffman—and other individuals with more moderate ideologies. This out-of-time white South, then, was not yoked to either a liberal or a conservative ethos. Part of its magnetism stemmed from its capacity to manage postwar cultural trepidations that eluded simple political categorization.

CHAPTER 1

The Many Faces of the South

National Images of White Southernness
during the Civil Rights Era, 1960–1971

"Beneath all the bad news that has come out of the South, and that may be expected to emerge for some time longer," a March 1966 issue of the *Nation* editorialized, "one can yet see the proof of this proposition." The proposition was "that of all forms of human ignorance . . . racial bias has the most superficial roots. . . . Prejudice does not breed discrimination; discrimination breeds prejudice."[1]

The left-leaning *Nation* made this comment on the possibility of altering racist thinking in "The Thaw in the South," an article that detailed the apparent slackening in white southerners' racial bigotry. The magazine's evidence for this unfreezing was thin. Drawing on a mere two news items—one story about white students' increasing acceptance of their black counterparts at the University of Alabama, and another profiling a white man in Schley County, Georgia, who positively related his experience serving as a foreman on an otherwise all-black jury—the piece's uncredited author concluded that "times change in the Southland, too."[2] The discourse utilized by the *Nation*, what might be termed the Changing South, depicted the white South in the midst of a painful rehabilitation. It left open the possibility that formerly intractable white southerners might be working toward setting aside their peculiar bigotry and achieving racial healing from which the rest of the nation might learn.

By mid-decade, as William G. Carleton noted that same year in an issue of the *Yale Review*, the South had "many moods."[3] The hopeful Changing South narrative was just one of three prominent discourses that highlighted the evolving and contested import of white southernness in the 1960s. The Changing South emerged as a response to the Vicious South discourse, a common trope in news media coverage of the civil rights movement. It focused on southern racism and cast white southerners as outsiders in the American dream of triumphant liberalism, and as antithetical to ideals of equality. A third discourse, best labeled the Down-Home South, celebrated the family ties, closeness to the land, and unaffectedness of such fictional characters as the Clampetts on *The Beverly Hillbillies* and residents of *The Andy Griffith Show*'s fictional small town, Mayberry, North Carolina. These programs delineated such "southern" traits as a refuge from cultural drabness, the supposed decline of traditional values, and rootlessness during the postwar era. While the Vicious South and Changing South suggested that race was integral to any portrayal of white southerners, the Down-Home South evaded contemporary racial troubles in the region and demonstrated that its black-white rift could be easily brushed aside or explained away when popular culture appointed white southerners as arbiters of lost, timeless American virtues.

These differing representations of the white South, even in the midst of its civil rights public relations disaster, granted Americans the opportunity to select the version of their choice at any given time without mandating their acceptance of any one of them completely or exclusively. In the 1960s, for example, American TV viewers tuning in Mondays could (and surely did) watch CBS's nightly news program (with Walter Cronkite beginning in 1962), where they saw reports on the latest wave of violence against civil rights activists in the South, and later in the evening catch the new episode of the highly rated *Andy Griffith Show*, a program that filled them with warm and fuzzy feelings for Mayberry's simple life and close familial connections. The massive success of both programs mitigates against there having been significant distinctions in their respective audiences. Americans who felt compelled to resolve their cognitive dissonance about the South usually needed a way to take race out of the equation; Down-Home South sitcoms did just that.

In the American imagination, the South was either a backward, mean, aggressively racist, foreboding, and yet tough and masculine locale (Vicious South); a region on the mend that reaffirmed a progressive story of American equality (Changing South); or a rural paradise, free of modern, technological, and racial anxieties (Down-Home South). These variants of white southernness would provide the raw materials for later imaginings of southern race relations and culture during the 1960s and 1970s that envisioned white southerners as possessing the tools for escaping the troubles of modern U.S. society.[4]

The Vicious South

The Vicious South discourse carried a dualistic purpose in its treatment of white southerners. On one hand, it closed off the South as a useful model of emulation for the majority of Americans. Certainly for nonsouthern liberals, this narrative reinforced the region as a place apart, the nation's embarrassing relative. Conversely, reactionary Americans, often supporters of the presidential candidacies of George Wallace, would later look to the whites who populated the Vicious South as paragons of toughness and manliness. National Wallaceites would draw on the symbol of the angry, resisting white southerner as an example for combating the disorder—racial and otherwise—that they wished to eradicate in the late 1960s and early 1970s. But this response could occur only after the news media and popular commentators helped to infuse the American consciousness with the image of a white South seething with anger and ready to commit racial violence.

TOURING THE VICIOUS SOUTH:
BLACK LIKE ME AND *TRAVELS WITH CHARLEY*

In 1959, white southern journalist John Howard Griffin set out on what should have been an impossible task for him: to document how it felt to live as a black man in the South. Under a dermatologist's supervision, Griffin took Oxsoralen, a drug that caused his skin to darken. He boosted the effect by exposing himself to natural and artificial light and dabbing his face and body with makeup. Once convincingly blackened, he traveled through the Deep South. *Black Like Me* (1961) presents what he discovered. It is an unsettling portrait of the white South: full of hate and pathologically committed to Jim Crow.

Griffin's journey through the southland brought him and his northern liberal audience face-to-face with the Vicious South. A constant theme throughout *Black Like Me* is the dehumanizing impact of southern racial practices on both blacks *and* whites. To Griffin, the "hate stare" comprised white southern cruelty at its most heinous. Practically everywhere he turned, the journalist faced this look. While waiting for a bus at a Greyhound station in New Orleans, Griffin encountered a respectable-looking white man who gave him the "stare." "Nothing can describe the withering horror of this," he wrote. "You feel lost, sick at heart before such unmasked hatred, not so much because it threatens you as because it shows humans in such an inhuman light. You see a kind of insanity, something so obscene the very obscenity of it (rather than its threat) terrifies you."[5]

Griffin thickened his description of white southern racism as he expounded on his adventures hitchhiking one evening from Mississippi to Alabama. White southern men, he found to his surprise, were often willing to give him a ride under the cover of darkness. Soon he realized that the reason had little to do with goodwill. On what seemed like "a dozen rides," he found his drivers' interests almost strictly prurient. "All but two," he remembered, "picked me up the way they would pick up a pornographic photograph or book—except that this was verbal pornography."[6] They bombarded and vaguely intimidated Griffin with questions premised on stereotypes of black men's sexual prowess and animalistic nature. This "ghoulish" dialogue went on incessantly ride after ride. One man tried to bait him into confessing that all black men lusted after white women. Another driver awkwardly noted that "he had never seen a Negro naked."[7]

Griffin construed the hate stare and sexual perversity as just two offshoots of the blinding hatred that afflicted many white southerners. He may have wished to use his book as a broader condemnation of national racism, but by providing his readers with a fly-on-the-wall account of the daily indignities faced by black southerners, he pegged their white counterparts as uniquely, if not bizarrely, racist. Indeed, he told *Time* before the book's publication, "I like to see good in the white man. But after this experience, it's hard to find it in the Southern white."[8] Griffin brought that viewpoint to millions of Americans through his best-selling book, as well as lecture tours and sympathetic advance television appearances with the likes of NBC's Dave Garroway and CBS's Mike Wallace.[9] Critical response to *Black Like Me* was strong. It enjoyed glowing reviews, which lauded Griffin's conclusions about the plight of blacks in the South and the brutality of their white tormentors.[10] His book served to popularize the Vicious South discourse and its claim of distinctive, obsessive white southern racism.

Shortly after Griffin began his perilous trek, John Steinbeck also tried to find the South; he uncovered more stories of white malevolence. The popular author had long been an observer of American life and landscapes. He was best known for a series of popular novels, including *The Grapes of Wrath* (1939), that chronicled the experiences of down-on-their-luck working people in his native California. *Travels with Charley* (1962) recounts his months-long trip around the United States in a pickup truck with a camper top during 1960. His only companion was his French standard poodle Charley. Steinbeck traveled from Long Island to the Pacific Northwest, down through California and across Texas, before concluding his journey in the Deep South. As his book's subtitle attests, he went "in search of America." If he located it anywhere, the reader is left to conclude, it was certainly not in the South. In his survey of the region, with few exceptions, he documented a backward, defiant white population clinging to its racial caste system. The real problem, the writer insinuated, was the rabid, working-class white southerner.

"I faced the South with dread," Steinbeck announced at the beginning of the book's southern section. "Here, I knew, were pain and confusion and all the manic results of bewilderment and fear. And the South being a limb of the nation, its pain spreads out to all America."[11] The region's racial malady, he surmised, infected the rest of the otherwise healthy nation. It was a sickness so severe and peculiar that he could not fully grasp it.

And yet he could not help but look. Setting out for New Orleans, Steinbeck was sucked in by news reports of the "Cheerleaders," a group of white women he had read about, known for berating black children at a recently integrated local school. "This strange drama," he recollected, "seemed so improbable that I felt I had to see it. It had the same draw as a five-legged calf or a two-headed foetus at a sideshow, a distortion of normal life we have always found so interesting that we will pay to see it, perhaps to prove to ourselves that we have the proper number of legs or heads."[12]

In Steinbeck's prose, the Cheerleaders personify the unhinged futility of defensive white southern racism. His rendering of them in *Travels with Charley* further underscored the usefulness of the Vicious South in absolving the rest of the nation of its race problem by condemning the apparently abnormal prejudice of the South. Employing a device common in civil rights reporting, Steinbeck contrasted peaceful, defenseless black schoolchildren with sneering, foul-mouthed white racists. For him, the Cheerleaders' behavior desexed and dehumanized them. He called "their insensate beastliness . . . heartbreaking."[13] One woman's "voice was the bellow of a bull."[14] "These were not mothers, not even women," the writer insisted. "They were crazy actors playing to a crazy audience."[15] Without stating it explicitly, Steinbeck argued, with liberal indignation, that Jim Crow transformed its white proponents into subhuman creatures.

Steinbeck's passages on the white South are not completely devoid of subtlety. For instance, after the Cheerleaders sequence, he related a conversation between him and an individual named Monsieur Ci Git. Steinbeck immediately indicated the gentleman's variance from the unrefined Cheerleaders. "He was a neatly dressed man well along in years," he recalled, "with a Greco face and fine wind-lifted white hair and a clipped white mustache."[16] The author was fascinated by this debonair individual who demonstrated a keen understanding of southern race relations and exhibited a glimmer of racial progressivism. "You're not what the North thinks of as a Southerner," Steinbeck told him. "Perhaps not," Ci Git responded. "But I'm not alone."[17] In the midst of so much dogged white racism, Steinbeck showed the Monsieur as the face of another South, one not invested in the racial hatred of the Cheerleaders. The fact that Ci Git exemplified southern middle-class refinement only lent further credence to the popular notion that white southern racism was most pronounced among the working-class rabble.

Other parts of *Travels with Charley* supplement this implicit class-based view of southern racism. After the Ci Git episode, Steinbeck described his experience picking up hitchhikers on his way from New Orleans to Jackson, Mississippi. The novelist reported the intense racism of one man who sounded like a cliché of white southern bigotry. When Steinbeck baited him and made it clear that he rejected the status quo of southern race relations, the man labeled him one of the "Commie nigger-lovers," who, he said, were "trouble-makers [who] come down here and tell us how to live."[18] In dramatizing this tense moment, Steinbeck reinforced the idea that Americans should fear the working-class white southerner. While scholar Allison Graham has shown that much popular culture during the civil rights era was invested in the rehabilitation of this figure, Steinbeck left readers with little hope that the Vicious South's snarling, often economically deprived, whites would ever change despite the presence of moderating influences like Monsieur Ci Git.

Almost without fail, the reviews of Steinbeck's travelogue dwelled on the book's southern section. Princeton historian Eric F. Goldman, one of the more complimentary critics, praised the book's racial liberalism. "Here is the most powerful writing in the book," he wrote in reference to the Cheerleaders episode, "stinging with the cold lash of outraged decency."[19] Other reviewers detected nothing revelatory in Steinbeck's exposé of southern racism. "This opportunity for high drama, for great sensitivity exposed in bitterness and horror," opined travel editor Kenneth Weiss in the *Washington Post*, "winds up in straight reporting with little new light shed."[20] While Weiss may had underplayed Steinbeck's gift for enlivening the New Orleans desegregation drama, he was correct that the author had offered virtually nothing that readers could not already see on a daily basis in the Vicious South narrative of civil rights journalism.

REPORTING THE VICIOUS SOUTH

The press corps's heavy reliance on the Vicious South trope deeply influenced its coverage of the southern civil rights movement. "Reporters in the South," scholar Sasha Torres has explained, "often ignored the journalistic imperative to neutrality."[21] There were good reasons for this, she judges, including the civil rights movement's "moral authority" and segregationists' obviously racist motivations even when using the language of states' rights.[22] Projects that strove for "balance" like the 1961 CBS documentary *Who Speaks for Birmingham?* often fell short. Torres points out that this particular documentary "ended with [reporter Howard K.] Smith calling on President Kennedy to 'restate' the laws of the land to recalcitrant [white] southerners."[23] Influenced by the movement's media savviness and its careful staging of protests—and, of course, by many whites' overt racial antipathy and violence—journalists typically presented white southerners as inimitably racist and correspondingly outside of the U.S. mainstream. Americans saw moving and still pictures of white southerners assaulting black and white protesters. News media frequently contrasted these ferocious whites with images of dignified, peaceful black civil rights protesters. For nonsoutherners, the message was clear: the South and its white inhabitants were abnormal and hostile to American ideals of equality.

Well before 1960, Allison Graham suggests, this subjective civil rights reporting had already established itself as a mixture of "literary and cinematic conventions."[24] News items often sketched the region as a sizzling and claustrophobic locality and their authors seemed to lap up Mississippi novelist William Faulkner's descriptions of a sweaty, benighted South as truth. In 1966, the *Nation*'s Dan Wakefield, for example, judged Sumner, Mississippi, "an eerie place. . . . The air is heavy, dusty, and hot, and even the silence has a thickness about it—like a kind of taut skin—that is suddenly broken with a shock by the crack and fizz of a Coke being opened."[25] Although some reporters recognized this imagery of the South as problematic, they often could not help themselves. In a 1962 report about trying to ensure journalistic standards in southern civil rights reporting, for instance, John Herbers of *Nieman Reports* referenced Faulkner's imagined South as reality. ("Today, Yoknapatawpha County . . . is undergoing rather drastic, externally wrought changes.")[26]

Even when not relying on overwrought prose, journalists tended to portray white southerners as strangely deformed, morally bankrupt residents of the margins of America. On television, the 1964 disappearance of three civil rights workers, Andrew Goodman, James Chaney, and Michael Schwerner, outside of Philadelphia, Mississippi, led Walter Cronkite's CBS News broadcast to contrast the admirable goals of the interracial movement with the intransigence of the white South. Alluding to the movement's achievement of framing noble protesters against angry white southern antagonists, David Farber argues that in this moment "America's leading newsmen made sure that Americans were aware of the Deep South's failure to create even elementary racial justice."[27] In print news reports as well, journalists frequently laid that "failure" at the feet of a weird, insular white South. Echoing Ole Miss professor James Silver's 1964 book-length denigration of Mississippi as a "closed society," that same year *Life*'s David Nevin called Philadelphia, Mississippi, "strange," and "its fear and hatred of things and ideas that come from the outside . . . nearly pathological."[28]

In other magazines and newspapers, Americans read reports designating the white South as "a wild mob of men and women" attacking journalists and freedom riders in Alabama in 1961, and as "a gap-toothed old man in a blue American Legion cap" who stood prepared to prevent black student James Meredith's integration of Ole Miss in 1962. "I'm ready for the kill," the man told a reporter, "are you?"[29] As in *Travels with Charley*, the opponents of desegregation came off as morally, and even sometimes physically, defective. *Newsweek*'s 1963 commentary "Case History of a Sick City" was written in the aftermath of Birmingham police attacking black protesters with snarling dogs and blasts from fire hoses, and the deaths of four black girls in the bombing of the 16th Street Baptist Church. The article blamed an obsessive commitment to hatred and white supremacy for the city's violent impeding of black civil rights. Using the words of a local white businessman, it condemned every white southerner who "spreads the seeds of hate" for creating a toxic stew of racial hostility and violence.[30]

Coverage of peaceful civil disobedience in Selma, Alabama, one of the most important sites of the black freedom struggle, only hardened the image of the Vicious South in the national mind-set. On 7 March 1965, news cameras rolled as state troopers and sheriff's deputies unleashed billy clubs and tear gas against nonviolent black marchers on the Edmund Pettus Bridge. Two weeks later, the national press followed the route of thousands of activists as they marched from Selma to the Alabama state capitol in Montgomery. The media reports from Selma often fit into the classic Vicious South mold, with villainous white southerners occupying an alien landscape juxtaposed against brave black protesters. Auto dealer Art Lewis and his wife Muriel were spot-on when they wrote in a March 1965 letter, "We were well aware that there was a perfect setup here with 'the villain' [Sheriff] Jim Clark, and when Martin Luther King arrived there was the hero."[31] White Selma's intense obstructionism, coupled with the news media's role as an agent in the creation of the civil rights movement's narrative, encouraged press reports to home in on that dichotomous portraiture of black agitators and white resisters. *Time* showed the social impact of the city's racism, noting that the majority black population represented only one percent of the city's voters. "The place has not changed much since" 1852, the magazine claimed, when Selma passed an ordinance allowing authorities to whip blacks convicted of "smoking a cigar or pipe or carrying a walking cane."[32]

Time's claims of the city's ingrained, timeless racism sounded tame compared to other journalists' commentary. Kentucky native Elizabeth Hardwick sprinkled her ironically titled "Selma, Alabama: The Charms of Goodness" in the *New York Review of Books* with nearly every southern literary cliché imaginable. She opened on "a sad countryside" with its "khaki-colored earth, the tense, threatening air, the vanquished feeding on their permanent Civil War—all of it brings to mind flamboyant images from Faulkner."[33] Throughout the article, she painted the white citizenry as degenerates. Sheriff Jim Clark's enforcers were "middle-aged delinquents and psychopaths."[34] She saved her most vitriolic words, though, for the poor whites—"these outcasts"—who "carry guns and whips and have power over senators and governors." Rather than pawns of the city fathers, Hardwick dismissed them as "a degraded and despised people."[35] Again demonstrating the civil rights movement's framing of heroes and villains, the journalist contrasted the city's whites with the "good people"—the black protesters fighting against the city's entrenched white power structure.[36] She lauded "the moral justice of the Civil Rights movement" waged by "good, clean, downright folk in glasses and wearing tie clasps."[37]

In the hands of the press corps, white southerners occasionally appeared as akin to the worst evils of the twentieth century. Southern fascism in Selma, some reports proposed, was as bad as, if not worse than, the brutalities of Nazi Germany. One black activist told the *New York Times*, "I fought in World War II, and I once was captured by the German army, and I want to tell you that the Germans never were as inhuman as the state troopers of Alabama."[38] Writing for the *Nation*, George B. Leonard, another native southerner, recounted his leaving San Francisco to join the movement in Alabama. He opened his article with scenes from the German death camps and scattered his writing with comparisons of Nazism and Deep Southern white supremacy.[39] Compounding the indictments of bigoted southerners, editorial cartoons responding to the Selma violence proliferated in nonsouthern newspapers. According to *Time*, in these cartoons "[Governor George] Wallace, Alabama law-enforcement officers and Selma's red-neck hoodlums were caricatured as fascist bullyboys, Neanderthal dimwits or lumbering ogres from a horror movie."[40]

The overwhelming presence of the Vicious South in the national media during the early to mid-1960s helped to fuel support for the southern civil rights movement and hostility toward its white adversaries. In its posing of debauched racists residing in a peculiar homeland against dignified blacks battling to assert their humanity, the Vicious South powerfully—and convincingly—interpreted the region as backward. The trope placed this bigoted and ignorant South against the non-South, the representative of what Joseph Crespino has referred to as "modern, open America."[41] The Vicious South discourse told Americans that the southland had nothing to offer the rest of the nation, for it was everything that America was purportedly not: racist, unequal, hateful, and violent. But, in fact, this view of the white South was vitally important to the nation's self-image. By encasing virtually all of the nation's social evils in one imagined space, and by marking the South as abnormal, it encouraged nonsoutherners, particularly liberals, to feel secure in their feelings of regional superiority and in their own sense of American exceptionalism. Although some citizens would come to identify with the anger and violence of the Vicious South, especially later in the 1960s, most Americans would begin to perceive that "otherness" as a positive trait only once they possessed tools to reassess the imagery of white southerners. This reassessment started even as the Vicious South discourse flourished, with alternative ideas about the region emerging that questioned if white southerners were truly racially deviant figures in an otherwise equalitarian country.

The Changing South

By the mid-1960s, with the civil rights movement still shaking the region, commentators—novelists, filmmakers, and journalists—had begun tinkering with the image of the South. Some of these individuals expressed guarded optimism for the ability of the region and its white inhabitants to adjust to racial change. Whereas the Vicious South stressed the region's obstinacy, this Changing South narrative discerned evidence of progress. Emerging as federal legislation dealt blows to institutionalized southern discrimination, the Changing South argued for the readiness of white southerners to heal themselves of the social sickness of racism. It cast them in another light, one that pictured them and their region on the path to national reconciliation and perhaps capable of teaching the country a few lessons of its own. Rather than seeing white southerners as forever destined to function as the nation's bigoted cousins, the Changing South presumed that they could be brought back into the fold as rehabilitated, full Americans who were knowledgeable about dealing with persistent social problems. This discourse rejected the idea of white southern racism as an uncorrectable regional problem and national embarrassment, while vowing that white southern bigotry was either on the wane or no worse than the prejudices of the rest of the nation. By reevaluating the pervasiveness of white southernness's most negative trait, the Changing South laid the groundwork for a frequent component of later imaginings of the white South: its maintenance of traditions supposedly wanting in modern American society.

The "surprising" aspect of the apparent white racial reform that was characteristic of the Changing South depended on the ubiquity of the Vicious South view of white southerners. In the 1950s, as it began its initial desegregation process in relative peace, Atlanta dubbed itself "The City Too Busy to Hate." Even in the early 1960s, when it became clear that the city's racial problems were more serious than initially reported, Atlanta continued to benefit from its comparison to other southern communities like Birmingham. In February 1964, the *Washington Post* addressed that juxtaposition in an editorial titled "Tale of Two Cities." While they acknowledged that "there are still pockets of segregation in [Atlanta]," the newspaper's editors insisted that "the distinction between Atlanta and Birmingham is a vital one. It is the distinction between reason and bigotry, between adjustment and conflict."[42] By drawing a line between the good South and the bad South, the Changing South discourse advised Americans that racial oppression could ultimately be conquered in the region and that, in contrast to the Vicious South narrative, white southerners might be able to salvage their sense of decency and equality and rejoin the nation.

Other pieces of journalism focused less on specific locales like Atlanta but still found reason for optimism throughout the South. *Newsweek* posited in May 1965 that "like a ray of spring sun, the changing [racial] attitude is creeping across the Southern landscape."[43] The magazine's competitor *Time* expanded on this view a few days later in an uncredited 1965 essay, "The Other South." Published in the aftermath of the Pettus Bridge violence in Selma, "The Other South" embodied a hopeful message about race relations in the region while admitting to the difficult work that lay ahead. Referencing the Vicious South outlined in much civil rights reporting, the essay stated, "To much of the nation and the world, the South is Selma."[44] *Time* advanced that racial tension and violence between blacks and whites would not vanish soon. Still, "another South" had become increasingly visible in the midst of the civil rights movement. This version, the piece's author postulated, was "a region of quiet, solid, if often agonizing, progress. That other South, all too easily overlooked, was not created this year or ten years ago; it was not brought into being only by an act of the Supreme Court or only by the exertions of the civil rights movement. It has long existed in the hearts of some men. But only lately has it begun to take over in reality and to make its true weight felt in the balance of events."[45] This Other or Changing South coexisted with the Vicious South; however, the magazine pointed to recent events to proclaim that national understandings of the region should be framed not by its very real white resistance, but rather by that "agonizing," and often reluctant, "progress" to which white southerners themselves were increasingly acquiescing.

Time clarified that the changes in the South "often seem heartbreakingly and absurdly slight."[46] Indeed, as the magazine noted, the sight of blacks being served by white bellhops in newly integrated hotels or segregationist Arkansas Governor Orval Faubus's wife inviting black women to tea may have struck readers as superficial, "but taken together, and given the South's unique history, such signs tell of an entirely new climate."[47] This guarded optimism came with a belief that troubled race relations were still bound to plague the South. *Time* declared that much of the problem lay in white southerners' apparent inability to transform as quickly as the civil rights movement demanded rather than in some inherent commitment to racism. "The Southern white man's old paternalistic and patronizing affection for the Negro has largely disappeared," the essay read, "but has not yet been replaced with a new friendship based on equality."[48] Continuing to qualify its analysis, as if groping to make sense of the new southern social landscape wrought by several years of strife, *Time* looked favorably on the increasing numbers of white southerners who supported the goals of the black freedom struggle. White supremacy in the South may not have been broken, the article's author suggested, yet an apparently unstoppable shift in southern life was occurring. Part of the test that lay ahead for black and white southerners was in redefining their relationships. White southerners would furthermore need to reconsider their own identities in an environment in which their social dominance had been challenged. This Changing South of *Time*'s imagination was the Vicious South on the wane, due in large part to the impact of federal legislation and business interests. "Perhaps, as regional differences fade," the essay concluded, "the South is finally approaching the point where it will cease to be an epilogue to tragedy and begin being merely a problem."[49] As the focus of civil rights activity (and its analogous journalistic coverage) moved away from the towns and cities of the Deep South to urban centers in the North, such fantasies became increasingly plausible.

Other popular publications during the mid-1960s confirmed the Changing South discourse's robustness as an alternative to the "othering" qualities of the Vicious South. An April 1965 special supplement to *Harper's* represented one of the most sustained versions of the Changing South narrative. Commemorating the one hundredth anniversary of the end of the Civil War, the magazine featured writings by southerners, most of whom were white (with contributions by two black writers and one British author). Their opinions on the South, its national image, and its race relations ranged from frustrated to melancholic to hopeful to delusional. The *Harper's* issue certified the vitality of the Changing South discourse just one month after the violence at Selma.

Harper's editor Willie Morris, a native Mississippian, enlisted participants and approved the supplement's content. Morris set a balanced tone for the magazine's southern issue in its foreword. He noted the intense national focus on the region, contending that "the South today is more important and perhaps more obsessive than it has been at any time in the last century." Wishing to primarily capture "the South as it has become," Morris introduced the varying subjects and perspectives covered by his contributors. In all of their articles, though, he uncovered "a dominant human theme": the continuing racial struggle between blacks and whites in the region. That theme "lies in the personal, the institutional agonies, the subterfuges and cruelties which have in the past prevented or discouraged Southern whites and Southern Negroes from recognizing one another as 'fellow Southerners,' as children and victims of a common heritage."[50] The southern future, Morris implied, would be measured by how well whites and blacks came to comprehend that heritage.

As writers, journalists, and historians debated this question in the *Harper's* special supplement, they portrayed a wide variety of Souths that were capable of invoking emotions ranging from fear and attraction to optimism and disappointment. But the dominant concept was possibility. In a portrait of his hometown of Valdosta, Georgia, for example, black journalist Louis E. Lomax concluded that "the whites themselves are slowly changing," and they were willing to accept blacks' challenges to white supremacy if it meant that peace could be maintained.[51] White novelist Walker Percy went a step further. While he thought post-*Brown* Mississippi society "insane," he also specified that the state was "even now beginning to feel its way to what might be called the American Settlement on the racial issue."[52] Although he saw in this transition "less a solution than a more or less tolerable impasse," Percy joined Lomax in squeezing out the essence of the Changing South: a sense of optimism about the capacity of the white South to redefine its associations with its black neighbors and restore its value to the nation.[53] By envisioning a way out of the southern racial dilemma, the Changing South presaged cultural productions that both displayed white southern racism as part of a national problem and held up white southerners as oracles of time-honored, but discarded, wisdom and values in an increasingly soulless U.S. consumer society.

THE CHANGING SOUTH IN LITERATURE AND FILM:
TO KILL A MOCKINGBIRD AND *IN THE HEAT OF THE NIGHT*

Two popular novels (and subsequent films) about race and the South— Harper Lee's Pulitzer Prize–winning *To Kill a Mockingbird* (1960) and John

Ball's *In the Heat of the Night* (1965)—delivered the Changing South image to a wide audience. What unites these novels' often very different Deep South milieus is their contention that white southerners had the capability to act morally and change their racist behavior. These novels aligned with mid-1960s journalism that posited the white South's ability to reinvent itself and its relationship with its black neighbors and the nation. More powerfully, they encouraged the belief that the key to southern racial reform was the middle-class white southerner who refused to give into old hatreds and instead courageously blazed the trail for both his and his region's racial redemption. In short, they determined that white southern racism was an individual, not a systemic problem. Individual conversion rather than serious structural changes to society was all that was needed to escape the region's trap of racial bigotry.

To Kill a Mockingbird, later made into a 1962 Academy Award–winning film starring Gregory Peck as the quietly crusading lawyer Atticus Finch, is set in fictional Maycomb, Alabama, during the Great Depression. Lee draws this fictionalized version of her own Monroeville, Alabama, home as "a tired old town."[54] "People moved slowly then," she writes. "They ambled across the square, shuffled in and out of the stores around it, took their time about everything." It was a place indeed where "there was no hurry."[55] The author lulls the reader into a warm tale of Atticus's daughter Scout and his son Jem's adventures in the first half of the book. The children's biggest concern is trying to make their reclusive neighbor Boo Radley emerge from his decaying, shuttered home. Aside from paying tribute to her father AC—like Atticus a fairly (if somewhat less) progressive lawyer in small-town Alabama—Lee's reason for writing the novel seems clear: somewhat disillusioned by the experience of living in New York City and nostalgic for a return to her roots, she re-created the world of her childhood (with Scout serving as her stand-in). As biographer Charles J. Shields presupposed, "Perhaps writing about the red dust and sweet tea of her Deep South also comforted her."[56] A few years after the book's publication, Lee remarked tellingly, "I would like to be the chronicler of something that I think is going down the drain very swiftly. And that is small-town middle-class southern life." While pointing to the uniqueness of this lifestyle, she also trusted there was "something universal in it."[57] One might logically extrapolate that Lee found it a welcome respite from an encroaching modern order characterized, in Shields's estimation, by an accompanying desire for "life set in simpler, pre–cold war times."[58] Literary scholar Eric Sundquist also beholds this escapist element in Lee's choice of time period, writing that "the novel harks back to the 1930s . . . to move the mounting fear and violence surrounding desegregation into an arena of safer contemplation."[59]

Although Lee's Maycomb is no Philadelphia, Mississippi, racial division is ever present in the town. It is this discord and its importance to the narrative that makes *To Kill a Mockingbird*'s imagined South the product of the civil rights era rather than the post–civil rights era. In the second half of the novel, Atticus defends Tom Robinson, a local black man accused of rape by the poor white teenager Mayella Ewell. In court, Atticus shows that Mayella had propositioned Tom and that he had refused her advances. He also reveals that when Bob Ewell, Mayella's father, discovered the attempted seduction, he beat Mayella and fabricated the rape allegation. Atticus's virtuosic closing statement includes a condemnation of southern racial injustice and of the cynicism of the people who perpetuate it. He implores the jurors to abandon the falsehood "that *all* Negroes lie, that *all* Negroes are basically immoral beings, that *all* Negro men are not to be trusted around our women."[60] Despite Atticus's efforts, Tom is convicted and sentenced to the penitentiary. He is subsequently shot and killed while making a run for the prison yard fence.

To Kill a Mockingbird thus balances a seductive portrait of southern small-town life with a nod to the corrosive effects of southern racism on both blacks and whites. Lee's black characters are noble in the face of prejudice, yet the reader learns little about them. The author explores whites in more detail, especially the racially liberal Atticus. The middle-aged lawyer is no crusader; he only reluctantly honors the local judge's request to take the case. But he believes in fairness and equality regardless of one's skin color. For him to think otherwise would call into question his authority and basic humanity. As he tells Scout, when she asks him why he took Tom's case, "If I didn't I couldn't hold up my head in town, I couldn't represent this county in the legislature, I couldn't even tell you or Jem not to do something again."[61] It is, in short, a question of honor, which Atticus couches in a defense of middle-class respectability. His decision to represent Tom already differentiates him from the hateful, unreasonable—and very real—whites of *Travels with Charley* and *Black Like Me*. Lee contrasts Atticus with these people by making him a man for whom both reason and gut instinct dictate that blacks deserve to be treated with dignity. It is a remarkable contrast with the Vicious South's white southerner, one that encourages readers and viewers of *To Kill a Mockingbird* to envision this figure as capable of racial tolerance and as worthy of emulation rather than derision. *Commonweal*'s Philip T. Hartung rightly observed, in a review of the film adaptation, that "'Mockingbird' says as effectively as any propaganda that there *are* [white] Southerners on the side of justice and tolerance, that there is hope for a country in which lawyers like Atticus are guiding their children along the right path."[62]

The villain of *To Kill a Mockingbird*—the drunken, ranting, and loathsome Robert E. Lee Ewell—on the other hand, is the Vicious South in the flesh. He is not only a virulent racist but also Atticus's social inferior. For all of Lee's intimations of structural southern racism, like much civil rights coverage and *Travels with Charley*, the epicenter of white southern bigotry in *To Kill a Mockingbird* is located in the individual members of the lower class. Lee rues the short-fused, drunken Ewell as "a little bantam cock of a man" with a "face . . . as red as his neck."[63] He rules over his disease-ridden family of debauched, pathetic white trash with a sense of misplaced pride that stems from his unshaken belief in white supremacy. Bob Ewell clearly lacks Atticus's dignity and social respectability. His aberrant behavior is most visible when he attacks Scout and Jem after the trial, as they walk home from their school's Halloween pageant. Ewell is indicative of "the cracker from hell" in 1960s popular culture that requires suppression by more upstanding white southern characters.[64]

Despite Tom Robinson's unjust conviction and lonely death, Lee forecasts redemption for a Changing South that goes beyond Boo Radley's justifiable killing of Ewell during his assault on Atticus's children. The essence of that redemption lies in the actions of courageous white southerners who dare to stand up and chart a new path. Just as important, though, are those whites who will behave commonsensically and fairly, like Atticus, instead of mindlessly attempt to maintain their crumbling racial caste system. So despite Lee's treatment of the systemic roots of southern racism, for her, as Joseph Crespino has argued, southern "racial change . . . would occur through the leadership of people like Atticus Finch—in other words, through elite southern white liberals."[65] Atticus is the face of this southern white racial liberalism, a man who represents the possibilities of a new South. Indeed, he serves as a forerunner of white southern figures like Jimmy Carter, who would present himself as a racial healer to American voters during the 1970s. Atticus is confident that the white South's efforts to mend itself and to restore its claim to the American creed of equality will be a hard-fought conflict. With a sly wink to the contemporary civil rights turmoil in the Deep South, the lawyer describes Maycomb as a town at war with itself over the racial issue. "This time we aren't fighting the Yankees, we're fighting our friends," he tells Scout. "But remember this, no matter how bitter things get, they're still our friends and this is still our home."[66] Atticus thus identifies himself as one of the people who will presumably show the Bob Ewells of the region the error of their cracker ways. Lee's relative indifference toward the inner lives of her black characters makes the redemption to which she alludes largely a white awakening, gradual though it may be.[67] For instance, the Finches' white neighbor Miss Maudie is disappointed by the jury's verdict against Tom Robinson, but she also thinks that "we're making a step—it's just a baby-step, but it's a step."[68] By condemning Maycomb's racial "disease," as Atticus terms it, and making the jury deliberate for longer than usual before inevitability convicting a black man based on the word of a white man, she believes that Scout's father has pushed the town in the direction of progress.[69] Through the character of the brave attorney, Lee leaves her readers with the assurance that the white South of the 1960s may be able to overcome its reliance on its claims of racial supremacy and exhibit its inner goodness once it contains its lower-class riffraff. Her novel hints at an uncertain, yet guardedly optimistic, forecast of the region's future: the "disease" may be cured only if the South's Atticus Finches dare to rise up and expose the lies that undergird the increasingly wobbly Jim Crow system. In this way, the novel fits the mold of what Thomas F. Haddox has labeled the "white civil rights novel" of the 1940s, 1950s, and 1960s. Works in this genre are marked by their "treat[ment] [of] political change as the sum of individual changes of heart rather than as a systemic transformation of policies achievable by collective action."[70] The limits of such politics are clear: Lee's work, for example, is more about the awakening (and reformative nature) of Atticus Finch's white South than the liberation of Tom Robinson's black South.

The cautious hope for this bright, enlightened future of the white South— and an individualistic understanding of how racial change will occur— that inhabits *To Kill a Mockingbird* is furthered in John Ball's *In the Heat of the Night* (and the subsequent film directed by Norman Jewison, winner of the 1967 Academy Award for Best Picture). The community in the story (Wells, somewhere in the Carolinas, in the book, and Sparta, Mississippi, in the film) seems almost a caricature of the racist southern small town. Gone are the unassuming attributes of Lee's Depression-era Maycomb. While Lee's 1930s town is sleepy, Ball's contemporary rural small town is decaying and torpid. His opening lines echo the most purple imagery of civil rights reporting: "At ten minutes to three in the morning, the city of Wells lay inert, hot and stagnant. Most of its eleven thousand people tossed restlessly; the few who couldn't sleep at all damned the fact that there was no breeze to lift the stifling effect of the night. The heat of the Carolinas in August hung thick and heavy in the air."[71] The antiracist characters in *To Kill a Mockingbird* like Atticus and Miss Maudie are missing. Ball's white characters, regardless of class, are deeply racist. At the beginning of the novel, the author wastes little time before imparting the bigotry that infects the town. Police officer Sam Wood converses with a diner employee who bemoans the dominance of blacks in the sport of boxing. Sam claims that their skills are due to biology. He says, "They haven't got the same nervous system. They're like animals."[72] Later in the novel, a local white councilman raises the familiar white southern refrain against outside agitators. In response to a proposed *Newsweek* profile of a local murder investigation, he scorns the magazine as a meddling "bunch of nigger lovers" trying to impose their views upon the town's whites.[73]

Like *To Kill a Mockingbird*, this highly racist backdrop drives the drama of *In the Heat of the Night*. As one reviewer of the film contended in 2008, the latter "relies on its audience's belief—prejudice, really—in the complete backwardness of the American South."[74] The unsubtle case for white southern racism nevertheless resonated with many critics and audience members. A scant two months after white law enforcement officers attacked peaceful black protesters in Selma, the *New York Times* asserted that Ball "handles the racial situation with detailed perception."[75] The fictional South of *In the Heat of the Night*, like much nonfiction of the era, renders the region as aberrational. In the film version, a nonsouthern liberal asks, "What kind of people are you? What kind of a place is this?"[76] Allison Graham rightly asserts that these were "questions begged by a decade of news footage."[77] But the overt racism of Ball's southern town is also a necessary construction to make some of its white characters' racial progress look all the more stunning, lending an almost romantic quality to the supposed ability of white southerners to transcend their bigoted environment.

While in *To Kill a Mockingbird*, brave white southern moderates, if not liberals, are entrusted with reforming race relations in the South, in *In the Heat of the Night* this task falls to an outsider—a *black* nonsoutherner, no less. This "outside agitator" is Virgil Tibbs (portrayed by Sidney Poitier in the film version). The drama begins when Tibbs is arrested at the local train depot, after an officer confiscates a wallet packed with cash from him. Tibbs, it turns out, is a Pasadena (Philadelphia, in the film) police detective. After the truth is confirmed, Tibbs assists Chief of Police Bill Gillespie (played by Rod Steiger in the picture) in investigating a murder—in the film, of a Chicago businessman who planned to build a factory in town, and in the novel, of a conductor putting on a local music festival. The expected racial tension between Tibbs and Gillespie, the town's all-white police force, and white locals ensues. Eventually, Tibbs's coolness and competence begin to win over Gillespie and Sam. Near the end of the novel, when a café manager refers to Tibbs as "a nigger," Sam demonstrates his racial epiphany. "Virgil isn't a nigger," he corrects the man. "He's colored, he's black, and he's a Negro, but he isn't a nigger. I've known a lot of white men who weren't as smart as he is."[78] After the case is solved, Gillespie shakes the black man's hand, a first for him. "You're a great credit to your race," he says to the detective in the novel. "I mean, of course, the human race."[79] Gillespie even allows Tibbs to sit on the "white" bench on the deserted train platform. Jewison avoids such heavy-handed sentiment. There is no inkling of Sam's transformation in the film, and although Gillespie is far less effusive, at the train depot he lugs Tibbs's suitcase for him, offers him a quick handshake, and a "bye, bye," before he tells the northerner, "You take care, you hear," followed by the men sharing a long, pregnant gaze. Signaling perhaps that he has undergone a deeper change, Gillespie's sly grin turns into an expression of pensiveness. Jack Temple Kirby has classified the film "in many respects . . . [as] a fine example of neoabolitionism."[80] The argument holds true for the novel, and while Jewison's film is clearly a work of racial liberalism, the relatively subtle portrayal of the Tibbs-Gillespie relationship appears to have little to do with the moral fervor characteristic of the neoabolitionist genre.

Critics appreciated that subtly and honed in on the change in the relationship between Gillespie and Tibbs. *Time* commended the way in which the film's characters "break brilliantly with black-white stereotypes" and lauded Jewison, who "has shown . . . that men can join hands out of fear and hatred and shape from base emotions something identifiable as a kind of love."[81] *Life*'s movie reviewer, Richard Schickel, highlighted the film's refusal to overstep plausibility. "They do not suddenly become brothers under the skin," he wrote, "put down their old prejudices, or vow to be better men."[82] The meaning of the change in Gillespie is nevertheless apparent from the knowing smiles on both men's faces as Tibbs boards the train. The seemingly impregnable barrier of Jim Crow that Ball and Jewison outline at the beginning of their respective versions is showing cracks.

Gillespie's transformation is all the more fantastic because he sounds and looks like one of the belly-protruding, khaki-suited white southern sheriffs who personified the Vicious South in the popular press. Jack Temple Kirby once pointed out that Rod Steiger "has a chilling resemblance to Sheriff Rainey who had been implicated in the 1964 murders of" Goodman, Chaney, and Schwerner.[83] *Newsweek* called Gillespie "a two-bit Bull Connor," and indeed Jewison later stated that he conceived Steiger's police chief more as an homage to the infamous Birmingham Commissioner of Public Safety.[84] Regardless, by the end of the film (and the book), Gillespie, after developing a close working relationship with Tibbs, could not be further from the racist white southern lawmen of civil rights coverage on television and in print.

The movie and novel left audiences with the unmistakable impression, similar to that in *To Kill a Mockingbird*, that even the most hardened southern racists—including Bull Connor types, no less!—might be capable of redemption. In Lee's work, white southern racism is a fundamental "disease" that cannot be easily eradicated. Historian Aram Goudsouzian posits that, likewise, "*In the Heat of the Night* never pretends to cure racism" or "an immoral social structure."[85] While these productions do allude to the hardened framework of white bigotry in the Deep South that affects all strata of society, the fact remains that they primarily focus on the possibility of individual change, at least when courageous white southerners or stately, competent black men are available to demonstrate the bankruptcy of southern white supremacy. For many Americans, particularly liberals, who looked upon the South with dread, the revelation that white southerners were capable of revising their racial views opened the way to more positive imaginings of the South in the late 1960s and 1970s.

As national audiences consumed the Changing South on the screen and on the page, they watched yet another discourse on white southernness play out week after week on 1960s network situation comedies. This Down-Home South characterized white southerners as close to the land, familial, and unaffected by consumer culture. It would influence a variety of Souths imagined by entities as different as the hippie counterculture, Jimmy Carter, and George Wallace. In contrast to the Changing South narrative, the Down-Home South ignored southern racism, thus offering another potent rendering of the region: traditional, simple, decent, and virtually lily-white.

The Down-Home South

Two of the most popular television shows of the 1960s distanced themselves from the southern racial unrest of the era, enabling them to display a wholly celebratory version of white southernness. *The Andy Griffith Show* (CBS, 1960–1968) and *The Beverly Hillbillies* (CBS, 1962–1971) inhabited worlds completely removed from the racial turmoil playing nightly on national news reports about the South. *The Andy Griffith Show* tells the story of Andy Taylor, a folksy, widowed sheriff who is raising his son in the fictional rural small town of Mayberry, North Carolina. *The Beverly Hillbillies* is based on a more outlandish concept: Ozark mountaineer Jed Clampett strikes oil on his property and transplants his nouveau riche family (sassy Granny, fetching Elly May, and simple-minded Jethro) to the land of "swimming pools [and] movie stars." The Down-Home South of *The Andy Griffith Show* and *The Beverly Hillbillies* idealized white southerners—especially those who made their homes in small towns or the countryside), holding them up not as villains, but rather as admirable individuals who possessed deeply rooted, traditional values abandoned by most Americans in their ill-fated modern, consumerist quest. This discourse differentiated itself from other civil-rights-era narratives by presenting an admirable South that was devoid of racial strife (and sorely lacking in nonwhites). The hit ratings of both shows demonstrate that even the powerful Vicious South discourse could not crowd out flattering views of the region and its white inhabitants in the 1960s. Furthermore, their popularity indicates that Americans were capable of holding different versions of the South in their mind simultaneously—and for different reasons—without being overwhelmed by the cognitive dissonance. For Americans alienated by feelings of rootlessness, these two comedy series were perfect; they were all about roots: the roots deeply planted by rural and small-town white southerners that reputedly immunized them against the empty promises of modernity, the anomie and personal dangers of urban life and the blandness of suburban life, and the beckoning of postwar "progress," while inculcating them with the comforts, joys, and nobility of a more authentic lifestyle.

THE DOWN-HOME SOUTH IN MAYBERRY: *THE ANDY GRIFFITH SHOW*

Millions of Americans read the April 1965 article "A Southern Sheriff Faces Some Problems." The title called to mind any number of the southern sheriffs staging rearguard actions to defend white supremacy in their counties. But the piece was not about them; it was instead a *TV Guide* profile of Andy Griffith, the comedy megastar whose eponymous series about a southern sheriff and the people of Mayberry was ending its fifth season, ranked fourth in the Nielsen ratings.[86] Writer Marian Dern phrased the titular "problems" as questions: What was Griffith to do now that Don Knotts, who played his popular sidekick, Deputy Barney Fife, had left to pursue film roles and Jim Nabors, who portrayed mechanic Gomer Pyle, had exited to star on his own popular program, *Gomer Pyle, U.S.M.C.*? Big dilemmas, no doubt, but hardly something on which the fate of an entire region rested.

The article's head-fake title was clever. In the national imagination of the 1960s, two lawmen, Eugene "Bull" Connor and Andy Taylor, stood for contrasting versions of the South. Connor, a real-life Birmingham, Alabama, law enforcement official, ordered his officers to violently protect the racial order in Birmingham. "He possessed the sensibility of a billy goat," *Newsweek* scoffed, and a blind, buffoon-like dedication not to "segregate no niggers and whites together."[87] Andy Taylor offered a stark alternative to the Birmingham Commissioner of Public Safety. In caring for his town's citizens on TV, he exhibited strength, humility, restraint, and humor, as well as a connection to the assertedly empowering qualities of the land. Unconsciously addressing the feelings of rootlessness that pervaded current U.S. cultural discourse, Donald Freeman of the *Saturday Evening Post* referred to the character as "a relaxed, highly competent son of the soil."[88] In other words, Sheriff Taylor is a man almost literally rooted in (and to) his locale. Indisputably, Bull Connor was the more "authentic" of the two—for better or worse, a real person—while Taylor, embodying positive claims about the white South, was born of Hollywood's imagination. Fantasied ideas of a bucolic white South obviously lent themselves to fictional representations. With Vicious South–focused reporting on Connor's state-sponsored violence and other real events unfolding in the region, Andy Taylor's fictional town was a secure terrain upon which these imaginings could be explored.

As scholar Phoebe Bronstein has found, "Andy's masculinity drew from a long lineage of the 'good southerner,' whose good nature becomes visible via his juxtaposition against bad southerners like Bull Connor."[89] Although both Taylor and Connor were white southern lawmen and wielded paternalistic control over their communities, they lived in decidedly different Souths. Connor encountered (and oppressed) a large black community. Andy, meanwhile, rarely sees black faces in Mayberry, and talks to only one black person, his son's football coach, during a single episode in the entire run of the series. Therein lay his powerful, if troubling, appeal: he is a white southerner whose attractive qualities enable him to exist without ever engaging with the racial realities of contemporary southern life. *The Andy Griffith Show*'s widespread popularity demonstrated that one could embrace its folksy, timeless South while keeping the Vicious South of Bull Connor at a safe cognitive distance.

The fictional Mayberry was modeled after Griffith's actual hometown of Mount Airy, North Carolina. Mayberry is miles away, both spatially and emotionally, from the turmoil of the Deep South. It is a place where race is not a problem (a conceit made easier by the near-total absence of nonwhite characters) and where tradition, a slow pace of life, and common sense triumph over the anxieties of the city and consumer culture. *The Andy Griffith Show* furthered its lack of relevance to contemporary events by inhabiting an alternate present. As Griffith told *TV Guide*, "We drive 1963 cars and we dress modern and all the stories seem to be takin' place at the present time, but there are overtones of a past era. It's this sense of nostalgia we create; it's this feeling that Mayberry is timeless."[90] Allison Graham mirrored the star's reflections: "It is this sense of a *remembered* community that is most striking about the series."[91] The distance from current events may have encouraged the sense that the show inhabited a mythical southern past, but nothing in the program hints that the characters exist in any period but the present. The dismissal of the race question was integral to Mayberry's preservation of its bucolic and communal South. Without it, Griffith's idealization of an imagined rural small-town South's purported superiority over the industrial and suburban world would have fallen flat.

The lack of black characters on *The Andy Griffith Show* allowed the program to present an agreeable image of white southernness in the era of civil rights unrest. The Vicious South simply does not exist in Mayberry. As James

Flanagan writes, "Everything that is troubling or volatile about America in the 1960s is not present in *Andy*. Even its fans would have to agree, given the show's era and geographical location, that Mayberry is a charming, folksy picture of pleasant patriarchy and benign whiteness."[92] Allison Graham makes much of the dearth of black characters on the program, arguing, "For a comedy series so intent on capturing an unusual level of emotional realism, the studied remoteness from the connotations of its [southern] setting was remarkable."[93] But the reasons for exclusion are not mysterious and have to do with both television network policy and the desire of the show's creators to maintain the authenticity of its southern mountain town. In large part, network standards mitigated against showing a biracial Mayberry. The three television networks—NBC, ABC, and CBS—carefully controlled the images that they beamed to their viewers. Even as the civil rights movement raised expectations for more inclusiveness on the small screen, executives remained apprehensive about putting blacks on TV.[94] In 1966, NAACP labor secretary Herbert Hill blasted *The Andy Griffith Show* for "never [having] shown a Negro on Camera."[95] The charge was technically untrue, because the show had incorporated some nonspeaking black extras for crowd scenes from the beginning, and a black character would have a major speaking role the following year, the only time this happened in the history of the series. It is also important to note that although the black population of North Carolina was roughly 25 percent in 1960, in Surry County, the site of Mount Airy, blacks made up less than 6 percent.[96] Still, Hill spoke an important truth: this was a show fundamentally about white people in a region (the South) that in reality was both white *and* black.

Griffith responded to the minor racial flap somewhat awkwardly, claiming, "We're not trying to avoid anything," while suggesting that introducing race into Mayberry would open the door to troubles in the town. "In a series like *Dr. Kildare*, for instance, you can have any number of Negro doctors," he said. "It's logical; it's a big hospital in a big city. But put a Negro doctor in a town like Mayberry and the people most probably wouldn't go to him. A story like ours, which is set in a small Southern town, just naturally leaves itself open for problems—especially when the show is comedy."[97] Griffith understood that a series about white southerners that featured black characters would have undermined the pleasantness of his televisual and bucolic South. To rehabilitate white southerners during the civil rights era, the easiest solution was to remove the black people they menaced each night on national news broadcasts.

In other important ways, *The Andy Griffith Show*'s Down-Home South created an out-of-time sensation for 1960s viewers. For one thing, it offered them an alternative to the supposedly corrupting influences of other contemporary TV programs. "The networks are so full of shooting, fighting, and killing," grumbled Chicago's Delores Perry, "that it is a pleasure to view this easy-going type of show."[98] More broadly, *The Andy Griffith Show* marked "an illusory return to innocence," stated Donald Freeman, "to a time and place slipped forever out of reach."[99] Freeman may have been referring to the show's soothing magic for the volatile Griffith, but he insinuated that it played similarly for its millions of viewers. The show's producers sympathized with many of the era's cultural commentators in their critique of America's urban violence, suburban blandness, and social anomie. But they did so in such a way that did not seem preachy. The show enveloped viewers in its tightly knit southern community and its residents' lives. These folksy characters enticed Americans fascinated by the fabled "good old days," as Griffith well understood when he discussed the role of nostalgia in building adoration for the show. As *Variety* noted in its review of a 1963 episode, the program was tailored to viewers who "like to look backward sentimentally and escape the complexities of life as it has been lived and is being lived."[100]

This escape was made possible, fundamentally, by the sheriff's benevolent and fair personality. In nearly every episode, he helps the townspeople to avoid questionable situations, saves the hapless Deputy Barney Fife from (greater) embarrassment, and selflessly gives others credit for his ideas. The show's producer called Griffith's character "Lincolnesque," an interesting adjective for a white southern character. The description fit, though, because there is no mistaking Andy's southernness. After all, he is a *good* southerner, the kind from whom nonsoutherners could learn a thing or two. In the words of *Baltimore Sun* critic Donald Kirkley, Sheriff Taylor is "a shrewd, easy going man with a keen sense of humor and a wonderful tolerance for the faults of his neighbors."[101] (To be fair, Andy does lose his cool on occasion, but only after Barney or other townspeople have annoyed him incessantly.) He is also a *good* American then—just as all-American, kind-hearted, and wise as Lincoln. In addition to the upright and eminently honest Andy, Mayberry is populated by southern stock characters whose personalities are presented as emblematic of their rural and small-town background.[102] These characters include the country rubes Gomer and Goober Pyle; the nervous, bumbling Barney; the doting, domestic goddess Aunt Bee; and the precocious Opie. Viewers alternately laughed with and at the residents of Mayberry. For instance, they could chuckle along with Andy, and admire his keen insight into the human condition, as he attempts to counter comic foil Barney's delusions of authority and overzealousness in performing his duties.

Even when using them for laughs, the series treats its characters in a warm-hearted manner and as decidedly superior to more "modern" Americans. The show's writers, for example, frequently penned story lines in which an outsider—often a city dweller—visits Mayberry and learns an important lesson about the virtues of the small town and its values. According to Gustavo Pérez Firmat, such "intruder" episodes (composing roughly a third of the series) highlight one of the fundamental traits of the town's residents: their resistance to change.[103] Often the fast-talking, frequently scheming visitors who dropped in from week to week represent the modernity that Mayberrians spurn. In other cases, they signify a general rootlessness. Episodes revolving around drifters explicitly designate outside society as lacking in direction and continuity. When a vagabond named Dave Browne (played by Buddy Ebsen, later Jed Clampett in *The Beverly Hillbillies*) passes through Mayberry, he proves to be a bad influence on young Opie, who opts for the fishing hole over the schoolhouse ("Opie's Hobo Friend"). Andy tells Browne that he must cease his friendship with his son. The hobo replies that the choice belongs to Opie, leading to the following exchange:

ANDY: No, I'm afraid it don't work that way. You can't let a young'un decide for himself. He'll grab at the first flashy thing with shiny ribbons on it. Then when he finds out there's a hook in it, it's too late. Wrong ideas come packaged with so much glitter it's hard to convince them that other things might be better in the long run. All a parent can do is say, wait, trust me. And try to keep temptation away.

MR. DAVE: That means that you're inviting me to leave.

ANDY: That's right.

MR. DAVE: Well, you're wearing the badge, so I'll leave. That wasn't so difficult. Your problem's solved.

ANDY: That's where you're wrong. That boy thinks just about everything you do is perfect. So my problem is just beginning. You left behind an awful lot of unscrambling to be done.[104]

With this brief scene, episode writer Harvey Bullock managed to sum up the series' consistent critique of an aimless, consumer-oriented society that was corrupting Americans, who, like Opie, were all too willing to "grab at the first flashy thing with shiny ribbons on it."

The episode "Man in a Hurry" (1963) offers another prime example of *The Andy Griffith Show*'s antimodern, anticonsumerist, antiurban ethos. The story involves a businessman from the city who is stranded after his car breaks down outside Mayberry. He becomes annoyed when repairs are delayed and he is forced to endure the company of the easygoing townspeople.[105] Although initially reluctant, he eventually comes around and heeds the residents' invitation, according to scholar Don Rodney Vaughan, "to try to relax and enjoy the simple things."[106] The obvious celebration of rural, small-town values at the expense of urban bustle and agitation is undeniable, with the businessman fabricating another car problem so he can stay in town an extra day. The episode ends with the man fast asleep in a rocking chair on Andy's front porch. A partially peeled apple rests in his hand. He has finally succumbed to the take-your-time ethos of his newly beloved Mayberry.[107]

The power of *The Andy Griffith Show* in the 1960s lay not in its realism but rather in its presentation of "southern" authenticity apparently lacking in the rest of contemporary American culture. Show chronicler Richard Kelly has written more recently of the importance of Mayberry in counteracting "our middle-class, technological society" in which people feel detached from their fellow humans and community.[108] Indeed, the series' themes acted as a counterweight to the nation's consumerism and increasing reliance on technology. *The Andy Griffith Show* is most certainly escapist, but it carries an unequivocal critique of modernity in its celebration of rural and small-town southern life. After the program's immensely popular original run ended in 1968, it continued in syndication. A 1970 national survey revealed reruns performing better in nonsouthern than in southern urban markets.[109] This popularity suggests the mythic clout of Mayberry's pastoral southernness as a safe zone from the rootlessness at the core of American life.

THE DOWN-HOME SOUTH MEETS SUNNY, DECEITFUL CALIFORNIA:
THE BEVERLY HILLBILLIES

The Beverly Hillbillies conveys a similar message about the value of an inveterate southern existence—this time exclusively rural. But whereas Griffith and his collaborators strived to create a semiveracious TV version of white southern life, verisimilitude seemed of little concern to creator Paul Henning and his team. The white southerners of the *Hillbillies* are caricatures, although many Americans probably unthinkingly accepted them as fairly authentic representations of little-understood southern mountain people. It is ironic that a show that critiqued the banality of postwar American life was itself a prosaic, modern creation. Such was the power of the Down-Home South.

Like *The Andy Griffith Show*, the near total absence of black characters on *The Beverly Hillbillies* made the show's southernness more viable to its millions of viewers. It taught them that erasing was easier than confronting the weighty problem of white southern racism. Even if Granny occasionally discusses the "War between the States," and in one episode confuses the nearby filming of a Civil War movie with the actual reigniting of the conflict itself, the show is nearly silent on the issue of race.[110] A notable exception is the 1970 episode "Simon Legree Drysdale." Mr. Drysdale is the Clampetts' banker and next-door neighbor. While staying at the Clampett mansion, one of Mr. Drysdale's secretaries, Jean (played by black actress and *Playboy* playmate Jeannie Bell in one of her five appearances on the show), decides to help out with the chores. During a visit, her brothers see her performing menial tasks wearing old-timey garb and jump to the conclusion that Mr. Drysdale has—that is right—enslaved her. More misunderstandings ensue, as expected, and Mr. Drysdale ends the episode locked in a cage.[111] Although the episode works only if one has knowledge of American slavery and its title references the vicious slavemaster in Harriet Beecher Stowe's 1852 abolitionist novel *Uncle Tom's Cabin*, its racial politics are clunky and tasteless. "Simon Legree Drysdale" does not have anything—let alone anything serious—to say about race or race relations. Jean's supposed "enslavement" was simply more goofy fodder for the show's writers.

"Simon Legree Drysdale" stands out for its unusual, by *The Beverly Hillbillies'* standards, inclusion of prominent black performers and allusions to racial concerns. By taking the Clampetts out of the South, their distance from the southern civil rights anguish of the era was less noticeable—if one were willing to forget about West Coast raced-based incidents like the 1965 Watts Riots that played out near the fictional Clampetts' new home. After all, in contrast to the blatant discrimination carried out by whites against blacks in the South, the deep and—for many Americans—difficult-to-grasp structural inequalities that undergirded urban rebellions outside of the South in the mid- to late 1960s did not lend themselves as easily to the scapegoating of racist individuals or groups. Making the Clampett clan an Ozark family also mitigated against viewers comparing them to the angry Deep South whites who were ubiquitous in Vicious South television and print coverage. Mayberry is nearly uniformly white. Similarly, the mountainous Missouri Ozarks of the Clampetts has traditionally been considered a bastion of whiteness.[112] Regardless, it is conspicuous that a show casting white southerners as clownish, but ultimately lovable and wiser than their nonsouthern counterparts, enjoyed an unprecedented popularity, premiering as it did during the Ole Miss integration crisis.

The *Hillbillies* episodes occur mostly outside of the South, far from Oxford, Mississippi, and other sites of the civil rights struggle. The sitcom functions as a fish-out-of-water comedy, with the rural foibles of the main characters differentiated from the actions of snooty Southern Californians who often lack the hillbillies' common sense. The show does offer viewers an opportunity to laugh at the outsized mountain people stereotypes as manifested in Jethro's stupidity and Elly May's animal husbandry skills. Audiences in the 1960s could also find humor in the always overzealous Granny's use of their mansion's swimming pool, or "ce-ment pond," as a giant washtub, or the family's confusion of the pool table for a dinner table.[113] Still, the characters, or "nature's noble savages," as *Washington Post* columnist Lawrence Laurent termed them, are not simply punch lines.[114] Paul Henning suggested as much in describing the apparent care with which he researched Ozark culture and, according to the *Saturday Evening Post*, his desire to implant an "ancient authenticity" in his characters.[115] He failed decidedly in this task, but he achieved something much more significant: he and his writers consistently presented the Clampetts' rural ways as superior to the practices of their rich, citified neighbors.

Despite the show's silly antics and Henning's claim that "there's no message except 'have fun,'" *The Beverly Hillbillies'* critique of 1960s society, along with its accompanying greed and materialism, is clear.[116] The upended Clampett clan might at first glance appear to suffer from the same rootlessness as the rest of society. But, as the series demonstrates, despite their best efforts, the people of California cannot change these Ozark folks. They remain people of the soil—like Andy Taylor and his fellow Mayberrians—firmly entrenched in their traditional rural values of hard work, simplicity, honesty, and, above all, commitment to family. As David Farber has argued, "In both *The Beverly Hillbillies* and . . . [The] *Andy Griffith Show*, the moral integrity of a consumer-based lifestyle—as against a rooted way of life—was sharply and unceasingly mocked."[117] Jed and his clan enjoy a sudden, dizzying transition to prosperity, one to which they never fully adjust over the course of the series. They continue to hold fast to their way of life, except for fleeting moments like when Jethro briefly finds himself the anointed leader of the Sunset Strip hippies, which results in the show lampooning the counterculture's supposed ridiculousness and vacuity.[118]

Importantly, *The Beverly Hillbillies'* rejection of technology and consumer culture fit into widely held cultural concerns and anticipated later imaginings of the South that censured modern U.S. society. Jed's family never loses its identity and always triumphs over its Southern California neighbors, who are often the epitomes of deceitfulness and consumerism. For instance, the Drysdales are money grubbers who condescend to the "peasant" hillbillies. Mr. Drysdale soothes his ragged nerves by smelling a stack of cash. Other outsiders to the southern mountain tradition constantly seek to defraud the hillbillies, thinking that the family's lack of sophistication indicates an innate stupidity. Yet the joke is on them, as the Clampetts, particularly the commonsensical Jed, always stifle their schemes. "The program therefore presents modern America, at least superficially, as venal, boorish, materialistic, and, ultimately, ethically and spiritually hollow," Anthony Harkins explains in his study of hillbilly iconography.[119] This portrayal of the white South, particularly its rural areas, and accompanying negative depiction of the contemporary United States defines the former's values as morally superior to those of the rootless non-South.

Not surprisingly, many television critics lambasted the program's broad comedy as pandering to the lowest common denominator. United Press International (UPI) wrote that "the series aimed low and hit its target," while the *New York Times* bewailed its "rural no-think."[120] "The more harsh critics of the TV scene," surmised *Los Angeles Times* columnist Hal Humphrey, "say such low-brow corn [as *The Beverly Hillbillies*] is proof positive that a majority of home viewers are little better than morons."[121] Some viewers were equally unimpressed. William R. Kimball of Ogden, Utah, reproved it as "the trashiest, most inane TV show that one could imagine."[122] Such vitriol did not seem to exist for *The Andy Griffith Show*. In part, this must have had to do with the more believable characters that populated Mayberry and a premise based on Griffith's own upbringing. "For a half hour each week," a 1963 *TV Guide* article on *The Andy Griffith Show*'s popularity claimed, "viewers can feel warm and comfortable in a dream town," but one that the likes of *The Music Man* composer Meredith Willson claimed was locked into the reality of small-town life.[123]

The obvious silliness of the *Hillbillies* hardly held back the show, which quickly shot to number one in the ratings, and it had its defenders, too. Kansas City's Paul E. Robinson parroted fans of *The Andy Griffith Show* who appreciated the *Hillbillies*' wholesomeness and refusal to "exalt moral degeneracy" (perhaps he had missed Elly May in her tight jeans, which, *Time* mused, actress Donna Douglas "somehow wears . . . as if they were a bikini").[124] Fans like Robinson were not alone in praising the show, with some reviewers appreciating Jed and his cohorts' *Andy Griffith*–like critique of modernity. Arnold Hano recognized *The Beverly Hillbillies*' antiurban bent and its proposal for "a return to . . . natural ways." Robert Lewis Shayon, writing in the high-brow journal *Saturday Review*, called it a "challenge to our money oriented value system" and "valid social criticism."[125] The show's cornball factor, then, did not fully obscure its cultivation of supposedly authentic rural southern characteristics.

Like the slew of other rural-oriented sitcoms, including *Green Acres*, *Petticoat Junction*, and the *Andy Griffith Show* spinoff *Mayberry R.F.D.*, *The Beverly Hillbillies* fell victim to declining, if still respectable, ratings, particularly among urban viewers. CBS President Bob Wood responded by tearing apart the schedule, initiating the "rural purge" of 1970–1971. "They cancelled every-thing with a tree," quipped *Green Acres* actor Pat Buttram, "including *Lassie*."[126] Replacing these programs were ones deemed by the network as more socially relevant, such as the urban-centered comedies *All in the Family* and *The Mary Tyler Moore Show*. Anthony Harkins infers that the declining popularity of shows set in or near the country—and "hillbilly vogue"—stemmed from "the country los[ing] interest in Appalachia as a 'problem region.'"[127] The actual reason was probably more simple: viewers had overdosed on formulaic rural sitcoms and now longed for something else. As Harkins notes, near the end of its run, *The Beverly Hillbillies* had drifted from its rock-solid premise: "Whereas the Clampetts were once emblematic of both rustic farce and bed-rock American virtue, they now increasingly stood only for the former."[128]

While they lasted, *The Beverly Hillbillies* and *The Andy Griffith Show*'s "southern" values were prized by many viewers worried about the state of modern society. The imagined Souths of these television programs embod-ied antithetical values to those promoted in the rapidly expanding, urban-based consumer culture of the time. Their creators combined escapism with trenchant social analysis, allowing viewers to name, but also to defuse, their prominent cultural anxieties in the dreamed-up worlds of Mayberry and a Beverly Hills invaded by the Clampetts.

It would be easy to argue that these TV comedies' rendering of the Down-Home South was completely adversarial to various media manifestations of the Vicious South; however, a closer look at these series' near erasure of nonwhites disturbingly suggests a kinship between the two narratives for those Americans interested in making the connection. One could interpret the shows' racial omissions as implying that black southerners were the cause of the South's racial problems, since apparently only by shuttling them to the background and making them almost completely voiceless could southern life on TV achieve a state of wholesomeness bordering on perfection. This undercurrent surely fed some whites' unrealistic and damaging nostalgia for a supposedly tranquil pre–civil rights movement America and South, before black southern "agitators" upset this "Down-Home" peacefulness. Along these lines, Phoebe Bronstein has detailed the racist connotations of *The Andy Griffith Show*, helpfully drawing on cultural theorist Stuart Hall's notion of "inferential racism," a surreptitious bigotry that "enable[s] racist sentiments to be formulated without ever bringing into awareness the racist predicates on which the statements are grounded."[129] As Bronstein writes, "Mayberry remained a world constructed by white supremacy and longing for a time that never was."[130] Although not overtly racist like the Vicious South, the benign characterizations of the white South on *The Andy Griffith Show* and

The Beverly Hillbillies carried a similar and equally pernicious meaning and message: white southerners were committed to a white supremacist society in which they would prefer to keep blacks in the background or out of the picture entirely.

Conclusion

The three most prominent discourses about the South during the 1960s civil rights movement—the Vicious, Changing, and Down-Home Souths—served specific cultural needs while also providing the raw materials for imaginings of the South during the next decade and a half. The Vicious South narrative, while perhaps most familiar to Americans during the period, did not preclude these other prevalent views. The Vicious South offered liberals a worthy scapegoat for American racism. It largely identified those problems as peculiarly the fault of white southerners, whom popular media showed departing from mainstream American values. At the same time, the Vicious South's othering of white southerners also cast them as manly, violent figures who refused to give into (for some whites) unwanted social change. That faith in white southern virility would form the centerpiece of politically and culturally conservative Americans' use of the Masculine South discourse in the late 1960s and early 1970s. The Changing South trope, in contrast, lent hope to the possibility of attaining the elusive goal of national unity and triumphing over racial division without abandoning the Vicious South's idea that the region's primary problem was racist whites. The Changing South would influence future imaginings by allowing liberal Americans to think of racism as more than simply a white southern problem. In other words, it helped to mitigate the biggest flaw in the South's image. While racial problems infused the Vicious and Changing South discourses, they were totally absent from the Down-Home South narrative as played out on popular television comedies in the 1960s. Even at the height of black-white turmoil in the Deep South, the immensely popular *Andy Griffith Show* and *Beverly Hillbillies* celebrated a white South far removed from contemporary racial unrest. The programs' antimodern critique of postwar U.S. consumer society and celebration of an idyllic—and dyed-in-the-wool—small-town and rural white South anticipated many future manifestations of the imagined white South.

These different Souths obviously functioned in very different genres. Although certainly the Vicious South would appear in fictional representations, it remained most powerful in nonfictional coverage. Why? Namely, because, despite media distortions, it told a true story about white southerners' campaign to preserve the Jim Crow order. Plus, much of the on-the-ground reporting (whether by news outlets or by writers like Steinbeck and Griffin) was visceral in such a way that it could not be replicated as powerfully by fictional treatments, both serious, like J. Lee Thompson's *Cape Fear* and Roger Corman's *The Intruder* (both 1962), and trashy, such as the rash of 1960s southern exploitation films.[131] Comedic approaches to such material would have simply been inappropriate. The Down-Home South, on the other hand, reveled in comedic fantasies, in part as a necessary step in distancing its white southern characters from those shown denying black southerners their civil rights on the front pages of newspapers and on televised news reports.

Comedy, coupled with convenient plot devices (placing Mayberry in the white-dominated mountains of North Carolina and moving the Clampetts out of the South to an ultra-wealthy white enclave) gave viewers license to consider white southerners in an environment in which race did not seem to play a role. The redemption narrative behind the progressive Changing South was too centered on past (and present) racism to allow for uniformly laudatory treatments of white southerners. Race had to be practically obliterated in order for Americans to embrace the beguiling features of an imagined (and frequently rural) South. For this task, the Down-Home South was perfectly suited.

By the end of the 1960s, the image of the white southerner stood available to meet the cultural needs of a variety of Americans. Drawing on the Changing South's fairly nuanced understanding of white southern bigotry and the Down-Home South's celebration of rural living, elements of the hippie counterculture cradled white southernness as a collection of noble, long-forgotten values, perfectly suited to their critique of an impersonal, rootless, and technocratic "Amerika." Their primary vessel was a strange musical hybrid: country-rock.

CHAPTER 2

"This World from the Standpoint of a Rocking Chair"

Country-Rock and the South in the
Countercultural Imagination

In March 1968 the Byrds flew south to Nashville—a city the band's bassist Chris Hillman called "the motherland" of country music—to record tracks for their upcoming Columbia Records album.[1] The LP that emerged in part from those sessions, *Sweetheart of the Rodeo*, marked the first major effort by a rock act to fuse rock 'n' roll with country and western. Was this the same folk-rock sensation that had extolled the virtues of traveling "Eight Miles High" two years earlier? Whereas that song had rocketed to number 14 on the *Billboard* Hot 100, *Sweetheart of the Rodeo* peaked at a disappointing 77th on the magazine's LP chart.

The album also was a dud among traditional country music audiences. This failure was foreshadowed in the Byrds' negative reception on the Grand Ole Opry. Not long after the *Sweetheart* Nashville sessions began, the group's manager convinced the program's producers to place the Byrds on the 15 March bill. During the performance at the historic Ryman Auditorium, some in the crowd greeted the—by Nashville standards—long-haired performers with catcalls of "tweet, tweet" and "cut your hair."[2] The band heard some clapping—although that may have been due to the show's electronic applause signs—as it made its way through a Merle Haggard tune and an original by new member Gram Parsons. The Byrds exited the stage and were quickly accosted by hostile producers and musicians, angered by Parsons's refusal to stick to the prescribed set list.[3] "They don't fancy rock groups down there," bandleader Roger McGuinn later told the countercultural music magazine *Rolling Stone*, "not on [the] Grand Ole Opry."[4]

The Byrds may have not captured the attention of the Nashville establishment or national country and pop audiences with *Sweetheart of the Rodeo*, but they joined an all-star roster of rock artists experimenting with country music in the late 1960s and early 1970s. At this time, Bob Dylan, Buffalo Springfield, the Flying Burrito Brothers, Linda Ronstadt, Dillard & Clark, the Band, and numerous others infused their music with a country sound, dubbed country-rock by the music press. While some of these acts enjoyed strong overall sales, they found some of their biggest supporters in a niche market: the hippie counterculture.

What was this counterculture? Attempting to reconcile various scholarly views, one historian usefully classifies it as "nothing less than the desire by lots of people, a great many of them young, to gain a greater sense of personal authenticity in less rigid circumstances without being restrained by prior social hierarchies and belligerent geo-political claims."[5] To discuss the views of the overwhelmingly white counterculture, I am relying primarily on writings of the "underground press." These publications emerged in mostly urban centers throughout the country in the mid- to late 1960s. They represented a merging of New Left and countercultural sensibilities.[6] In my analysis of these publications, I prefer to use the terms "counterculture," "countercultural," and "hippie" to discuss hip youths' reactions to country-rock music and southernness, as it reveals an investment in cultural rebellion against the confines of modern, "technocratic" society most strongly tied to hippie culture. But in doing so, I am also able to track the sentiments of New Left adherents writing for the underground press, engaged in what historian Doug Rossinow has termed a "countercultural turn," or an adoption of the cultural strategies and goals of the counterculture.[7] My less distinguishing treatment of "New Left" and "countercultural" views is necessary, and only acknowledges what was already obvious by the late 1960s: that these publications were a hybrid voice of the New Left and the counterculture and that the two movements themselves were increasingly difficult to distinguish.[8]

Counterculturists were not the only new audience for country music.[9] By 1968 its popularity had spread far from the cradle of the South, with the genre enjoying a sizable blue-collar audience and heavy radio airplay throughout the country. It remained, though, for many Americans—hippies included—a deeply southern cultural expression. When the Byrds performed in Nashville, they crossed cultural lines in two ways: they publicly merged rock and country styles, and they brought together a West Coast countercultural ethos and white southern culture. The Byrds were hip, but not hippies; they were wealthy rock stars recording for a multimillion-dollar conglomerate. Their largely countercultural audience, however, many of them already suspicious of the blanket condemnations of the South à la the Vicious South discourse, welcomed country-rock as an opportunity to explore new musical terrain and the enticing—and deeply rooted—culture of an imagined white South.

The countercultural interest in country music makes little sense if one considers it as simply the music of a backward, racist people. Although some hippies certainly felt this way, others saw in both country and the largely white southern culture from which it sprang tools for their fight against the stagnancy of so-called mainstream American society. Still others, reflecting the viewpoint adopted by some young left-wing politicos in the late 1960s, believed the musical style could act as a point of commonality in their effort to ally themselves with white working-class Americans. As alternative sounds, country music appealed to counterculturists who felt burned out by what they saw as the chaotic condition of U.S. society, where political unrest and race riots had become all too frequent. Envisioning the white South, then, was another variation of "dropping out" for interested hippies.

Countercultural newspapers regularly contained snippets of the Down-Home South discourse, celebrating the white South as a rural refuge from the problems associated with rootlessness and soul-sucking modern practices and technologies. But while hip supporters of long-haired country typically rejected the Vicious South portrait of white southerners that most of them grew up watching on TV news coverage of the civil rights movement, they did not ignore white southern racism. Rather, according to underground press accounts, they cast racism as an *American* problem, not a distinctly southern one. Hippies, like fans of Down-Home South sitcoms during the 1960s, thus freed themselves to invoke a traditional (and in this case predominantly rural) South in their critique of Amerika, in which white southerners were no more responsible than white nonsoutherners for the country's racial ills.

To be sure, not every counterculturist was enamored of country and country-rock music. Some flayed country-rock as "a hype started by the [music] industry to sell some more records."[10] Others, as one hip record reviewer claimed, could not find an entry point into something so "culturally foreign" as country music.[11] Through their frequent embrace of country-rock, however, underground press writers espousing countercultural values frequently imagined white southernness as a celebration of community, family connections, closeness to the land, and, perhaps most importantly—and nebulously—authenticity in a rural setting. All of these characteristics were connected to the desire to recover "roots." "The new left's search for authenticity," Doug Rossinow asserts, "was expressed most often as a conflict between the *artificial* and the *natural*."[12] The same holds true for the counterculture's own "search for authenticity," which simultaneously rejected the commercialized culture of what historian Lizabeth Cohen has termed the Consumers' Republic.[13]

Country-rock was important culturally for two major reasons. First, it provided a powerful avenue for hippies to utilize mythical white southern traits as part of a critique of modern American society. Second, the widespread popularity among hippies of the Byrds and other bands that were even more focused on presenting backwoods southern sounds and imagery—especially *the* Band—reminds us that the countercultural vision of the South was not simply an antimodern tool against the technocracy; some hippies also deemed it an escape from the real and imagined political and social turmoil and rootlessness of the late 1960s and early 1970s. It was part of a similar impulse in mainstream U.S. society, the one that led Americans to idolize *The Andy Griffith Show* and *The Beverly Hillbillies* and gaze hopefully at a Changing South. The sounds of country-rock and its accompanying response among hippies and straight Americans represented another important demonstration of the South of the Mind's pull.

The Southernness and Authenticity of Country Music

In recent decades, scholars have granted country music considerable attention, frequently concluding that its reputation as a strictly southern art form has been overstated. James Gregory notes that "country music historians typically stress the music's close connection to the culture of the rural and working-class white South, and while acknowledging the importance of New York record companies and other commercial structures, they are happiest telling the story of Jimmie Rodgers, the Carter family, Roy Acuff, and other great musicians who reshaped the sounds and styles of country music while remaining in the South."[14] Scholar Gerald W. Haslam has gone further, suggesting that "the fertile crescent" of country music is not the Deep South, but rather central and western Texas and Oklahoma, which "escaped reb[el] homogeneity in their populations and music."[15] Haslam argues that while the South has played a major role in creating and nurturing country music, the "southernness" of the genre has been exaggerated in large part because of Nashville's consolidation of commercial country music in the mid-twentieth century. His *Workin' Man Blues: Country Music in California* makes a convincing case for the strength of country music outside of the confines of Music City.

Haslam's book holds important implications for the study of country-rock's creators, many of whom grew up absorbing the ample country-themed television and radio offerings broadcast on Golden State stations after World War II. For example, Chris Hillman of the Byrds and the Flying Burrito Brothers first took up the mandolin and got his start playing in bluegrass bands.[16] By the early 1960s, Bakersfield, California, had emerged as a western home to country music, an alternative to Nashville. Popular artists like Buck Owens and Merle Haggard launched the Bakersfield Sound, a response to the slick, orchestrated Nashville Sound of the 1950s and 1960s, that featured the distinctive twang of Telecaster guitars, a heavy backbeat, and prominent pedal steel guitars. Rock artists who dabbled in country music, virtually all of whom were connected with the California music scene, often preferred—and deemed as more authentic—Owens's and Haggard's harder edged recordings over the current "countrypolitan" Nashville style, and "claimed to be heirs to the Bakersfield Sound," in musicologist Olivia Carter Mather's estimation.[17] As the Grateful Dead's Jerry Garcia claimed, "We're kind of on the far fringe of it, but we're part of that California Bakersfield school of country-and-western rock 'n' roll—Buck Owens, Merle Haggard."[18] Chris Hillman added, "Without [Buck Owens] . . . there might not have been . . . that country-rock left turn so to speak."[19] Even so, country-rock musicians also idolized the older traditional styles of southern country artists, who they saw as helping to form the core of country music, and covered their songs alongside those of Haggard and Owens. In the liner notes of his 1970 album *Magnetic South*, former Monkee and country-rock pioneer Michael Nesmith reflected on his relationship to country music. He cited Jimmie Rodgers, Hank Williams, and rock 'n' roller turned country star Jerry Lee Lewis—all southerners—as "to me something of a musical triumvirate. Somehow I always get back to them."[20]

By molding a southern musical form to relate to a West Coast context, country-rock musicians invented a brand of country music that encouraged counterculturists to similarly bend the image of the South to fit their needs. Indeed, prior to 1968 and the proliferation of country-rock recordings, hip youths and country music rarely mixed. Pamela Des Barres, famed groupie and dedicated Flying Burrito Brothers fan, conjured visions of southern rednecks when she recalled, "I had always thought of country music as lame and corny, played by backwoods guys with crew cuts."[21]

The relevant question is not whether country music was primarily southern, but whether counterculturists—not the artists themselves—interpreted it in this way. The conventional wisdom of the 1960s and 1970s (and later), as Haslam admits, portrayed this music as southern. Nashville's hold on the country music industry after World War II and its delicate exhibition of the genre as universal yet distinctly (and distinctively) southern contributed to this popular view.[22] In his seminal study *Country Music, U.S.A.*, first published in 1968, historian Bill C. Malone, added another reason for the perception of the music as southern: its origins in the southland. "Commercial country music," he reasoned, "developed out of the folk culture of the rural South."[23] As late as 2002, Malone would claim that "although country music has reached out to the world, it has nevertheless preserved a special relationship with the South."[24] There is no doubt that in part due to the increasingly smooth sounds of Nashville, country music had gone national by the end of the 1960s, gaining outstanding popularity with nonsouthern working-class audiences. But in identifying the music's ongoing romance with the South, contemporary commentators also maintained that country music remained rooted in a southern milieu. Southern journalist Paul Hemphill's 1970 book *The Nashville Sound: Bright Lights and Country Music* detailed the many shifts in modern country and western, from its nonsouthern popularity to its dynamic sound. For Hemphill, though, one could not disconnect country from its origins. "Country music has always been the soul music of the white South," he wrote.[25] And, as Chris Hillman and his fellow Byrds well knew, "Nashville is and always has been the spiritual home of country music," a glitzy urban mecca for a rural southern form.[26] Other observers, like sociologists John D. McCarthy, Richard A. Peterson, and William L. Yancey, held that even by 1972 country's fans remained "predominantly southern and white."[27]

Many writers in the nation's hundreds of underground newspapers, awash in a mixture of New Left politics and countercultural ideas, argued along similar lines. The *Berkeley Barb* described the southern and rural tilt of "the traditional country and western market."[28] Baltimore's *Harry* stated that country was perceived negatively by "non-Southern, non-hip listeners."[29] Country music, then, was strongly connected to southernness in both popular and countercultural imaginations. By visualizing the music as southern, counterculturists were free to interpret it as a window into the region's culture and values.

Country, Rock, Country-Rock, and the Counterculture's Quest for Authenticity

Country music—and its southernness—could not (and cannot) be extricated from questions of authenticity. Counterculturists' mission to live free of artifice could assume multiple forms, including, as David Farber elaborates, lifestyles that were about "creating institutions, vocations, enterprises, and opportunities built not on stoned indifference but on active social engagement and community-oriented hard work."[30] Hippies' forays into country music represented an attempt to make the countercultural lifestyle function using the music of the rural white South. Hippies drew upon the notion, later supported by the research of Bill Malone, that the connection between working-class white southernness and country music was inescapable. Analyzing the southern expression "don't get above your raisin," Malone calls it "a rebuke to pretense and snobbery, and a plea for respect for and loyalty to one's roots."[31] Here one can see the concept of community, familial closeness, and strong bonds that counterculturists found so lacking in the postwar United States. "This egalitarian philosophy," Malone continues, "has been a central facet of the thinking of southern working people, and it has long been a unifying, but hard to maintain, theme of the music that they have bequeathed to the world."[32]

It is of course ironic that in attempting to recover the values of rural white southerners, country-rock musicians and counterculturists bobbed to the beat of a highly commercialized, technology-driven form of music. Then again, hippies had managed to rationalize their embrace of similarly fraught rock music. According to historian Michael J. Kramer, while hippies wrung their hands over fears of cultural co-optation, they also looked to new forms of communication and technology as channels through which to explore untapped avenues of community and citizenship.[33] As a result, it is inaccurate to label the counterculture "anti-technology." In analyzing Ken Kesey's "Acid Tests," freak-out events in the 1965 and 1966 San Francisco Bay Area that combined LSD, acid rock, film projection, bizarre PA announcements, and a general "let-your-freak-flag-fly" mentality, Kramer concludes, "the goal was to repurpose the tools of electronic technology that seemed to be dominating and deadening postwar life. If the wavelengths of mass-mediation were beamed down to the people by the mainstream forces of Cold War America, if the spaces of associational life in the country were dominated by unidirectional messages from centralized powers, then at the Acid Tests the ambition was to realize a culture of participatory democracy by putting the multi in multimedia."[34] Granted, 1960s country music was no less commodified or technology-reliant than acid rock, but its traditional connections to rural working-class southern life surely mitigated similar hippie concerns about more psychedelic sounds.

Even if counterculturists were generally accepting of the commerce and technology that abetted acid rock, some of them longed for other, more "authentic" sounds. Country could be a viable substitute. Acid rock acted as an accompaniment to the use of hallucinogenic drugs. Bands performing in this style relied on long, drawn-out songs and guitar solos and light shows to enhance the experience of tripping on LSD, mescaline, or other psychedelics. (It is no accident that San Francisco's acid rock innovators the Grateful Dead were frequent participants in Kesey's Acid Tests.) As early as the end of 1967, just months after San Francisco's Haight-Ashbury hippie scene had reached its pinnacle, some counterculturists were growing tired of the psychedelic style. The inaugural issue of Philadelphia's underground publication the *Distant Drummer* was blunt: "The entire drug/music scene is wretched. Psychedelic sounds are simply dreadful; musically and chemically." The author also bemoaned the scene's exploitation by market-driven "hucksters" and designated it as "phony" and "false."[35] "Nowadays," Ithaca's *First Issue* complained, "the average high school rocker reads charts with fifteen polyrhythmic changes and is expected to cut all the standard Coltrane and Stravinsky licks."[36] Simply put, psychedelic-drug-fueled music was overly complicated and lacking in authenticity. Several underground press writers looked to country-rock as a remedy. In February 1969, *First Issue* praised the "humility and conservatism" of rockers like Dylan, the Byrds, and the Band, all of whose recent records had drawn on country and western.[37] Likewise, the *Berkeley Barb* commended Dylan's twangy *Nashville Skyline* for recovering the simplicity of early rock 'n' roll.[38] It also explicitly advised readers to abandon worn-out sounds and head for the fresher pastures of country-rock: "If you're tired of clumsy psychedelic bands and synthetic folk, it's time to give [country-rockers] Commander Cody [and His Lost Planet Airmen] a listen."[39]

The term "country-rock" bears no stable meaning. Most of its practitioners despised the label, with Gram Parsons calling it a "plastic dry fuck."[40] Linda Ronstadt characterized the genre's sound more charitably as "weld[ing] country music songs and harmonies to a rock-and-roll rhythm section."[41] That usually meant the use of country instrumentation like pedal steel guitars, banjos, and fiddles with a heavier emphasis on bass and drums. Still, such definitions are inadequate. Consider, after all, the rock-influenced and, to use Richard Peterson's term, "hard-core" (i.e., country music perceived to be more traditional and authentic than the pop orientation of "soft-shell" country like countrypolitan) sounds of Merle Haggard and Buck Owens that listeners nevertheless universally recognized as country music.[42] The most accurate, but also the broadest, definition of country-rock is music played by long-haired musicians, typically from a rock background (and perhaps before that a folk background) that mostly eschewed the slick production stylings of the Nashville Sound. This definition covers the many (and mostly) West Coast bands that introduced country music into their repertoire in the late 1960s and 1970s. Regardless, most country-rock acts were not interested in purely replicating the sounds of country music recordings. Like the name of the genre indicates, they were looking to wed rock 'n' roll with traditional country music. But that led to a highly diverse sonic approach: listen to the polished sounds produced by Music City's studio musicians on Dylan's *Nashville Skyline* (1969) versus the bluegrass excursions of Dillard & Clark, for example.

Countercultural audiences, as one might expect, had authenticity on their minds when they listened to country-rock. As referenced earlier, though, they did not form a consensus about what constituted authentic country music when hip musicians played it. Some hippie critics suggested that country-rock bands should be just that—purveyors of country that maintained an orientation toward rock. In this vein, the *Great Speckled Bird* criticized *Sweetheart of the Rodeo*'s "academicness," dismissing it as "a country version of the white blues purists mimicking B. B. King's every grunt." At the same time, the publication applauded the artful fusion of rock and country on the Flying Burrito Brothers' 1969 debut *The Gilded Palace of Sin*: "an album rich in everything that makes rock and country music a goodness [*sic*].[43] The Austin *Rag* disagreed with the *Bird*'s take on *Sweetheart of the Rodeo*, labeling it "pure country rock at its best," although it shared the idea that rock artists should not abandon their identity when playing country music.[44] Holding to that definition, Steve Rosen, a writer for the *Spectator* of Bloomington, Indiana, chided Poco for being "merely interested in making their music sound country and nothing more." He credited the recently split Dillard & Clark, in contrast, for their "experimentation with country music and their rock background."[45] A seeming minority of countercultural scribes favored country-rock that came as close as possible to country music. In September 1968, *Rolling Stone* published the article "Country & Rock" by Jon Landau, a contributor to the Liberation News Service, a kind of underground version of the Associated Press, in which he highlighted a few of the major rock bands that had gone country. Landau held up Roger McGuinn's group for special praise: "The Byrds have approached country music as an entity in itself and have aimed for a greater degree of fidelity to the rules of the style." Somewhat inaccurately, he claimed that McGuinn had "deliberately abandoned other aspects of his regular [rock or folk-rock] approach just to see how he could do within the confines of this particular idiom."[46] Without negating the country-rock fusion that the *Great Speckled Bird* saw the Flying Burrito Brothers undertaking, underground writer Mike Bourne stressed the band's countryness. Although not averse to artists adding pop elements to country music, he lavished particular acclaim on the Burritos for "coming on like a hip Buck Owens." They "are still essentially purists in one sense," Bourne concluded, as "their country orientation is heavy but hardly multi-directional."[47]

The counterculture, like traditional country audiences, also invested itself in what constituted authentic country music. In actuality, it seemed to have little trouble sorting the wheat from the chaff. Clearly deplorable was what one Philadelphia underground writer called the "plastic finesse" (read: inauthenticity) of the Grand Ole Opry, then a beacon of Nashville's "soft-shell" countrypolitan style.[48] But countercultural enthusiasts of country-rock appeared equally comfortable with a wide range of other current and past performance styles. The key was whether they fell under the "hard-core" category (although they did not use this term, hippies clasped onto its characteristics).

Hippie-approved country was fairly diverse, ranging from the rock-influenced contemporary sound of Bakersfield's Buck Owens to the Appalachian bluegrass that many San Francisco–area bands like the Grateful Dead drew on to the Byrds' plan of "a complete, almost outdated country album"—that is, "not modern country, . . . [but] 20-years-ago or 15-years-ago country," which brought to mind the music of Hank Williams and other southern artists.[49] Judging by their attraction to bands that experimented with various country styles, hippies were cognizant of country music's myriad influences and constantly fluctuating presentation. As non-hippie Paul Hemphill wrote, "Let the Country Music Association and the scholars talk all they want to about country music being the only pure form of American music; what they should say is, country music is the purest *hybrid* music we have in America. If it was simple and moving and earthy, country music borrowed from it."[50] Counterculturists accepted country-rock as merely another amalgamated form of an already amalgamated music. Their limited wrangling over the authenticity of country-rock's country sources was not symptomatic of the counterculture lacking investment in what was "real." Far from it. It had to do more with a newly emerging—and predominant—definition of authenticity.

Historian Grace Elizabeth Hale has argued that ideas about authenticity were in flux in the postwar era. Thanks in large part to the folk revival of the late 1950s and early 1960s, it was transitioning from a concept based in experience or background to one centered on feeling. The obvious problem of white middle-class youths performing the music of southern black and white "folk" while lacking any connection to these people's hardscrabble, rural existences necessitated this modification. "Being alike on the inside, as people who shared emotions and the need for self-expression," Hale reveals, "replaced being alike on the outside, as people who shared a history of oppression and isolation. Emotionalism replaced materialism."[51] This innovation not only allowed affluent white college kids to play "real" folk music but also facilitated the formation of a youth community. "Feelings," Hale explains, "not historical connection or faithful reproduction, created the new community of outsiders."[52] A similar process occurred for many counterculturists, who through this new understanding of authenticity could claim a connection to imagined white southern folk through country or country-rock music, just like their older hip counterparts had done with folk music earlier in the 1960s. Seizing the opportunity to borrow from multiple forms of "hard-core" country music, country-rock musicians could invigorate rock 'n' roll with country traditionalism—and produce entirely new sounds—while allowing their listeners to tap into the emotionalism of white southern culture without requiring any experience with the conditions that birthed this culture. In the second installment of a three-part series on the country genre, the *Spectator*'s David Satterfield stamped country music as steeped in the Populist tradition (at least until about 1900) of interracial cooperation between poor whites and blacks in the South and dripping in the authenticity of a proud, hardworking, striving, and even exploited, culture. "Country music, like Black music," Satterfield contended, "has often spoken for those [poor white southerners] who are forced to exist by selling their labor power—labor which is embodied in products not their own, which are taken from them and sold as a commodity in the fetishism of American 'affluence.'"[53] For a counterculture searching for authenticity, such descriptions signaled that many hippies assessed country music as ripe for the borrowing, serving as an accessible entry point into the roots and perceived realness of traditional white southernness. As long as counterculturists could "feel" the music, they could tap into a wellspring of borrowed authenticity.

A line from *Rolling Stone*'s review of Linda Ronstadt's second album further illustrates this point. Referring to her rendition of "Lovesick Blues," a country staple and a major hit for the hard-core Hank Williams in 1949, Alec Dubro speculated, "I'd say that most people would not be able to tell whether this was a 'real' Country singer or a hippie chick singing Country."[54] No matter that Ronstadt came from an affluent Arizona family, nor that Dubro did not much enjoy this particular song. For him, she nailed the music's feel, and was therefore authentic, by managing to sound like a purveyor of pure country sounds. In short, she offered insight into the rural white South, a place that in the countercultural imagination was family-oriented, antimodern, deeply authentic, and free of artifice. In the cultural mathematics computed by some hip youths, country-rock equaled country, country equaled the (largely) rural white South, and the (largely) rural white South equaled the cure for rootlessness. Like similarly tortured calculations used by hippies to fetishize African Americans and Native Americans, that proved a useful equation for a cultural movement intent on dissenting from and living outside of mainstream U.S. society.

The South and Race in the Countercultural and Country-Rock Imagination

The South largely played an imagined role for hippies, but not always. Hippie enclaves existed all over the country, including in the South.[55] As elsewhere, they tended to form in college towns like Durham, North Carolina, and major cities like Atlanta, where underground publications helped to promote countercultural values. Some hippies, whether native to the South or not, also came into contact with the region through the Back to the Land movement of the late 1960s and 1970s, which showcased countercultural dissatisfaction with urban life and a desire to pursue "right livelihoods" on their own self-sufficient terms.[56] One of the most notable hippie rural communes, The Farm, was formed by San Franciscan Stephen Gaskin and his disciples in 1970 in Tennessee.[57] Other migrants ventured to southern Appalachia. Jinny A. Turman-Deal's work on the Back to the Land movement in West Virginia reveals that back-to-the-landers, many of whom considered themselves "ex-hippies," were drawn to the mountain South with visions of live-and-let-live white southerners. "Mountaineers were popularly known to be independent, self-reliant, and industrious," she writes, and some back-to-the-landers envisioned them as "fairly open-minded."[58]

For most counterculturists, though, the South remained fairly abstract. Given the appreciable media attention devoted to the 1960s southern civil rights movement, race played a relatively small role in country-rock and its reception. Influenced by the Vicious South discourse, underground press accounts typically acknowledged the pervasiveness of white southern bigotry, but counterculturists broke from that narrative by postulating that white working-class southerners were themselves, ironically, constrained by a racist society. They were not the problem; rather, their views were symptomatic of the nation's larger racial ills. Youth radicals, regardless of whether they valued politics or culture more as methods of resistance, frequently decried nonsoutherners who disparaged white southerners as racists while denying their own prejudices.[59] This belief in collective responsibility for the American racial dilemma allowed many counterculturists to look past their fears of white working-class southerners to idealize them as proud, honorable people whose values were antithetical to those of modern society. That is what country music represented to many hippies, so it is not surprising that they were attracted to rock artists who mined this southern musical tradition. For example, in a review of a 1969 concert by the Flying Burrito Brothers, the *Distant Drummer*'s Frank Gruber praised the band's music in words that recalled the allure of Mayberry: These were "songs [that] make you and the whole world simple. By no means hicks, the group persuades you to take a walk in the country and yearn for small-town America. I like it."[60] The absence of racial commentary accompanying the discussion of country-rock in the counterculture speaks to the power of this vision of white southernness, which many in the movement regarded as an invigorating challenge to stifling modernity.

Certainly, some counterculturists refused to excuse the region's racist past (and present) or to evince optimism at its potential for reinvention. Such individuals received their anthem in 1970, with sometime country-rocker Neil

Young's release of "Southern Man." With its relentless beat and blistering guitars, the song is a full-out rock assault on the southern past. Jim Cullen tags the tune as "one of the most passionate denunciations of the white South that has ever been recorded."[61] The first verse lambastes hypocritical white southerners who have failed to rectify their painful, brutal legacy of oppression. "How long? How long?" Young sings after recounting a terrifying cotton South landscape of racial violence, full of "crosses . . . burning fast," "screamin'," and "bull whips crackin'."[62]

Young's song spoke a larger truth about the tortured legacy and continued torment of southern racism, yet "Southern Man," like the Vicious South discourse it aped, lacked any subtlety or nuance. Its racialized and anachronistic imagery had more in common with the South of 1870 than of 1970. (Young would later concede that he had overreached in the song.)[63] The artist's use of the masculine singular as a surrogate for the whole of the region's racial transgressions shared the tendency of other nonsoutherners to scapegoat individual southern rednecks during the civil rights era, rather than address the more elusive problem of institutionalized racism.[64]

Hippies frequently viewed the South and white southerners through a different lens while waging a wider cultural critique of American society. In line with their appraisal of the systemic problems plaguing the country, ranging from overconsumption to social anomie, many writers in the underground press promulgated a deeper commentary on southern racism. Counterculturists were apt to find "rednecks" or "hillbillies" loathsome, yet often they discerned this bigotry as part of the broader structure of American racism. In other words, the white southerner was, to paraphrase Bob Dylan's civil-rights-era song, "only a pawn in [Amerika's] game."[65]

Underground newspaper reviews of the film *Easy Rider* (1969) document hippies' ability to view white southerners as something other than the violent, racist maniacs of the Violent South narrative. During the movie's climax, a shotgun-toting Louisiana redneck in a pickup truck kills the two main characters, the freak-looking Wyatt (aka Captain America) and Billy, whom the locals had earlier disparaged as "refugees from a gorilla love-in."[66] The underground response to the dual death scene was overwhelmingly negative. Reviewers blasted the easy scapegoating of an entire region as peculiarly racist and violent. "Of course, there's rednecks around who wouldn't mind blowing the head off some long-haired communist Yankee queer," read a review in Houston's *Space City News*. "But those people aren't the system; they're the sick products of a sick culture, and to one degree or another every one of us is infected with that same sickness."[67] Nonsouthern publications laid out similar critiques. Providence, Rhode Island's *Extra* called the film "a lie because it makes the South the villain without making it clear that this whole nation is going insane."[68] A *Distant Drummer* reader disseminated this perspective, too, admonishing that bigotry was a national, not a regional, predicament. "My experiences indicate that the only difference between Southern prejudice (or Western) is that it is easier to express it in the South," he concluded.[69] (Interestingly, the underground press typically focused on the southern rednecks of the film's conclusion rather than on Jack Nicholson's character George, an alcoholic southern lawyer, who before being murdered [by, yes, rednecks], joined Billy and Wyatt on their trek and personified the Changing South narrative and its assertion of white southerners' potential for decency.) These and other hippies excoriated racism not as a parochial southern problem, but as indicative of the moral failings of modern American society. Hippies thus echoed one of the key takeaways of Howard Zinn's *The Southern Mystique*: southern exceptionalism was a nonsouthern fantasy and the North was complicit in the *national* sin of racism.[70]

When counterculturists did lash out at southern racism, they generally balanced their assessments with an affinity for the region's white culture. It was this compartmentalization of the good and the bad in their interpretation of the southern lifestyle that enabled many hippies to imagine the region's whites in idealized terms. In his 1970 book *Total Loss Farm: A Year in the Life*, Raymond Mungo, cofounder of the Liberation News Service, critiqued white southerners as backward and pathological, but he could not deny that there was something invigorating about their music, especially country, and their rural surroundings. In fall 1969 Mungo and a group of friends departed the East Coast on a westward trip. They swung through the Deep South along the way. Mungo's conflicted view of the region arose from his preconceptions, as well as his encounters with its landscapes and its people. "The South has nothing to do with anything," he insisted, "nobody you really love lives in the South, nothing you need comes from the South, you have identified with *Easy Rider* and centuries before that Goodman, Chaney & Schwerner."[71] Mungo may have seen the region as a cesspool of bigotry, yet he was still taken by its natural beauty. This dichotomy lay at the center of his judgment. For instance, he looked in wonder at the Alabama countryside. But while it was free of the "jackhammering" that accompanied so-called progress, he seemed haunted by its racist history. Its "universe . . . hangs always, like a man lynched," he wrote, "at the same suspended point in time and space."[72]

The South's dedication to—and one might say obsession with—its past, along with its agrarian landscapes, beckoned counterculturists like Mungo. He and his companions also admired the feeling of easygoing timelessness that he ascribed to its culture, such as the "good music" they dialed in on Nashville's country radio.[73] And they took comfort in the city's array of musicians "ingesting the sacrament."[74] Mungo spoke directly to the appeal of southern country music and its ability to inspire positive feelings in "a world so thoroughly fallen-apart as our own": "'We need a whole lot more Jesus and a lot less rock n' roll,' one song went, and rightly so; for the basic pulse of Nashville is neither existential or apocalyptic, but easy toe-tapping happiness."[75] Mungo was silent on whether he actually approved of the song's pro-Christian message; even so, his comment gave away his respect for the traditionalism that could produce such a song. His musings corresponded to hippies' views of the region that acknowledged its shortcomings while seeking to recover elements of perceived virtue. That is why, like Mungo, they could simultaneously "love the South, and fear it awfully."[76]

Similarly, country-rock artists could glorify the South while pointing out its alleged deficiencies. In the case of the Byrds, Gram Parsons sings of a beautiful rural setting "callin' me home" on "Hickory Wind," one of *Sweetheart of the Rodeo*'s standout tracks.[77] Elsewhere the Byrds took satirical aim at southern racism. On the curiously titled *Dr. Byrds and Mr. Hyde* (1969), the band included the Roger McGuinn–Gram Parsons composition "Drug Store Truck Drivin' Man." This comical song pokes fun at a white southerner who works as a late-night country music disc jockey and serves as "the head of the Ku Klux Klan."[78] Although the composition mocks the DJ's racism, it plays as less of an indictment of southern prejudice and more as an attempt to make the character appear ridiculous. "Drug Store Truck Drivin' Man" was, in fact, a thinly veiled brush-off to influential Nashville DJ Ralph Emery, a member of the country music establishment who had criticized the Byrds on the air when they came to play on the Grand Ole Opry in March 1968. The sardonic song satirized white southern bigotry without engaging in a blanket condemnation of the South's racial problems. The Byrds, like Mungo, could accentuate what they considered the strengths of the South without allowing the region's supposed drawbacks to overwhelm those traits.

Imagining White Southern Culture through Country-Rock

When imagining the South, country-rock artists mostly presented counterculture-pleasing, bucolic versions of the region; in short, a kind of timeless southern agrarianism. The cover of Linda Ronstadt's Nashville-recorded 1970 release *Silk Purse* frames her as a fetching hippie down on the farm. She sits barefoot in a pen surrounded by hogs. The artwork for the Beau Brummels's 1968 LP *Bradley's Barn*, also made in Nashville, features a red, slope-roofed country barn, a wooden fence, green trees, and colorful flowers. On the cover of his own Music City–recorded *Nashville Skyline* (1969), Bob Dylan assumes a country crooner persona, dressed in what Bob Proehl later termed "the 'authentic' clothes of a poor white southerner," backed by a blue sky and tipping his hat to the would-be listener.[79] Reflecting both the counter-cultural preoccupation with the West and the tradition of southern country musicians stretching back to the 1930s, other artists dressed in cowboy gear or employed western-style imagery in their album art (e.g., the cover and title of the Byrds' *Sweetheart of the Rodeo*).[80] The Flying Burrito Brothers were an exception, choosing instead to clothe themselves in the "Nudie suits" favored by establishment mainstream country and western musicians like Spade Cooley, Lefty Frizzell, and Porter Wagoner, albeit with some hip touches like the marijuana leaves and naked woman on Gram Parsons's costume.[81] By putting themselves in rural settings and cutting their records in the South's country music capital, these artists encouraged a linkage between the supposed authenticity of their country music and what they identified as the genuine pulse of white southern culture.

Country-rock's nostalgia for the region's purported timeless traditionalism extended beyond record artwork. Groups like the Everly Brothers and the Byrds generated wistful versions of the South in song. Don and Phil Everly were a Kentucky duo who had scored several country-tinged pop hits in the late 1950s and early 1960s. Despite the addition of such hip touches as wah-wah guitars, their move to country-rock in the late 1960s signified more of a commercial strategy designed to boost flagging record sales than a fundamental change in style or sound. In the Everlys' "Bowling Green," released in 1967, the Kentucky city is a place where "folks treat you kind" and "let you think your own mind."[82] The jaunty melody and tight Everly harmonies contribute to the portrait of southern purity. Bowling Green, the song suggests, is a place that boasts not only good-hearted people of the live-and-let-live variety, but beautiful natural surroundings, too. "Kentucky sunshine makes the heart unfold," the Everlys sing, and "the fields down in Bowling Green" are blessed with "the softest grass I've ever seen."[83]

Even though it describes a city of moderate size, the song follows the country tradition of idealizing the rural and small-town southern existence. One can easily detect the appeal of such descriptions for the counterculturally minded. On the aptly titled 1968 LP *Roots*, the Everly Brothers further emphasize their southern heritage, defining white southernness as family oriented. The album opens with an excerpt from *The Everly Family Show*, a 1940s and 1950s radio program. The voice of Everly patriarch Ike promises the audience some "family style and country style" tunes.[84]

On other recordings, country-rock artists constructed white southernness in a manner appealing to their largely hippie audience. The Byrds' "Hickory Wind" presents bucolic images of singer Gram Parsons's childhood visits to South Carolina, exemplifying the countercultural critique of cities "with a faraway feel."[85] Parsons's aching vocal and the interplay of a whining pedal steel guitar and fiddle add to the song's nostalgia for the South as a refuge from urban anxieties. Similarly, some country-rock artists lauded southern religiosity and the evidently unchanging traditions of southern culture that it represented. There is a certain degree of irony in the Byrds' renditions of Arthur Reid Reynolds's "Jesus Is Just Alright" (1969) and the Louvin Brothers' "The Christian Life" (1968). The same goes for Linda Ronstadt's cover of "We Need a Whole Lot More of Jesus (And a Lot Less Rock and Roll)" (1969), the song that Raymond Mungo had admired during his travels in the South. Occasionally, these efforts turned unintentionally parodic. On the Byrds' version of "The Christian Life," Roger McGuinn sings such lyrics as "my buddies shun me since I turned to Jesus" in what band mate Chris Hillman laughed off as an "awful [southern] accent." "He overacted, so to speak," Hillman said, implying that McGuinn was trying to make the song sound more authentic.[86] Many hippies evidently did not mind; those who took these religious songs seriously were receptive to the supposed genuineness of southern faith. *Rolling Stone*, for example, appreciated how the Byrds universalized the sentiments and communal spirit of southern religion. Critiquing a series of 1969 shows with the Flying Burrito Brothers, one of the magazine's correspondents wrote, the Byrds "extract, from what might otherwise be a dated Southern hymn, the joyfulness and optimism which is a part of all religion and they allow you to participate in it."[87] The reviewer's enthusiasm for southern piety is reflective of many hippies' embrace of not only Eastern but also Christian faith tradition. This trend is evidenced by the rise of evangelism and religious communes in the counterculture.[88] Authenticity for hippies did not preclude the existence of critical distance. Addressing Linda Ronstadt's covers of country songs like "We Need a Whole Lot More of Jesus," another *Rolling Stone* piece spotlighted the similarity of the singer's voice to respected country artists June Carter and Patsy Cline before explaining that "she obviously feels the music without entirely believing it."[89] Aside from reinforcing the connection between emotionalism and authenticity, the magazine advanced the idea that hippies could enjoy the "feel" of the South—its ties to family, rural setting, communalism, and religious dedication—while choosing to eschew its more conservative, even reactionary, qualities.

The emphasis on feel, or to put it another way, intuitiveness, fit with the countercultural valuing of experience over rationality. "Logical argument doesn't work," said Jerry Rubin. "People's heads don't work logically. People are emotion freaks. People are crazy."[90] Fellow Yippie Abbie Hoffman was more succinct: "Words are the absolute in horseshit."[91] Rationality promised to reveal universal truth, but hippies insisted that people could not access this truth via science and reason. Furthermore, it was "rational" planning that provided the logic for the war in Vietnam and that fabricated the banal world of suburbia, they stressed. It is little surprise, then, that in cheering an album like Dylan's *Nashville Skyline*, the *Berkeley Barb* would tell listeners to avoid overanalyzing it and to forget about the lyrics. "The music itself is the message," author "A. J." stated, "[and] we don't want to play any exegical games." More than a record of unaffected, jaunty country tunes, the album "is a celebration of our culture."[92] Soul over mind.

The values that counterculturists attached to the white South in the underground press all existed more in the realm of the spirit than in that of reason. The earthy and anachronistic construction of the counterculture's South clashed with the approach of technocrats who placed their unmitigated faith in objective truth. Southernness thus became an antirational tool against the establishment. This was remarkable; the fact that few southerners—or Americans for that matter—would have acceded to this assault on objectivity demonstrated the extraordinary flexibility of "the South" as an idea when handled by the imaginative (and frequently altered) minds of the counterculture.

Thinking the Unthinkable: Imagining a Countercultural–White Southern Alliance

In their responses to country-rock, hippies at times expressed their desire to concoct more robust connections with white southerners. Take, for example, the Flying Burrito Brothers' "Hippie Boy," the final song on *The Gilded Palace of Sin*, and the accompanying countercultural press response. The tune features an understated country backing track, an organ that lends the song a hymn-like feel, and spoken vocals by Chris Hillman. The narrator is a member of straight society who encounters a young male hippie on the street. The boy urges them to find unity in their common humanity despite occupying different stations. Later the narrator seems to agree with the sentiment and alludes to a basic similarity between "any hippie, bum, or hillbilly out on the street."[93] "Hippie Boy" underlines its theme of harmony by evolving in its concluding moments into the gospel tune "Peace in the Valley," a 1951 country hit for Red Foley and the Sunshine Boys. The reference to hillbillies obviously brings to mind white southern mountain people. In these admittedly tongue-in-cheek lyrics—Chris Hillman later dismissed the song as "stupid," the result of too much drinking—the Burritos nevertheless highlight the countercultural desire to reach out across the cultural divide.[94]

Rolling Stone tended to agree in its full-page featured review of *The Gilded Palace of Sin*. Referring to "Hippie Boy," music writer Stanley Booth remarked, "The album's ending somehow summons up a vision of hillbillies and hippies, like lions and lambs, together in peace and love instead of sin and violence, getting stoned together, singing oldtime favorite songs." Booth speculated that Burrito Gram Parsons's apparent southern "country" purity stemmed from his roots in Waycross, Georgia (Booth also hailed from there), where "Culture exists . . . only in the anthropological sense." This background provided Parsons with a unique perspective on "the strangeness and hostility of the modern world, but he speaks to and for all of us."[95] Besides shedding light on the song's evocation of countercultural-southern unity and suggesting that Parsons's southernness legitimized his artistry, Booth explicitly defined southern values as universally applicable but somehow lost to modernity. White southern culture then was a repository of authenticity just waiting to be tapped.

Elsewhere countercultural writers proclaimed the importance of hippies forging an understanding with white southerners. Gurney Norman's *Divine Right's Trip: A Novel of the Counterculture* (1972) was originally serialized in *The Last Whole Earth Catalogue* and chronicled a hippie's rediscovering of his rural Kentucky roots. The main character, D. R., travels from California and ends his journey at his family's Appalachian farm. During one sequence, he follows an old miner named Virgil through a strip-mined, ravaged countryside. As scholar Rob Holton writes, "This alliance between a rural blue-collar man such as Virgil and hippy such as D. R. unites the new alienated hip youth of the 1960s with an older tradition of working-class resistance."[96] Norman's meditation on the desirability of countercultural and rural southern alliances culminates in D. R.'s marriage to his companion Estelle on the farm. "Their wedding celebration," Holton argues, "unites rural Kentucky traditionalists with the young, rebellious urban youth who arrive for the party."[97]

In the underground press, much of the commentary about the hippie-southern fusion implied by country-rock centered on Bob Dylan's late 1960s abandonment of rock 'n' roll and subsequent move into country and western. Publications commonly ruminated on the artist's supposed effort to attract traditional working-class country audiences on *Nashville Skyline*. In a piece detailing Dylan's apparently changing politics, *Fusion* embraced his country turn, calling country perhaps "the one non-middle-class musical form that speaks for working people," and pondering whether *Nashville Skyline* collaborator and country star Johnny Cash could be, like Dylan, one of the youth movement's prophets.[98] Other counterculturists were not so sure. "Chris" of the *Washington Free Press* told a *Rolling Stone* reporter that he would have preferred that Dylan "do a duet album with Jerry Rubin instead of Johnny Cash. Like, you know where Johnny Cash stands," Chris said. "And it isn't for the revolution."[99]

In an article published the following month titled "The Politics of Country Rock," the *Berkeley Barb* fleshed out Chris's dim view of the Dylan-Cash collaboration. The article's author, "Tari," was not upset by Dylan's association with Cash; instead, Tari abhorred Dylan's perceived alliance with the country musician's audience, or "'Tennessee Studs' north and south of the Mason-Dixon line who hate niggers, hippies, commies, and jews."[100] Tari's inclusion of southerners and nonsoutherners in the country music audience not only recognized the reality of late 1960s country listenership but also reflected the countercultural sense that perhaps white southerners were no more bigoted than whites in the rest of the country. In spite of his or her vitriol, the author concluded with a plea for unity. Invoking the poor white southerners of Dylan's "Only a Pawn in Their Game," Tari formulated a political use for the white South beyond as a model for countercultural emulation. The writer insisted that hippies and their southern and nonsouthern antagonists must form an alliance, which sounded ironic in light of his or her criticism of Dylan's association with Cash. "We are their victims," Tari wrote, "and if we don't get them off our backs soon, and get together with them, the machine's survival instinct will have won."[101] Tari's assessment of country-rock led the commentator to trumpet countercultural calls for harmonious relations between people and to attack the perceived human-crushing American technocracy. Atlanta's *Great Speckled Bird* echoed the *Barb*'s petition for intergenerational and interregional harmony. The paper pictured "the roots of Cash's music" as "the warmth, vitality, community and stubborn stick-to-it-ness of the rural South" and suggested that, particularly in the South, country music could serve as a point of commonality for hippies and rednecks.[102]

At least one account conveys that some young rebels saw Dylan's countrified songs as a resource to help unite youth and working-class cultures in America, even outside of the South. In the late 1960s, the New Left began organizing in white working-class neighborhoods. Students for a Democratic Society (SDS), in the midst of its "cultural turn," had merged countercultural sensibilities with its focus on creating a social revolution based on "participatory democracy." Joseph Ferrandino, a graduate student at SUNY-Buffalo, recalled the story of an SDS activist finding a point of unity with the residents of an unspecified white working-class neighborhood in their shared enjoyment of *Nashville Skyline*. "The excitement of this common experience provided the catalyst that helped get his organizing project off the ground," Ferrandino stated.[103]

Ferrandino saw Dylan along with groups like the Rolling Stones and the Band as practicing "cultural subversion" capable of spreading radical messages to the white working class. It was "Dylan, who has extended his hand as a representative of a particular new working class background—the college educated urban youth—to other working class people young and old, and to American roots—country people, Johnny Cash, etc. (as in *John Wesley Hardin* [sic] and *Nashville Skyline*)."[104] Ferrandino's vignette perfectly supports Doug Rossinow's assertion that in the increasingly counterculture-sympathetic New Left of the late 1960s, "radicals came to believe that cultural activism was their most certain path to creating significant political change in the United States."[105]

Writing in New York's *New City Free Press*, Stephen Bloomfield and Robin Shaikun argued for the necessity of such partnerships from the hippie side. These authors castigated stereotypical media images like those of the vicious rednecks in *Easy Rider* because they created "false mistrust . . . among groups of people who ultimately have common interests."[106] They specifically described a needed coalition between "silent majority" Americans and hippies, but in referencing the negative depictions of southerners in *Easy Rider*, they insinuated a more narrow partnership between counterculturists and white southerners, too. White southerners and hippies, Bloomfield and Shaikun intimated, were a good match because the American system exploited both of them.

The dream of uniting hippies and rednecks was mostly unrealized, but for a brief time in the early 1970s, this unwieldy grouping coalesced around the emergence of "progressive country" music in Austin, Texas. The city housed the conservative main campus of the University of Texas system and, by 1966, the *Rag*, the first underground newspaper in the South. In the early 1960s, disaffected youths, including Janis Joplin, began gathering at Threadgill's, a local establishment that catered to and encouraged their love of blues, folk, and country music. By 1967, Austin had its first countercultural music space, the Vulcan Gas Company. The hippie-redneck combination became visible once Eddie Wilson, the manager for the Vulcan's house band Shiva's Headband, founded the Armadillo World Headquarters in 1970.[107] The Armadillo focused on booking acts that fell under the new progressive country label. The genre's boundaries were somewhat hard to define. As Jan Reid, annalist of the Austin music scene in the 1970s, explains, "What mattered was not the identity or hair length or philosophy of the singers, but the kind of instruments that accompanied them. If anything remotely country could be discerned in a recording, it qualified."[108] The symbol of progressive country was the "cosmic cowboy." This figure dressed like a cowboy, but wore his hair long and smoked pot. In a place like Texas, hippie identification with cowboy imagery was in one sense ironic, but it also served a deep—and logical—cultural need for hip youths. "The hippie-redneck trope developed," writes historian Jason Mellard, "because many Anglo-Texans in town grew up in settings that made the markers of traditional Texas culture, 'redneck' culture, second nature. While they may have rebelled against the politics or mannerisms of their home culture in adopting a countercultural lifestyle, the rejection could hardly be total."[109] Mellard also ties the rise of progressive country and the genre's fascination with "place, the past, craft, and the pastoral . . . to a certain seventies sensibility that prized rootedness and tradition." This was a mind-set that both hippies and working-class white Texans could embrace.[110]

This common ground shared by these uncommon folks resulted in diverse crowds for shows at the Armadillo by such artists as Jerry Jeff Walker, Michael Murphy, Commander Cody and His Lost Planet Airmen, and Willie Nelson, the last of whom was the most visible personification of the redneck-hippie connection. The alliance, although certainly hyped by the media, did truly exist for a time in the early to mid-1970s. But some counterculturists worried about its meaning and depth. Jeff (Shero) Nightbyrd, former editor of the *Rag*, was one of them. Writing in the *Austin Sun* in 1975, he bemoaned the all-too-easy adoption of the cosmic cowboy identity by "any young dude" without having to adjust his outlook: "Particularly, it doesn't require any changes in attitude like being a hippie in the sixties did. You don't have to know anything about the war, give a damn about race, tussle with psychedelics, or worry about male chauvinism."[111] Cosmic cowboys, he lamented, could be even more misogynistic than their redneck counterparts.[112] These were the perils of integrating two radically different groups of people on the basis of an easily co-opted, commercialized cultural product.

Regardless of its impracticality and limited showings, creating solidarity with working-class white southerners, whether deep in the heart of Texas or elsewhere—even if only in their heads—appealed to many hippies. In an analysis that also brings to mind progressive country, historian Jeff Cowie draws on *Rolling Stone* cofounder and publisher Jann Wenner's contention that country-rock "was [in Wenner's words] 'the music of reconciliation,' an attempt to fill the gap between the rock 'n' roll Left and the country Right, between the grand designs of the youth movement and the grit of people who worked for a living."[113] Most of the time, though, hippies and country-rockers themselves were content to fantasize about the white South from a distance.

The Band's South: Outsiders Looking In

The musical act that best embodied countercultural imaginings of an out-of-time white South was the Band, a group frequently identified as playing country-rock. Whereas other country-rock acts often sang tangentially of the South, the Band presented a direct portrait of the region's white inhabitants. The group's perspective, in its sympathetic and anachronistic portrait of the region and its people, paralleled writings on the South in the underground press. An analysis of the Band's South and its countercultural and mainstream responses deepens our comprehension of the counterculture's fascination with the region, and perhaps more importantly, it demonstrates that hippies' constructions of the white South held considerable appeal for straight Americans, too. This endeavor necessitates a thorough parsing of the attributes of and influences on the Band's imaginings of the South, as well as countercultural and mainstream reactions to their music.

When sixteen-year-old Jaime R. "Robbie" Robertson stepped off the train in Fayetteville, Arkansas, in spring 1960, his head must have been spinning. He was in a new universe. The Toronto-born Robertson had met Ronnie Hawkins, a wild rock 'n' roll showman from Arkansas, when Robertson's band the Suedes had opened for Hawkins and his backing group the Hawks at a gig in Ontario. Hawkins was so impressed with the kid's guitar playing that he offered him a shot at joining the Hawks. The Arkansas trip marked the first time Robertson had ever been to the South, and yet he had been dreaming of it for years. After a boyhood dedicated to soaking up the white and black music of the region on vinyl, Robertson would now encounter its people, music, and culture firsthand. He spent time at the family farm of fellow band mate Levon Helm, the Hawks' drummer. Helm's family hailed from eastern Arkansas. Robertson was captivated by this place, where black and white musical styles fused and laid the groundwork for the integrated rock 'n' roll sound that provided the soundtrack for his imaginings of the South. The guitarist and songwriter began to formulate the tale of a struggling, honorable white southern people that he would perfect in song once the Hawks morphed into the Band in the late 1960s. That story was shaped by Helm's relatives and their neighbors, who impressed Robertson with their strong sense of community; music brought them together and crossed generations.[114] Robertson's South of the Mind was further influenced by his later reading of works by William Faulkner and Tennessee Williams, which added a touch of the tragic to his songs of hardworking, striving people who lived close to the land.

As music journalist Robert Palmer observed in 1978, "The songs Robbie ended up writing came out steeped in the South's bottom lands and shacks and cotton fields, steeped in the Baptist and Holy Roller churches where folks in the throes of religious hysteria invented the duck walk and all the other classic rock & roll moves."[115] Robertson's initial wide-eyed love affair with the South tempered somewhat, but he never lost the feeling that the region was a world apart. His version of the myth of southern distinctiveness dovetailed perfectly with countercultural musings in the underground press. The South as Other did not mean racial aberration for Robertson, or for hippies, necessarily; instead, it signified a repository of lost values. The sepia-toned southernness explicated by Robertson on record existed out of time. It was a refuge from modern ills: urban anomie, suburban blandness, and inauthenticity.

The Band reached a broader audience than just the counterculture. (Its second album, featuring an actual sepia-toned cover, hit number 9 on the *Billboard* charts in 1970.) The Band's success betrayed, in part, the extent to which countercultural perspectives had influenced straight America, as well as the broad appeal of a tradition-preserving white South in the national imagination. For less hip Americans, Robertson's South could serve as an antidote to the perceived breakdown of modern society and the social unrest driven by riots, debates over the Vietnam War, and changing mores that gave the 1960s era its off-kilter feeling. In short, the Band represented what a *Rolling Stone* cover story on the group referred to as "the search for a calmer ethic."[116] Perhaps most powerfully, in the music of the Band, the South promised, for those who encountered it, healing of—or at least a retreat from—racial and political strife. In analyzing Robertson's fascination with the South in his 1975 book *Mystery Train*, Greil Marcus captured this sense of the South as a land with rich lessons to teach. "Here was a different world," he mused, "with more on its surface than Canada had in its abyss; you could chase that world, listen to it, learn from it. Perhaps you could even join it."[117]

A prime component of the Band's allure to counterculturists lay in its communal ethos. Its members—Robertson, Helm, Garth Hudson, Richard Manuel, and Rick Danko—exhibited this trait in their personal lives and it was a key aspect of their aural sketches of southernness. They first gained the reputation as a tightly knit unit due to their association with Bob Dylan. After breaking away from Ronnie Hawkins but while still known as the Hawks, they toured the United States and Europe with Dylan in 1965 and 1966 as he tried his hand at electric rock 'n' roll. When he retreated to Woodstock, New York, after a near-fatal motorcycle accident, Dylan and the group recorded several album sides' worth of material (known as *The Basement Tapes*) at the Band's home, dubbed "Big Pink," in nearby West Saugerties. The Band's communal living arrangement there attracted hip youths intent on recovering their humanity in a society stricken with the disease of rootlessness. Robertson and his musical colleagues devised an alternative lifestyle. The group's biographer Barney Hoskyns has portrayed the musicians as "a kind of microcosmic community, a potent model of the early American pioneer settlements."[118] The members played together, ate together, and lived together, establishing their own commune of sorts in rural New York. Underground newspapers often praised their communal spirit.[119] Importantly, the Band's togetherness and rural hermitage appeared to youths as deeply rooted, and not simply a marketing pose. After the release of the group's second album, *Time* interviewed Amherst College students about the Band. One student remarked on the naturalness of its iconography: "You listen and you just know that's no group of johnny-come-latelys from the suburbs who've gone off to a commune while Daddy foots the bill."[120]

The Band's perceived sense of community was bolstered by a vibe of familial connectedness, which roped in audiences craving roots. The group's persona was one of sons and brothers who had not forgotten from where they came. The Band exemplified this spirit in the artwork for their 1968 debut *Music from Big Pink*. One photograph, titled "Next of Kin," features the group's members surrounded by their families in Ontario. The faces of multiple generations stare out at the viewer. The message is simple: these are men who have not turned their backs on their loved ones or their traditions.

The photograph lent credence to the Band's counterintuitive contention that its members found little in common with young cultural and political rebels. After the release of *Music from Big Pink*, in an interview with the Toronto underground newspaper *Egg*, Robertson groused about the "punky attitude" in current music and youth culture. He objected to the tendency to "hate your mother and stab your father." As Robertson explained, "We don't hate our mothers and fathers."[121] Drummer Levon Helm agreed, later declaring in his autobiography, "Hell, we loved our families!"[122] In Robertson's and Helm's formulations, counterculturists and other young people had a slash-and-burn mentality when it came to the past and their kin. Indeed, few hippies seemed interested in maintaining the kind of biological familial connectedness that informed the Band's imagined South. Many counterculturists dissented from the views of their parents and distanced themselves from traditional notions of family; hippies frequently created alternative kin groups. Robertson, Helm, Danko, Manuel, and Hudson had themselves formed such a connection with each other, and it was this communal brotherhood with which many hippies could identify.

The Band, like its countercultural devotees, fetishized "roots" and a return to simplicity, and both entities looked to the South as a major repository of "lost" values. The group never laid claim to any political agenda and denied any intent to release political songs. "Besides," Robertson said in 1970, "who can write *songs* about all this garbage that's happening now, wars and revolution and killing? I can't."[123] The Band claimed that it just wanted to play good music that avoided the excess and empty flash of much contemporary rock music. Both mainstream and underground publications picked up on this defining feature of the group. The *New York Times'* Mike Jahn commended the Band in December 1969 for its ability to simultaneously recover both the simplicity and the depth of feeling in southern music. "The musicians," the journalist advanced, "still play like five friendly old coots picking away in the back of some Kentucky barroom. Their songs, even when cryptic and wordy, after the style of Bob Dylan, sound like old family favorites."[124] Counterculturists concurred, commenting on the "aura of authenticity" that ran through the Band's music. While alluding to the deep-seated southernness of its songs, Houston's *Space City News* referenced this aura and praised the "gaping agelessness and placelessness" that infused the group's tunes.[125]

And yet the Band was firmly entrenched in one place in particular. Its songs may have denied any political agenda, but the group's frequent promotion of an antimodern, rural white South spoke to its members' view of this mythical region as a worthy alternate social model. While conveying the power of old southern music, Robertson and his band mates also wielded potent ideas about the South. The group's most sustained treatment of the region can be heard on its second LP, 1969's *The Band*. Barney Hoskyns has scrutinized the record as a kind of concept album about the South.[126] Although not every song is about the region, Robertson clearly wished to interpret seriously the white southern experience, or what Hoskyns designates "the things Southerners themselves took for granted," on the record.[127] Robertson's visions of the South assumed an impressionistic tone. He, like other country-rock artists and countercultural enthusiasts of the white South, was most concerned with the *feel* of the region and its people. Thinking back to his early visits to Arkansas, Robertson explained his methodology of writing about the South: "There'd be a little shack out in the middle of a field at night, and I'd wonder who was in there. Not that I wanted to knock on the door, because I preferred to use my own imagination, but that's what kinda led me to this songwriting style."[128] The Toronto native composed as an outsider—Hoskyns calls him "a Yankee with his nose pressed up against the window of the South"—and nonsouthern counterculturists and other Americans could plainly relate to Robertson's search to pinpoint and shape the dynamic images that he perceived as uniquely southern.[129]

As heard on *The Band*, the group's vocalists—Manuel, Danko, and Helm—sing about Robertson's South in the voice of nostalgia. The album's concluding track, "King Harvest (Has Surely Come)," tells a sympathetic tale about a besieged southern farmer who sees his union membership as his only salvation from hard times. The time period in the song is indeterminate, although the narrative reads like something out of Steinbeck's Great Depression–era novel

The Grapes of Wrath, except set not in Oklahoma and California, but amid the "magnolia trees" and the "rice" fields of the Deep South.[130] On "Rockin' Chair," the geriatric sea dog narrator sings wistfully of his southern homeland. "Oh, to be home again," the old man pines, "down in old Virginny," where he can smell the air, enjoy the tobacco, and "have no care[s]."[131] The funky "Up on Cripple Creek" tells the story of a truck driver trying to get back to Lake Charles, Louisiana, to see to his "little Bessie," who provides him with myriad pleasures—sexual and otherwise. Although Lake Charles is a small city with a population around seventy-eight thousand according to the 1970 census, Cripple Creek is probably an imagined locale; it remains possible that Robertson was referencing a real place in the southwestern Virginia portion of Appalachia.[132] Cripple Creek is where Bessie "sends" the narrator and "mends" him when he "spring[s] a leak."[133] Greil Marcus has theorized that "Cripple Creek is like the Big Rock Candy Mountain, a place where all fears vanish beyond memory."[134] Viewed in light of the decidedly southern focus of *The Band*, it is fair to conclude that Cripple Creek functions as a bucolic, rural southern sanctuary in the narrator's mind, further reinforcing the album's celebration of the region.

Aside from its occasional nods to modernity (e.g., truck driving and Spike Jones in "Up on Cripple Creek"), the group envisioned an archaic South, a place where white people lived simple, meaningful, interconnected lives, often in the face of great hardship. Musicologist David Emblidge rightly argued that "there is plenty of good humor in the ill-fated romances they recount; yet they also treat the pain, suffering, loneliness and hard work inherent in rural life."[135] As the underground newspaper *Harry* similarly noted in 1970, overstating things somewhat, "The Band's world is a rural, country one where one faces the stark forces of nature and existence alone."[136]

"The Night They Drove Old Dixie Down," the centerpiece of *The Band*, and its most "southern" song, documents the most challenging era in southern (and American) history: the Civil War. It is a deeply political track that investigates the collision of war, working-class values, and a mythical southern past. Robertson's "Dixie" features an unusual, jerky chord progression and melody. Playing an early version for Helm, Robertson "flashed back to when [Levon] first took me to meet his parents in Marvell, Arkansas, and his daddy said, 'Don't worry, Robin—the South is going to rise again.'"[137] To write the lyrics, Robertson supplemented his memories with historical research at the Woodstock library aided by Helm.[138] In the finished composition, a poor Tennessee soldier named Virgil Caine narrates the Confederacy's demise. He describes the fall of Richmond, the death of his brother, and a fleeting vision of Robert E. Lee. "Dixie" presents Virgil as an honest man fighting to overcome forces beyond his control. In the face of adversity, he sticks to rural, working-class values of hard work and simplicity. "Now I don't mind choppin' wood," he says, "and I don't care if the money's no good." The culture of acquisitiveness is alien to Virgil. "Ya take what ya need and ya leave the rest."[139] The song's lyrics and mournful tone, enhanced by Garth Hudson's anguished-sounding melodica and Rick Danko's lonesome high harmonies, create a sensation of despair for a region and people who have succumbed to the Yankee invaders. Helm's lead vocal, with its flat southern inflection, further heightens the powerful message of "Dixie." Jim Cullen finds parallels between the tune's message and attempts by former Confederates to reinterpret the war's meaning during and after Reconstruction. "Ironically," Cullen elucidates, "a sober contemplation of Southern defeat shaded, almost imperceptibly, into a celebration that did little to examine the underlying causes of that defeat by anything other than overwhelming numbers."[140] By telling the story of the Civil War at a microhistorical level, the Band avoided the uncomfortable and central matter of southern slavery and racism.

The song's Lost Cause content received little attention from countercultural and national commentators. What seemed most compelling and powerful about "The Night They Drove Old Dixie Down" was how, as one Band chronicler later pointed out, it "gives voice to several thousand anonymous people's stories."[141] Many listeners said that these stories challenged their preconceived notions about the region and caused them to look upon the South not as a bastion of racism, but rather as a storehouse of welcome, uncommon traits. Jonathan Taplin, the Band's tour manager, was astonished when he heard "The Night They Drove Old Dixie Down" for the first time. "It was just the most moving experience I'd had for, God, I don't know how long," he remembered. "Because for me, being a northern liberal kid who'd been involved in the civil rights movement and had a whole attitude towards the South, it was a very cathartic experience. It was like having it all wrapped up in three and a half minutes, the whole sense of dignity and place and tradition. It brought tears to my eyes."[142]

"Dixie's" perspective, as Cullen indicates, was hardly new, but rarely had the Civil War's consequences for ordinary white southerners been presented so powerfully and appealingly. By focusing on the white working class, Robertson's tune left no room for mulling the war's impact upon the South's enslaved black population. His songs about the South like "Dixie" fit with the common countercultural view that the South was not singularly responsible for the country's racism, and that, actually, its traditional white culture had much to offer the technocratic North. Had the Band tried to recover the regional black perspective, it would have complicated—if not undermined—its imaginings of the South.

The Band's evocation of the white South in "The Night They Drove Old Dixie Down" received lavish acclaim in *Rolling Stone*. Echoing Jonathan Taplin's feelings of cultural discovery and reevaluation, the magazine's co-founder Ralph J. Gleason, a middle-aged man but also a reliable espouser of countercultural views, asserted, "Nothing that I have read . . . has brought home to me the overwhelming human sense of history that this song does. . . . It has the ring of truth and the whole aura of authenticity," so much so that "it seem[s] impossible that this isn't some oral tradition material handed down from father to son straight from that winter of '65 to today."[143] For Gleason, the triumph of Robertson's songwriting in "Dixie" was its apparent reality. And if this song was reality, then most nonsoutherners' understandings of the Civil War and of white southerners' racial guilt must have been wrong. More than that, Gleason's reading of the track reflected a belief in the greater authenticity of the white southern experience—an experience steeped in history and moored to traditions of labor and family.

Both countercultural and mainstream publications moved beyond song analysis and sought to explain the larger meaning of the Band within the context of their imagined South's supposed cultural utility. It is in this effort that the *national* power of an out-of-time, fantasied South in the late 1960s and early 1970s is clearly demonstrated. The group developed a reputation in underground and mainstream press circles for creating music that offered a refuge from the decade's social upheavals—race riots, political assassinations, war, and protests—which formed the basis of the popular conception of America in turmoil. The countercultural *Los Angeles Free Press* attested that the Band's "lyrics paradoxically reflected the troubles of these times with the backwoods flavor of the music."[144] In other words, theirs was not simply old music, applicable only to the southern past; the Band had taken tradition and made it relevant to the milieu of 1960s America. There was a sense among countercultural observers that by returning to the traditions of the southland, the Band had crafted a musical and cultural world that veered away from the modern unrest wracking American society. *Rolling Stone* contributor Ed Ward would later remember "that *The Band* helped a lot of people dizzy from the confusion and disorientation of the '60s feel that the nation was big enough to include them, too."[145] Although the Band's South featured struggle and both actual and anticipated violence, it also knitted a durable, unchanging safety net of community and family support that often felt missing in modern America. As Ward put it, Robertson wrote about a world that touched on the counterculture's profound sense of alienation from its political and cultural environment.

This appraisal—that the Band promised refuge from a tumultuous America through its imagined white South—was even more pronounced in the popular press, revealing the power of the group's southernness to dialogue with many mainstream Americans. Titling its 1970 profile "The Band: Music from Home," *Look* magazine contrasted the performers with overtly political musicians and cited Robertson's aversion to mixing music and politics. The article's author, John Poppy, did not state it outright, but his descriptions of the Band's music underlined their songs' deeper cultural politics. He singled out *The Band*'s "The Night They Drove Old Dixie Down," "Up on Cripple Creek," "King Harvest," and "Rockin' Chair" as proof of the group's ability to write songs that "tell stories of things we may not have experienced directly but still feel in our blood, bits of our collective life on this continent."[146] Note the similarity between Poppy's and Ed Ward's analyses: together they proclaimed that the Band was teaching Americans about themselves and helping them to recover their true identities. It is telling that Poppy selected the four songs from *The Band* that are most explicitly about the South. Like others, he detected both authenticity and universality in the artists' sonic expeditions into the region. "The Band," Poppy certified, "seems to be recording an American history—of earth, humor, muscle, emotion—that could stand with *Let Us Now Praise Famous Men* for truth."[147] Ralph Gleason made the same literary connection in his review.

Journalist Jay Cocks drew similar conclusions in a 1970 *Time* cover story, "Down to Old Dixie and Back." The author considered, among other things, Americans' increasing search for roots as key to the Band's commercial vigor. Cocks placed the group within the country-rock movement, associating the genre's birth with artists' desire to return to musical simplicity. He went further, though, to analyze the music's larger cultural meaning: "Country rock is also a symptom of a general cultural reaction to the most unsettling decade the U.S. has yet endured. The yen to escape the corrupt present by returning to the virtuous past—real or imagined—has haunted Americans, never more so than today."[148] Few hip or straight journalists made this claim as unequivocally or as eloquently as Cocks. Addressing the "commercialized, McLuhanized, televised, homogenized world" in which the Band made its music, Cocks maintained that Robertson's southern-focused songs collectively functioned as a salve against the artificialities of the modern, workaday world.[149] "What The Band has worked out," he explained, "is something that countless other Americans hope for, a sort of watchful, self-protective truce within the encroaching world of noisy commerce."[150]

The very title of the *Time* article proposed that the Band had located in the South valuable alternatives to the status quo that were capable of regaining the type of authentic lived experience negated by the contemporary American existence. By embracing a South that was old and traditional, Cocks articulated, these four Canadians and one Arkansan were not only performing interesting music and paying tribute to white southern rural people but also building a refuge from the unpleasant realities of the present. Cocks concluded his piece with a quote from Robertson that demonstrated the musician's grasp of the escapist appeal of his group: "Live outside what's going on? Well, look what's going on. You almost have to live outside or you lose it. You lose everything. You become your own joke."[151] The Band's popularity among both the counterculture and the larger record-buying public suggests that its imagined white southern sanctuary found many willing adherents.

Although Cocks and other media personnel grouped the Band with other country-rock acts, its sound never fit with the country experimentations of acts like the Byrds, the Everly Brothers, the Flying Burrito Brothers, and Linda Ronstadt. Its influences were too diverse—the Band likely owed as much to Ray Charles as to Hank Williams—to be easily categorized. Still, country-rock was the name that stuck. "We hated it," Helm said of the label.[152] Aside from the sound, Robertson felt little in common with California-based country-rock performers, who he thought likely had more of a direct familial connection to southern music and culture.[153] Regardless of Robertson's attitude, in terms of its fantasies of the South, his outfit had much more in common with other country-rock acts than he acknowledged. No band better exemplified the views of hippies who embraced the rural, working-class, white South than *the* Band, a group of mostly nonsouthern outsiders whose songs' imaginative and imagined handling of the region showed the continuing allure of eternal, unchanging white southernness in the 1960s, not only for hippies, but for straight Americans as well.

Conclusion

As the 1960s gave way to the 1970s, the counterculture continued to borrow from the South to critique straight America. West Coast country-rock trod a different path, moving away from its southern roots. The most popular artists like the Eagles and Linda Ronstadt did not try to incorporate "hard" country into a rock format. They opted instead for slight country touches (a banjo here, a dobro there) to sweeten the sound of their easy-listening pop-rock songs. In her analysis of country-rock, Olivia Carter Mather draws parallels between commentators' identification of the Deep South with the larger Sunbelt in the

1970s and the Eagles' deemphasis of the "southernness" inherent in country music. "While previous country rock projects relied on southern culture and its myths (i.e. Gram Parsons as 'gothic')," she argues, "the legacy and success of the Eagles rests on how they were able to take regional modes of behavior and un-regionalize them, or at least apply them to a wider geographical experience."[154] The reference to Parsons is poignant. In 1973, the year after the release of the Eagles' debut album and the same year as the Byrds' breakup, the twenty-six-year-old Parsons's life of excess caught up with him; he died of a drug overdose. The golden era of southern-centric country-rock was over.

The counterculture was in eclipse, too, with some hippies still doing their best to maintain their values as rural communards, largely away from the public's (and the media's) view. While they lasted as a cultural force, hippies carried with them two complicated imaginings of the South that met at the confluence of the Changing South and the Down-Home South. On the one hand, they saw a region wracked by racism, full of obtuse, oppressive whites trying to keep blacks and other challengers of tradition in their places. In this version of the South, hippies tended to write off white racism as symptomatic of national bigotry, while accepting that it may have been more pronounced below the Mason-Dixon Line. Another strand of thinking shaded the countercultural reception to country-rock music: the South was a repository of needed values overlooked by mainstream American society. The two views were not mutually exclusive, and therefore, counterculturists could embrace both outlooks simultaneously. As a result, the stereotype of the vicious rural white southerners of *Easy Rider* could coexist with the noble farmer/Confederate soldier of the Band's catalog.

Like so many Americans, numerous hippies saw in country music's "three chords and the truth" an entry point into white southern culture. This cultural legacy appealed to both musicians and counterculturists dissatisfied with the emotional distance of contemporary rock music. By fashioning their own version of country music, country-rock artists reinterpreted the genre for their mostly countercultural audience. But the sound of country-rock mattered less than what it embodied. Like the country music and the white southern culture from which it derived, it meant honesty, simplicity, family, and authentic, rooted living, away from urban and suburban problems. Hippies idealized the South as one of the last places where these values existed in unadulterated form. Of course, their conception of southern authenticity was based on a location that did not currently exist and had never quite existed. That was largely irrelevant, though. Hippies were not interested in documenting the reality of the South; they desired its symbolism. In the southland and in country-rock music, they saw instruments to buttress their condemnation of modern, technocratic American society. Counterculturists used what they admired about the South for this larger purpose, ironically connecting them with the increasingly mainstream tendency to employ the imagined white South to express one's dissatisfaction with the modern United States.

It is notable that hippies searched so broadly to locate resources for their critique of the alleged oppressive plasticity of America. More than a simple acknowledgment, this recognition necessitates a more complicated approach to comprehending the cultural revolution and the malleable uses of southernness in late 1960s and 1970s America. Just as counterculturists found alternatives to contemporary life in imagined Native American and Eastern cultures, as other scholars have noted, they also encountered them in the South, the land of both the Band *and* George Wallace. As the next chapter demonstrates, Wallace exemplified a very different South (think of it as a positive spin on the Vicious South narrative) that still maintained the sense of masculine self-reliance implicit in the counterculture's South. Wallace brandished his southernness on the national scene during his four presidential campaigns (1964–1976). He engaged in a discourse best termed the Masculine South, and he was far from its only purveyor. Although in many ways rejecting Wallace's perspective, popular productions like the novel and film *Deliverance* (1970, 1972) and the movie *Walking Tall* (1973) shared the Alabama politician's argument that the white South, especially the rural white South, offered an elixir for the nation's supposedly flagging virility in the late 1960s and early 1970s.

CHAPTER 3

"When in Doubt, Kick Ass"

The Masculine South(s) of George Wallace, *Walking Tall*, and *Deliverance*

In 1974 *Creem*, a music monthly that distinguished itself as a more purely rock-oriented publication than *Rolling Stone*, dispatched a team of non-southern writers to travel into the South. There they interviewed locals and provided readers with an updated, tongue-in-cheek version of W. J. Cash's *The Mind of the South*. The magazine's mostly young white male readership learned about southern men's sexual proclivities, Atlanta's drag queen scene, and the enduring legacy of racism. *Creem* trafficked in an overtly salacious and visceral presentation of southern life. Editor Lester Bangs called it a place with "an abiding and unaffected warmth, and a raunch that can't be belied."[1] For him, white southern traditionalism comprised not only hospitality and communalism but also a penchant for violence. Borrowing a line from a bar patron he met in Macon, Georgia, Bangs summed up what he considered this shoot-first-ask-questions-later attitude of the South: "When in doubt, kick ass."[2]

The freewheeling spirit that floored Bangs and his *Creem* colleagues resembled what W. J. Cash had identified as the epitome of unrestrained white manhood: the "hell of a fellow." He lived "to stand on his head in a bar," Cash described, "to toss down a pint of raw whiskey in a gulp, to fiddle and dance all night, to bite off the nose or gouge out the eye of a favorite enemy, to fight harder and love harder than the next man, to be known eventually far and wide as a hell of a fellow."[3] This understanding of white southern manliness underwrote a key part of imaginings of the South in the popular and political discourses of the late 1960s and 1970s: white southernness as housing the violence necessary to stem the supposed decline of masculinity during the period.

Freed from the ubiquity of the Vicious South narrative, beginning in the late 1960s, the Masculine South, often but not exclusively cast in rural terms, proved to be a popular discourse among many culturally and politically conservative Americans. This concept allowed them to explore the perceived attributes of the white southerner who exerted a *regenerative* violence capable of bolstering the masculinity necessary to achieve social control over the alleged softness and social permissiveness that pervaded the sixties era's cultural and racial liberation movements.[4] Trent Watts has astutely stated that "in the years since World War II, the American South has exhibited a variety of models of white manhood and masculinity."[5] The Masculine South, of course, was not exactly the "real" South any more than its unruly cousin the Vicious South; it was another aspect of the South of the Mind suited to a time in which the national conversation fixated on centers of social unrest largely outside of the South. Like the Vicious South, it treated white southernness as inherently violent, but in contrast, this fantasy cast southern-derived restorative violence as transformative, not pathological, and worthy of national emulation. Three manifestations of the Masculine South stand out for their popularity in the national consciousness, and for their varying politics: George Wallace's national campaigns for president (1964–1976)—especially his 1968 third-party run—the highly grossing low-budget film *Walking Tall* (1973), and the even more profitable novel (1970) and movie (1972) versions of *Deliverance*.

George Wallace constructed the South as a place where white men still ruled without question and would defend themselves with force if necessary. In contrast to allegedly lawless northerners, he argued, southerners used violence to maintain their masculine prowess, which in turn helped to preserve the social and racial order. As a "based on a true story" account of Sheriff Buford Pusser's attempts to collar bootleggers in McNairy County, Tennessee, in the 1960s, *Walking Tall* mythologized a South similarly reliant on regenerative violence, yet it invoked nonsouthern fables of the southland as a rural and masculine refuge while sidestepping Wallaceite racial animosity. Meanwhile, in their respective versions of *Deliverance*, southern novelist James Dickey and British director John Boorman detailed four Atlanta suburbanites' search for manhood in the terrifying Georgia hinterland. Dickey and Boorman identified the rural white South as a locale with a distinctive predilection for brutal aggression; to varying degrees, they deemed it a useful tool for overcoming the emasculation of suburban life. Each of these popular representations simultaneously provoked and embodied powerful imaginings about the capacity of the rejuvenating violence supposedly inherent in the white South—particularly in the rural white South. All three endorsed the Masculine South as an instrument for shoring up American manhood in order to smother the political, social, and cultural disturbances that were rattling U.S. society in the sixties era.

By the late 1960s, new challenges to standards of American masculinity emerged from previously marginalized groups, including blacks openly advocating for both civil rights and the rights of manhood. Simultaneously, the shaggy-haired men of the counterculture and members of the New Left pushed for new definitions of masculinity. In the Port Huron Statement (1962), SDS encouraged pacifism and utilizing "unfulfilled capacities for reason, freedom and love" and the "unrealized potential for self-evaluation, self-direction, self-understanding, and creativity."[6] By the early 1970s, frustrated elements of the radical Left would turn to bombings and other attacks on public property, but liberal/leftist calls for new formulations of masculinity generally rejected violence as a suitable manifestation of manly behavior. Instead, proponents of such views contended that violence demeaned both its purveyors and its victims. The most powerful critique of modern masculinity, though, came from the feminist movement, which called for women's emancipation from the oppressive patriarchy and for rethinking the normative "roles" of men and women.

Some popular observers looked favorably upon what Barbara Ehrenreich has termed the "androgynous drift" of the late 1960s and 1970s, with its acceleration of men turning "away from the rigidity of the breadwinner's role" using the feminist language of "liberation."[7] Men's liberationists latched onto works with titles like *The Liberated Man*, *The Hazards of Being Male*, and *The Male Machine*. These books favored a more fluid masculine identity and, like feminists, deemed the status quo as similarly detrimental to men's well-being. Making this point—with obvious exaggeration—psychologist Herb Goldberg, the author of *The Hazards of Being Male* wrote, "The male in our culture is at a growth impasse. He won't move—not because he is protecting his cherished central place in the sun, but because he *can't* move. . . . He lacks the fluidity of the female who can readily move between the traditional definitions of male or female behavior and roles."[8]

Not everyone was ready to leap into a new era of gender flexibility. Men's liberation, it was alleged, could be just as unsettling—and harmful—as women's liberation. For example, claims surfaced linking the abandonment of one's patriarchal responsibilities with a decline in productivity, prompting *Business Week* in 1977 to lambaste the "great male cop-out from the work ethic."[9] Who was to blame? Some commentators pointed fingers at weak men. Others saw a convenient scapegoat in feminism. In their 1974 book

The Male Dilemma: How to Survive the Sexual Revolution, Anne Steinmann and David J. Fox took the latter approach. "The publicity surrounding the 'women's lib' movement has been formidable," they stated, "but rarely, if ever, in the avalanche of words by or about women, has man been mentioned at all. He is told he must move over, but no one has bothered to tell him where or how. Like the establishment, he has become a symbol, a shadow."[10] Men, once unquestionably at the head of U.S. society, were now, such claims had it, ceding—willingly or unwillingly—their authority. Either way, alarmists cautioned, Americans had cause for concern.

Popular culture of the 1970s both referenced and fueled these debates about men's roles by displaying a host of sensitive, even broken, men. Films like *The Deer Hunter* and *Coming Home* (both 1978) centered on psychologically and physically wounded Vietnam veterans, shells of their formerly strapping selves. Record companies released albums by representatives of the "New Man," according to one scholar, "in the persons of lank-haired singer-songwriters like James Taylor, Jackson Browne, and Neil Young, with their miserable ballads about lonely men wandering dejectedly along the seashore."[11] Those effeminate hippies had had their way, or so it seemed.

Cultural conservatives, adding to a chorus of alarmist voices, looked for ways to restore traditional male behavior and dominance. Sounding like a pulpier, more misogynistic Steinmann and Fox, an advertisement for the men's magazine *True* promised readers "informative features that bring the American man and American values back from the shadows. Back from the sterile couches of pedantic psychiatrists. Back from behind the frivolous skirts of [women's] libbers."[12] Action, maybe even violence, was the key to restoring languishing masculinity, such antifeminist critics decreed. This mentality seeped through the surface of such popular film characterizations as Clint Eastwood's old-school cop in *Dirty Harry*, who with his almost comically suggestive long-barreled Smith & Wesson .44 Magnum, blows through municipal bureaucracy and civil liberties in the interest of bringing down an epicene, long-haired, and cowardly but deadly serial killer. The same year as *Dirty Harry*'s release (1971), ABC Pictures issued director Sam Peckinpah's controversial *Straw Dogs*. This time the effete man was the hero, an American mathematician who restores his manliness by killing off the ruffians terrorizing him and his wife in the English countryside with a variety of instruments, including a bear trap. The English countryside was very distant to Americans. Other proponents of regenerative masculine violence looked for solutions closer to home—in the Masculine South of their imaginations.

George Wallace: Violent White Southern Masculinity on the National Stage

In his 1970 book *DO IT! Scenarios of the Revolution,* Jerry Rubin depicted segregationist Alabama governor George Wallace as the personification of American imperialism and violence. "He is the symbol of the country which destroyed the Indian, enslaved the black, colonized Latin America, A-bombed Japan, invaded Cuba and napalmed Vietnam," sneered Rubin. "He is the Amerikan flag. He is the cowboy, the Marine, the Bible-toting missionary priest, the businessman and the cop-on-the-beat."[13] Rubin's use of the right-wing Wallace to represent Amerika's purportedly mean-spirited, foot-on-the-neck policies at home and abroad fit with the radical's larger leftist critique of the nation. The deeply masculine imagery that Rubin applied to Wallace was no accident. A major component of the iconography of the four-time presidential candidate lay in his manly demeanor and vigorous attacks on a host of social enemies supposedly plaguing working- and middle-class white American men and their families, from black welfare recipients to hippies and northeastern elites.

Rubin's conflation of Wallace with bullying Americanism was somewhat ironic given that no postwar politician was more identified with the South (that is, the *white* South) than the governor. A group of British journalists covering the 1968 presidential race termed him "a southerner to the end of his brilliantined hair."[14] Wallace said he was a "professional southerner," with a vocation not only to represent the white South but also to ardently defend what he saw as its interests.[15] He was born in the town of Clio in the southern Alabama countryside. The census of 1920, completed the year after his birth, put the population at 838. Wallace did not promote his rural roots as explicitly as Jimmy Carter would later, although he proudly told voters that his father was a "dirt farmer" and "as a youth he did chores on the farm."[16] The South for Wallace was more than farmlands. It was the anti-America, or perhaps more accurately, America's essence: a place in which white supremacy was still unquestioned, the common man could still get ahead, and manly, socially sanctioned violence was necessary. For him, it was exactly what the rest of the nation needed in the late 1960s and early 1970s.

As governor of Alabama, Wallace communicated as a patriarchal protector of the segregated southern way of life against an intrusive federal government. He, declared journalist Marquis Childs, was driven by "an almost Messianic sense of his own mission to free the South of the hated Yankee domination."[17] The governor did not overtly thump his chest for anything he called "southern masculinity." He did not have to. His image as a southerner and his constant references to the draconian tactics employed by Alabama law enforcement to keep the peace performed that work for him. With such hypermasculine rhetoric, the "pugnacious Southern bad boy," as Wallace biographer Dan T. Carter has called him, cemented a "basic bond" with "his audience . . . [that celebrated] a man's world free from the constraints of women and their weaknesses."[18] Wallace, then, helped to both form and reinforce the perception that southern manhood was a unique and ass-kicking counter to the feminization—embodied in an emerging culture of permissiveness—afflicting the larger society.

As a presidential contender, Wallace appealed to Americans who felt powerless in the face of confusing domestic and international transformations. These people included Chicagoans Ronald and Sally Hoppe, who spied in Wallace a mouthpiece for their beleaguered values. "The world [the Hoppes] were born to, a white world of upward mobility based on hard work, has been threatened by the storms of social change," reported *Time* in 1968. "They now find it an incomprehensible world of yippies and hippies, riots, crime and inconclusive war, and they long for solutions couched in phrases that they can understand and relate to themselves."[19] The Alabamian spoke to such presumed powerlessness, highlighting the value of "southern-style" violence as a tool for keeping the social and racial order in check and regenerating an allegedly depleted American manhood. Without real men, Wallace indicated, the country was in danger of succumbing to disorder at home and abroad. He stressed his own virility through his physicality on the presidential campaign trail, pounding podiums to underline his points and reminding voters of his early days as a boxer. In exploiting this pugilist image, the governor conveyed that he would protect "average" Americans from their enemies and also beat those enemies into submission with his fists, casually recommending for them "a good crease in the skull."[20]

Wallace's prejudices and gendered performances appalled critics. But they appealed to Americans who admired white southerners like him for holding the line on race and standing up for "rednecks," regardless of region, who felt ignored by party leaders. The candidate's macho, ferocious southernness constructed the region as a distinctive, masculine alternative to hippies, black protesters, feminists, government bureaucrats, and intellectuals, who he deemed as undermining the vigor necessary to maintain order in the midst of the political and social confusion of American society in the 1960s and 1970s.

In that effort, Wallace enlisted a malleable, transferable notion of energetic southernness rooted in the anger and backlash racism of the Vicious South. He searched broadly to locate support for his quest to maintain the segregated southern way of life against the orders of the federal judiciary. His first inaugural address as governor, delivered in January 1963, is best remembered for its vow, "Segregation today. Segregation tomorrow. Segregation forever." But Wallace surrounded that pledge with an entreaty to nonsoutherners to join the cause of white southern segregationists. After all, one did not have to hail from the South to be "southern." The governor proclaimed, "You native sons and daughters of old New England's rock-ribbed patriotism . . . and you sturdy natives of the great Mid-West . . . and you descendants of the far West flaming spirit of pioneer freedom . . . we invite you to come and be with us . . . for you are of the Southern mind . . . and the Southern spirit . . . and the Southern philosophy . . . you are Southerners too and brothers with us in our fight."[21] Wallace's attempt to redefine southernness as not contingent on birthplace or even region was cagey and born of self-interest. It was also necessary to support his contention, reminiscent of antebellum enslavers, that the South had maintained the true meaning of the nation's founding in liberty (*not* equality).

If the white South had preserved true American manhood, then, according to Wallace's logic, nonsoutherners who espoused these values must be "southern" too. Political scientist Joseph E. Lowndes has stated that during his presidential campaigns, Wallace furthered this sleight of hand. The Alabamian, Lowndes finds, took the "symbolic figure of the white southerner under attack from the federal government" and expanded it to "the more general 'Middle American' as the embodiment of the signifier *America*—the white middle-class male from every region who is pushed around by an invasive federal government, threatened by crime and social disorder, discriminated against by affirmative action, and surrounded by increasing moral degradation."[22] But for Wallace, southernness represented more than victimization; it also meant resorting to violence to punish what he considered the nation's victimizers. And lower-class and middle-class white males would remain victims, in the governor's view, until they unleashed their full manhood. "Southern" violence, therefore, was a trait that he presented as worthy of transregional emulation.

Beginning as a presidential candidate in 1964, Wallace contrasted his toughness and fondness for purposeful violence with the imagined effeminacy of his political and social targets. He focused much of his rhetoric on vilifying Washington's institutions, which he claimed were run by weak, ineffectual men. In 1967, he told the conservative *National Review*, "The people are going to be fed up with the sissy attitude of Lyndon Johnson and all the intellectual morons and theoreticians he has around him." Elsewhere he denounced the hostile press corps as "sissy-britches intellectual morons."[23] Government bureaucrats, activist Supreme Court justices, and "pseudo-intellectuals" (i.e., professors and supposed policy experts who would be better served by using a little common sense) were running down the entire country, he insisted.

They were robbing states, municipalities, and individuals of independence and self-reliance, both qualities of manliness he associated with the South.

At rallies, Wallace mocked the long-haired and bearded protesters who dared to shout insults or hold signs with trolling slogans like "Seig Heil, Ya'll" and "Weirdos for Wallace."[24] He carefully honed his responses, and he used them repeatedly. The governor offered to autograph protesters' sandals, and in response to hippie-looking hecklers, he would joke, "Now, take it easy *honey*. Oops, it's a he; sorry I thought it was a she."[25]

With lines like these, Wallace contrasted himself with the feminized opponents of his good, decent, orderly, patriarchal society. He positioned himself as the perfect masculine foil: tough, combative, and always ready for a scrap. Observers consistently referred to Wallace's early days as a two-time bantamweight Golden Gloves champion to underline his cantankerous personality and political style. During his 1972 presidential run, Wallace's campaign further played up this iconography, selling wristwatches with a caricature of the candidate as a boxer. For conservative pundit James Jackson Kilpatrick, Wallace was "a man in constant motion," who, while being interviewed, "is constantly bouncing on the ring ropes and shuffling in the corner, shadow boxing, skipping rope."[26] The governor also had swagger. "He can," wrote Kilpatrick, "strut sitting down."[27]

Wallace's pugnacious image derived from his deftness at ducking and weaving around difficult questions; he also preached fierce retribution against those whom he deemed perils to the country. For a working-class and middle-class white constituency wracked with feelings of feebleness, Wallace represented raw power.[28] Through his hypermasculine fantasy of governance, he spoke to these feelings of inadequacy. His politics largely consisted of "getting tough," but he offered few policy solutions. A 1969 *Esquire* article summarized the centrality of violence to Wallace's politics. "His message was simple, his rhetoric unvarnished," the article read. "Ghetto riots? 'People who riot ought to be bopped on the head.' Campus protests? 'We ought to grab some of those college students by the hair of the head and stick 'em under a good jail.' Law and order? 'Just let the police enforce the law.' Vietnam? 'We should go in and beat hell out of 'em or get out.'"[29] In one of his favorite lines, Wallace made plans to run over any anarchist who lay down in front of his car.[30]

Ronnie Van Zant, front man for the 1970s southern rock group Lynyrd Skynyrd, underlined the cathartic nature of Wallace's southern message, assuring the British magazine *New Musical Express*, "If any of them Russians or anyone call your queen a *whore*, he wouldn't let 'em get away with it."[31] Van Zant had obviously absorbed the Alabamian's linkage of violence, manliness, and feelings of empowerment. Like his program for barreling through domestic difficulties, through his constant willingness to spar, Wallace would help maintain U.S. preeminence as the democratic world's masculine protector, capable of withstanding the forces—communist and otherwise—that he identified as conspiring to undermine it.

Violence was central to both Wallace's allure and his ability to draw dividing lines between himself and his supporters and the forces they opposed. Although he never engaged in violence himself, *Newsweek*'s claim that "his appeal is metaphorically violent" turned a blind eye to the way that the candidate presented himself as personally ready for combat.[32] Frequently, his ugly rhetoric melded with violent action at his rallies. Joseph Lowndes has explained that "in his stand against federal authority, in his threats to run over demonstrators if they got in the way of his car, in his links to violent white supremacists, and in the fistfights at his rallies, Wallace and his supporters forged a new sense of us and them, drew new lines that defined new identities."[33] Wallace presided over the chaos, baiting protesters and at times menacing them. While stumping in the West in October 1968, the *New York Times* recorded, "He angrily challenged 'punks' to come to the platform."[34] The candidate generally kept his emotion in check despite such thunderous oratory. Instead, he let his supporters battle on his behalf. Presidential campaign watcher Theodore White, for example, discussed an attack on one anti-Wallace protester in Cicero, Illinois, the Chicago suburb where in 1966 angry whites had pelted black civil rights marchers, including Martin Luther King Jr., with bricks and bottles. White recounted seeing a woman, who had obviously internalized Wallace's gendered and racialized rhetoric, assault the anti-Wallace demonstrator. She "clawed [at the protester's] face, slapped it." She next "yelled, 'You nigger-loving homosexual!'" while other "approving" Wallace supporters spewed similarly hateful utterances.[35] Such occurrences were not uncommon and were well documented in the national press.

Not surprisingly, the violence lacing Wallace's speeches prompted critics to label him and his supporters as rednecks. The governor, of course, treated the redneck epithet as a badge of honor. "Well, there are a lot of us rednecks in this country," he told a nonsouthern audience in 1968, "and they don't all live in the South."[36] Like southern identity itself, Wallace reimagined "redneck" as a term applicable to any white American, regardless of class or region, who adhered to the candidate's principles. In doing so, he suggested that the nation would be in better shape if its leaders embraced their inner redneck and met social disorder with quick, retaliatory violence.

Wallace's siren song to the nation's rednecks carried with it obvious racial undertones. His weaving together of southernness and violence was a dominant feature of his dual effort to restore white masculine vitality and rescue the status quo from jeopardy. Nowhere was this more evident than in his antiblack rhetoric. As a presidential candidate, Wallace rarely spoke publicly in openly racist terms. He instead employed a coded racial language that identified many of the problems plaguing the nation in the late 1960s and early 1970s as largely black perpetrated. Through veiled phrasing, Wallace touted his southernness as an implicit marker of his willingness to use violence to maintain order and white supremacy. As one former Alabama senator put it, "He can use all the other issues—law and order, running your own schools, protecting property rights—and never mention race. But people will know he's telling them, 'A nigger's trying to get your job, trying to move into your neighborhood.' What Wallace is doing is talking to them in a kind of shorthand, a kind of code."[37]

Wallace's supporters were aware of the centrality of violence and racial suppression in his message. In September 1968, as the governor's third-party candidacy crested in the polls, a crowd of 150 whites, some wearing Wallace buttons and shouting the candidate's name, attacked a group of Black Panthers at a Brooklyn courthouse. *Newsweek* associated the incident with Wallace's own extreme speechifying.[38] In the same piece, the magazine quoted a Wallace supporter who touched on the candidate's link between forcefully maintaining racial control and his oath to restore calm and stability to American society. "He's gonna turn this country around," the man said, and in the same breath, "It's not that we dislike niggers—we hate 'em."[39] Other supporters believed that a Wallace presidency would result in a strongly enforced racial hierarchy like the one he tried, but failed, to maintain as Alabama governor. That same month, in 1968, *Washington Post* columnists Rowland Evans and Robert Novak interviewed a collection of Wallace voters in Warren, Michigan. One of them, a school janitor, spoke approvingly of the racial violence he saw at the core of Wallace's proclamations. "He'd crack the whip on the Negroes," the man said.[40] In each of these instances, the governor's supporters followed the logic of his politics of powerlessness that posited violence as crucial to restoring both racial and social discipline to beleaguered white Americans.

The prevalence of racism among Wallaceites was hardly surprising given how consistently the Alabamian attributed the crime and general unrest wracking American cities to riotous blacks. His authority to stop that disorder rested in part on the premise that he embodied a law-and-order South distinctive from the lawless North. For his audiences, Wallace imagined a South where authorities kept control with the threat of force and crushed unruly and criminal behavior, especially that exhibited by minorities. In the South, black offenders were not coddled, as he claimed they were in the rest of the country. He hollered that illegal disturbances must be met by righteous and overwhelming violence. "We don't have riots in Alabama," he told a packed Madison Square Garden crowd during the 1968 race. "They start a riot down there, first one of 'em to pick up a brick gets a bullet in the brain, that's all. And then you walk over to the next one and say, 'All right, pick up a brick.'"[41] The governor did not have to tell his listeners who "they" (i.e., blacks) were.

In an interview with journalist Robert Sherrill, Wallace further outlined his racialized distinctions between the purportedly orderly—and roughly policed—South and the crime-ridden cities above the Mason-Dixon Line. As detailed in the reporter's 1968 book *Gothic Politics in the Deep South: Stars of the New Confederacy*, Wallace attested that blacks actually enjoyed greater protection in the South than in the North.[42] He added that both black and white southern neighborhoods were safe. "We know how to live together down here," he boasted. "You can walk through the nigger section without fear. A nigger can walk through the white section. We've got good law enforcement in Alabama." Wallace's hypocrisy was obvious. Sherrill editorialized that the governor made this statement in the midst of a series of black church burnings in Lowndes County, Alabama.[43]

For Wallace, violence was *the* basis of ensuring law and order. He called to mind what journalist Marshall Frady referred to as white southerners' "loosely leashed readiness for mayhem."[44] Wallace would not have necessarily disagreed; it was the target of the mayhem that made it justified. Although the Alabamian claimed to deplore violence, he excused it—and even fostered it—when it was used against demonstrators, rioters, nonwhites, and other enemies of his hypermasculine South. Using rough tactics to maintain law and order was one of the characteristics that Wallace felt distinguished the South from the rest of the country. Nonsoutherners seemingly did not have the fortitude to properly enforce the law. While en route to New Hampshire in late 1967, Wallace judged the state's people as "kind of overbred," meaning in part that they lacked the toughness and instincts for the warranted violence he considered central to the character of white southerners.[45] In an interview with the *New York Times*' Tom Wicker, he implied that this northern overrefinement led to a failure to crack down on social disorder. At one point, Wallace articulated his desire to "smash one of these federal judges in the head and then burn the courthouse down. But," he told Wicker, "I'm too genteel."[46] The politician then went further, pledging that Americans would benefit if only he could cut loose a group of reactionary white southerners on the nation's racial and social problems: "What we need in this country is some governors that used to work up here at Birmingham in the steel mills with about a tenth-grade education. A governor like that wouldn't be so genteel. He'd put out his orders and he'd say, 'The first man who loots something [that] doesn't belong to him is a dead man. My orders are to shoot to kill.' That's the way to keep law and order. If you'd killed about three that way at Watts the other forty wouldn't be dead today."[47]

Wallace's claims of the South's relative safety and the benefits of a violent southernness were clearly self-serving and obscured continuing racial conflict in the region. But they presented an enticing, if superficial, portrait of law enforcement for like-minded Americans: to recover its masculinity, the effeminate North just needed to embrace severe force and punishment. Then criminals would be running for the shadows instead of terrorizing city residents while impotent public officials looked on.

As his hypothetical regarding Birmingham steel workers revealed, a faith in gut-level instincts born of anti-intellectualism drove the logic of Wallace's violent southernness. The candidate celebrated the "commonsense" thinking of masculine, hardworking nonelites whose solution was to lash out rather than to engage in the touchy-feeliness he bemoaned in the measured judgments of the country's "pseudo-intellectuals." The people he called "the folks" (i.e., those who supported him) intuitively knew how to deal with a problem; pseudo-intellectuals, said Wallace, used unmanly overanalysis. "Any truck driver'd know right off what to do at the scene of an accident," he fumed, "but you take a college professor, he'd just stand around lookin' and gettin' sick."[48] "The folks" had much more sense, he bragged, than these so-called experts. With populist and anti-intellectual zeal, he said he deferred to the judgments of barbers, steelworkers, textile workers, autoworkers, firemen, policemen, and beauticians. For instance, the *Washington Post*'s George Lardner wrote that Wallace, a former taxi driver, hyped cabbies as "a fount of the right kind of knowledge, an exemplar of instinctive wisdom."[49]

Wallace pinpointed the common folks—his token inclusion of beauticians aside—as robust, patriotic men, willing to take vigorous action against America's enemies in the nation's cities as well as in Vietnam. His theme of restorative, retributive violence lay at the heart of his oft-said line during the 1968 campaign that the police should be allowed to run the country for two years in order to suppress domestic crime and anti-Americanism.[50] When he made this statement, the Alabamian was surely thinking of individuals like the Philadelphia cop and self-described potential Wallace voter who told pollster Samuel Lubell of his quick turn to physical brutality when he witnessed a black man assault a fellow police officer. "Well, I'll tell you I got extreme," he admitted. "I chased that nigger for three blocks and when I caught up with him I beat his ass off."[51]

The Alabamian questioned liberal experts' policy decisions that favored careful deliberation and explanation over blind action, particularly when assessing the high crime rates in urban ghettoes and other social problems. Wallace sometimes blasted such solutions with racist enthusiasm. At a speech in Los Angeles's "Little Dixie," he derided the liberal tendency to search for underlying social factors as the root cause of crime. Their excuse? "The killer didn't get any watermelon to eat when he was 10 years old," he said.[52] In short, Wallace prescribed less thinking and more gut-level reaction for the nation. He placed his faith in the cop and the cabbie, who were real men because they responded to problems with muscular action. The methodical ruminations of the effete professor and public policy planner, the candidate asserted, sacrificed manly vigor, leading to social chaos. Only by engaging in violent, hardheaded responses could Americans hope to regain their manliness and stifle the urban disorder plaguing their nation.

This anti-intellectual approach to governance was a case study in feel over facts. "Naw, we don't stop and figger," Wallace told Marshall Frady, "we don't think about history or theories or none of that. We just go ahead."[53] Frady, basing his judgment on Wallace as a "consummate political and cultural articulation of the South," concluded that the governor had little use for logic or rationality.[54] Likewise, leftist gonzo journalist Hunter S. Thompson suggested that the Alabamian touched "people on some kind of visceral, instinctive level that is probably both above & below 'rational politics.'"[55] Indeed, Wallace's adherents were more likely to laud the candidate for his ability to "tell it like it is" than for his sober analysis of policy issues. As one Wallaceite explained to Thompson at a 1972 rally in Milwaukee, "He don't sneak around the bush. He just comes right out and *says* it."[56] Part of Wallace's attractiveness lay in his ability to exploit the South as a place that eschewed the excessive thinking apparently plaguing the rest of the country. For instance, when southern blacks got out of hand, no one needed a government commission to explain their behavior, and there was always a brick (clenched by a white hand) ready to keep them in line. Both Wallace's presidential campaigns and his imagined South were largely about "kicking ass" as an antidote to the rational, expert-driven, coddling procedures that Wallace and his folks said were ruining the rest of the country.

One of the sad karmic consequences of Wallace's rhetoric of violence was that both he and his national ambitions would be felled by a would-be assassin's bullet. In May 1972, a pathetic white loner named Arthur Bremer shot and paralyzed the governor in Maryland during the Democratic primaries. After a torturous recovery, the now wheelchair-bound candidate attempted a fourth and final presidential run four years later and failed miserably during the primary season (see also chapter 5). *New York Times* journalist Robert Reinhold contended in 1976 that "the collapse of support for Mr. Wallace can be traced both to his crippled condition and to the relative unimportance of racial matters as issues. The governor's health seems to be the more important factor."[57] Undoubtedly, confined to a wheelchair, Wallace's go-to presentation of himself as a virile man willing to use violence to rescue white society was no longer tenable.

Even so, the viability of Wallace's message of socially regenerative violence did not rise and fall with his presidential candidacies. Discourses on southern-style law-and-order solutions outside of the Alabamian's orbit gained popularity, particularly in the realm of film. The best and most popular example is 1973's *Walking Tall*, a tale of vengeful justice in the contemporary South. It made $23 million at the box office (on an estimated budget of $500,000) and drew attention from critics.[58] While the film followed Wallace's argument that violent action affirmed masculinity and that a lack of force resulted in social disarray, its discourse notably differed in its treatment of race. In the rural South of *Walking Tall*, violence kept white men manly and society together without acting in the service of white supremacy.

Walking Tall: Skull Cracking and Racial Brotherhood in the Law-and-Order South

Walking Tall is a highly fictionalized chronicle of the life of Buford Pusser, the sheriff of McNairy County, Tennessee (1964–1970). This man followed the violence-as-creating-order philosophy, dedicating himself to rooting out vice (prostitution, gambling, and bootlegging) in his jurisdiction by kicking ass. At least that is the story the film tells. The cheaply made, but effective, biopic shows Pusser in almost superhuman terms; he survives being beaten, stabbed, and shot. Unlike the real-life sheriff, the movie character forgoes a gun in favor of an oversized hickory stick that he uses to beat on bootleggers and other lowlifes. The Masculine South components of *Walking Tall* quote almost word for word from the imagined South of George Wallace. Both the governor and Pusser were men who exerted power, order, and machismo through brutality. The film reflected, moreover, Wallace's contention that the "system" was broken; feminized authorities indulged criminals rather than jailing them. What might seem like policy brutality or vigilantism, then, was not only justified, but necessary, according to the film's logic. Besides criminals, *Walking Tall*'s villains similarly include a rule-bound and seemingly naïve judge—the bane of Wallaceites—and a sheriff (Pusser's predecessor) who refuses to take down the vice lords. The film condones the robust Pusser's extralegal violence and vigilantism. Its rendering of the politics of violence in the rural South and the coverage it received in the national press reinforced the popular tendency to identify the region as a uniquely antimodern space where the use of force against unruly elements fortified the vitality supposedly necessary to ensure social control.

At the beginning of *Walking Tall*, wrestler Buford "The Bull" Pusser returns to his hometown in McNairy County with his wife and two children after spending years away. (Note the similarity to Wallace's boxing background. These are men who were grounded in violent, manly pursuits.) Veteran action director Phil Karlson includes shots of the bucolic countryside that Pusser's parents call home, setting up an inviting and familiar portrait of the southern landscape. Danger, however, lurks underneath the surface. In town, Pusser meets up with an old friend, who is every bit the archetypal good ole boy. He takes Pusser to the bustling, ironically named local bar, the Lucky Spot. There Karlson bombards the viewer with images of debauchery, including prostitutes working out of trailers in the parking lot and rigged games of chance played in the crooked establishment's backroom. Pusser's friend is cheated during one such game, prompting Buford to protest. He is immediately seized, beaten, and stabbed several times, before being left for dead on the side of the road. After a long recovery, Pusser returns to the bar. Equipped with the belief that only force can stifle lawlessness, he exacts violent revenge on his attackers, busting limbs and skulls, armed only with his self-fashioned wooden club. The authorities prosecute him for his crime, but he successfully appeals to the jury by ripping open his shirt on the stand and displaying his disfigured chest.

Fed up with the local law enforcement and justice system's refusal to crack down on the vice industry, Pusser enters and wins the sheriff's race in the county and declares war on the criminal syndicate. An orgy of bloodshed ensues. Sheriff Pusser endures gunshot wounds (his jaw is nearly blown off at one point), and the gang murders his wife in an ambush. After her funeral, the lumbering protagonist drives his car into the Lucky Spot, killing two assailants. The film concludes as the townspeople, energized by Pusser's vigilantism, throw the bar's gambling tables and furniture onto a bonfire. While the movie's maudlin Johnny Mathis theme plays over the credits, the camera lingers on a bandaged Pusser as he is driven away from the scene. The viewer leaves with the message that righteous violence is the solution to restoring wounded masculinity and stemming social disorder.

The law-and-order aspects of *Walking Tall* and their ties to Wallaceite and Nixonian political rhetoric are undeniable. For Jack Temple Kirby, the film "had most of the ugly, majoritarian sentiments of Richard Nixon's 'law and order' reelection campaign [of 1972]."[59] Many commentators similarly levied a liberal critique of this connection in addition to the film's right-wing elements. Adopting a faux southern dialect in her review of *Walking Tall* in *New York* magazine, Judith Crist judged it "so durned Amurrican that only a quote from Nixon seems lacking from its publicity."[60] Similarly, a British film critic bemoaned the penultimate scene in which the townspeople ransack the Lucky Spot. It is, as the film defines it, the culmination and ultimate justification of Pusser's bloody vengeance and "a terrifying image of Nixon's silent majority at work."[61] Some liberal spectators went further. Echoing the Left's criticism of Wallace as a dangerous reactionary, *New Times*' Michael Robbin both admired the picture's aesthetics and labeled it a "fascist work of art."[62]

Commentators at times made explicit links between Wallace and *Walking Tall*. In a satirical March 1974 piece, the *Washington Post*'s *Potomac Magazine* categorized Americans into different groups ranging from "Just Folks" (aka Wallaceites) to "Plain Bureaucrats" and "Counterculture," and broke down their interests according to such distinctions as "Investments," "Furniture," "Birth Control," and "Bumper Stickers."[63] Under "Heroes" for the "Just Folks" crowd, the author listed George Wallace, along with Miami-born lieutenant William Calley (of My Lai Massacre infamy) and Buford Pusser.[64] By placing Wallace and Pusser alongside each other, *Potomac* disclosed their similar capacities for violence. Also notable: all three "Just Folks" heroes were unimpeachably masculine white southerners.

"Just Folks," or simply "the Folks," as Wallace envisioned the great mass of white American working people, saw much to legitimize their worldview and Wallace's own masculine southernness in *Walking Tall*. While there are no meddling "pseudo-intellectual" characters in the film, there are plenty of coddled criminals, and a judge concerned about following strict legal procedures even when it means releasing potentially dangerous individuals. Joe Don Baker as Buford Pusser puts Wallace's rhetoric into action, confirming that law-and-order violence is paramount in this Hollywood-created South. The masculine protector Pusser spends the film performing vigilante actions such as threatening to dynamite a turncoat cop if he does not reveal his duplicity, and avenging Pusser's own savage brutalization at the hands of the area hoodlums. The extreme breakdown of law and order in McNairy County only further justifies his actions in the film. The celluloid Pusser, therefore, brings to mind Wallace's contention that cities in the North and West would be better off if the police took over for a couple of years.

Far from a minor plot point, the southernness of *Walking Tall* is indispensable to its law-and-order discourse. Allison Graham, though, has contradicted the southernness of the film, stating that it depicts Buford Pusser "as an icon of upright *American*—not lawlessly southern—vigilantism."[65] Graham's reasoning for the universality of *Walking Tall* is valid on the surface. Remember, for example, Judith Crist calling the picture "so durned Amurrican." But the movie treats its setting as anything but generic. From the shots of bucolic rural surroundings to the familial closeness among the Pusser kin and the depiction of a strained interdependence between the white and black populations, Karlson's work could not exist outside of its imagined South. Graham fails to acknowledge that Pusser's tough southernness on screen functions as an example for the rest of the country. *Walking Tall* harnesses rural white southernness in the service of *American* masculinity by deeming it capable of reenergizing the nation's white men to tighten their grip on the loosening bands of society.

Set against an arcadian southern locale, albeit one beset by criminal forces, Pusser's good ole boy nature clashes, for instance, with Inspector Harry Callahan's nihilistic bent in *Dirty Harry* (1971), director Don Siegel's portrait of nonsouthern urban decay. *Chicago Tribune* contributors Jim Higgins and Shirley Rose Higgins ventured to McNairy County, Tennessee, shortly after *Walking Tall*'s release, where they marveled at the "scenic rural countryside where homespun towns and villages make a traveler feel he has rediscovered the tranquil America so frequently lost amid city bustle." Referencing the film's plot, the Higginses found "it . . . hard to visualize there is corruption" among such beautiful surroundings.[66]

Representations of the South, especially when cultural arbiters or politicians presented them as contrary to a corrupt status quo, could be utilized as both distinctly southern *and* fully American. George Wallace, after all, held up his home region as the embodiment of the country's presumably endangered values. Thus, the patriarchal Pusser is simultaneously universal and southern in *Walking Tall*. In other words, despite its genre elements, the movie is not simply a "Southern *Dirty Harry*." It hypes a Wallace-like southern model for using redemptive force to combat national dilemmas of violent crime and a purportedly creeping emasculation.

Some reviewers were quick to note the gravity of the film's southernness, principally in the portrayal of the tough Pusser. These critics largely considered his propensity for violence as central to the character's southernness. For the *Chicago Tribune*'s Gene Siskel, "Joe Don Baker plays Buford Pusser as a cross between Li'l Abner and 'Popeye' Doyle [the main character in the equally gritty 1971 urban crime drama *The French Connection*]. His enthusiasm for swift retributive justice is catching."[67] Pauline Kael, writing in the *New Yorker*, dug more deeply into Baker-as-Pusser's southernness, playing on the connection between white southerners and manly exertion in the public's mind: "He seems Southern redneck—a common man who works outdoors in the sun—to the soul. He has that heavy, flaccid look that Southern white men often get early in life; it goes with a physical relaxation that can fool Northerners like me, who don't always recognize the power hidden in the flab. As Baker plays him, Buford is a nonreflective hero who, when angered, tramples on his enemies uncontrollably."[68] Kael assessed the character as a kind of animal, a man who does not think, but merely reacts. Her analysis put a negative spin on the visceral brand of southern manhood parlayed by Wallace. She and other liberals may have been sickened by the Pusser character's violent, swift-acting, and anti-intellectual masculinity. However, Wallace and *Walking Tall* argued that these traits were essential to creating and maintaining "real men"—men who *acted*, and sometimes maimed and killed.

Although his film buttressed Wallace's Vicious South–influenced conceit that the region represented a bastion of rudely enforced lawfulness in the midst of national lawlessness, Karlson's depiction of Pusser's white southern manhood differed from Wallace's example. Race marked this point of departure and made *Walking Tall* a unique discourse on the meaning of the contemporary white South. Wallace's white southern masculinity was grounded in a tradition of racial antipathy that fired his race-baiting politics. *Walking Tall* breaks with this vision of white southern manhood. On the issue of black-white relations, the film implicitly contrasts Pusser with the Bull Connor school of southern lawmen. Pusser may look the part of the bigoted law enforcement officer, with his tight jaw and bulbous, hulking physique, but he is remarkably antiracist. Jack Temple Kirby astutely surmises the significance of the film's racial message in the context of Pusser's mission to be a man and "walk tall": "If the means of rising from the crawling posture seem frightening and quasifascist, the positive ends, for once, did not exclude people on the basis of color. Southern violence was redefined, and [W. J.] Cash's savage ideal, thriving still, was no longer quite so solidly based upon the Proto-Dorian bond of white supremacy."[69] In short, the Pusser character is a New Southern man, whose message of racial reconciliation would allow him to resonate with a broader national audience than Wallace, while still possessing the "loosely leashed readiness for mayhem" that Marshall Frady attributed to the southern mentality.[70] Karlson's version of the South, therefore, combined both reactionary and progressive elements: it spoke to national concerns about lax law enforcement and male weakness as it embraced a more enlightened approach to race relations.

Pusser's racial open-mindedness manifests itself most notably in his friendship with Obra Eaker, a young black man. Pusser first hires Obra to assist with his and his father's timber-processing operation and later makes Obra one of his trusted deputies. Obra and Buford are old friends; they recognize each other when the black man humbly arrives on Pusser's land looking for work. Buford's father Carl warns his son that Obra has been infected with "a raging case of that new social disease: Black Power." Buford laughs off the comment. "Is that all?" he asks, unconcerned by Obra's resistance to traditional black and white power structures in the rural South.[71] The younger Pusser and Obra feel a kinship that both acknowledges and transcends their racial difference. During their initial reunion, Obra says that they are "part of the oppressed minority."[72] He intends it partially as a joke, but both the characters and the film find truth in the statement. Southern white society has victimized Obra because of his skin color; Buford's oppression has come at the hands of a gutless law enforcement system that refuses to grant him justice after his vicious maiming at the Lucky Spot.

Walking Tall confirms the connection between Buford and Obra, as well as a sneaking sense of Pusser's white paternalism, through their collective use of violence against white and black offenders. After eight black civil rights activists die from drinking poisonous moonshine, the new sheriff is intent on bringing the responsible bootleggers to justice. He enlists the help of Obra, who is all too aware of the white authorities' typical callousness toward black victims of crime. He is reluctant to assist Pusser until the white man explains that he, unlike the old sheriff, thinks it important to investigate "eight dead niggers."[73] Obra agrees to help Pusser apprehend the bootleggers, who turn out to be black themselves. This scene affirms Buford's belief in enforcing justice harshly—but equally—across racial lines. Despite the white sheriff's kind treatment of deputy Obra, Pusser remains the dominant figure in their relationship. He convinces Obra of his good intentions in regard to the black community. The deputy is not allowed to voice his radicalism. When Buford assuages his father's concerns about the black man, he downplays not only Carl's fears about the social demands of militant blacks but also the seriousness of such demands in the first place ("Is that all?"). The countercultural *Great Speckled Bird*'s review of the picture recognized this paternalistic racial dynamic at work in the film's southern setting. It stated that the sheriff "shows [Obra] how to stand tall against the reprobates of the white world and those of his own color."[74] Pusser is the quintessential postwar racial liberal: concerned about the plight of people of color, yet more focused on his effort to save them than on creating conditions for their self-empowerment. He is Atticus Finch without the respect for legal strictures and alleged criminals' constitutional rights. The Changing South was still in progress, and, the creators of *Walking Tall* conjectured, racial enlightenment might coexist with (and receive succor from) a little ass kicking.

Pusser's racial philosophy marks him as an anomaly in the film's South. This imagined locale remains, in Karlson's judgment, deeply bigoted, which makes the sheriff's actions all the more noble for a man of his race and social position. In one scene, Obra is jumped by a gang of outwardly racist rednecks when he tries to arrest them. Spectacularly, he is able to subdue and drag them outside while a bemused Pusser looks on. The ringleader of the group later apologizes to Obra for his obnoxious behavior. It might appear that the film is dispatching a hopeful message about southern race relations. In this case, *Walking Tall* tells audiences that even hardened bigots are capable of reform. Furthermore, Pusser obviously treats both races fairly, or at least with equal brutality. But the feature's racial politics are actually more complicated. In a 1974 analysis of *Walking Tall*, film scholar Peter Biskind engaged in a rare analysis of those politics and articulated a major problem with the film's imagined South. In the picture, he admonished, "Racism is a minor annoyance easily amenable to a few knocks on the head, and clearly subordinate to such intractable problems as gambling."[75] For all of Pusser's railings against "the system," racism is not treated as an institutional concern. It is, rather, an individual deficiency with which the movie deals at "the primitive level of personal relationships," Biskind elaborated, "and then dismisse[s]."[76] Like the earlier southern crime drama *In the Heat of the Night* (chapter 1), with its Changing South narrative, *Walking Tall* advanced the liberal fantasy that individual blacks could eradicate white racism by simply proving their humanity to whites. The film's racial message was one that allowed the white South to serve as a model for liberal nonsoutherners. Although *Walking Tall* does not go as far as white southern politicians like Jimmy Carter who vouched that the region had already undergone a period of difficult racial healing unlike the North, it does present an alluring portrait of the South transcending its black-white troubles—at least in some instances. In racial terms, the film breaks with the Wallace model of traditional southern masculinity grounded in white supremacy. Yet without a serious challenge to the "system" of racism in the South, its questionable insights about racial change and race relations, while enticing, left little of use to nonsoutherners struggling to resolve the troubling legacy of prejudice in the 1970s.

The film's Masculine South instead functioned as a salvaging of the Vicious South—its violence, masculinity, and generally reactionary posturing—putting the emphasis on a brutal sheriff cleaning up his small town and the surrounding countryside, rather than on white dominance. This feature of *Walking Tall* is perhaps the only element distinguishing it from George Wallace's politics of regenerative violence. Dissimilarly, the novel and movie versions of James Dickey's *Deliverance* say nothing about race while further augmenting the idea of an exotic rural South in which violent exertion shored up the supposedly feminizing effects of urban and suburban living. Here again, cultural creators presented rural white southerners' apparent partiality for force as a useful antidote to a modern society that nurtured male weakness.

Deliverance: Seeking Masculine Regeneration in a Terrifying Rural South

"It is nothing new to say that *Deliverance* is a portrait of masculinity—or male relationships—in crisis," scholar Ed Madden has declared.[77] True, indeed. What makes southern novelist James Dickey's popular 1970 novel and its $46.1-million-grossing and Academy Award–nominated 1972 film adaptation (directed by Englishman John Boorman) significant as an example of the Masculine South discourse is its imagining of the white South as a violent, manly proving ground.[78] Notably absent from this vision are the law-and-order aspects and racial preoccupations of both Wallace's campaigns and *Walking Tall*. This is not the bucolic and familial South of *Walking Tall* nor the white supremacist refuge of Wallace's rhetoric. Referred to as "quintessentially a man's book" by the *Wall Street Journal*, *Deliverance* is a tale of four white, middle-class southern suburban men left to fend for themselves in the wilds of northern Georgia.[79] Before this experience, they have been made effete by their family life in the suburbs and white-collar work in the city. *Deliverance* identifies the rural white South as a distinctive locus of masculine rebirth, untouched by modernity and capable of helping these men overcome their softness through toil and bloodletting.

The movie's trailer describes the four protagonists not as southerners, but as "suburban guys like you or your neighbor."[80] This claim brands them as regular Americans; not true *southerners* by *Deliverance*'s standards. They are lacking in the only southernness that will matter in the film and the novel: the chutzpah to conquer the punishing local hinterlands and its wily inhabitants.

The story begins with Lewis Medlock, an outdoor enthusiast and faux survivalist, convincing his fellow white-collar friends—Ed Gentry, Drew Ballinger, and Bobby Trippe—to take a canoe trip down the fictional Cahula-wassee River before it is dammed and its wildness is lost forever. He impresses his friends, especially the novel's narrator Ed, with his studied knowledge of nature, and so they decide to go along. The journey will result in Drew's death, Bobby's rape by mountain men, Lewis's severe injury, and Ed's transformation from a spineless suburbanite into a primitive man who scales cliffs and kills in order to save the others.

Dickey prefaces Ed and his friends' harrowing experiences in the Georgia wilderness with vignettes of Ed's boring, coddled existence at work and with his family. In the beginning of the novel, Ed suffers from a nagging emptiness—a lack of masculine exertion. He recounts that his advertising "studio was full of gray affable men who had tried it in New York and come back South to live and die."[81] This is not the rural South. Ed's world is split between his numbing office job in Atlanta and the air-conditioned leisure of his home in a New Southern suburb. Although the handsome, fit star Jon Voight would portray Ed in the film, Dickey made the character balding and overweight. He is a man who has allowed his lifestyle to sand away all of his hard edges.

Dickey couples this description of Ed's masculine side with the well-muscled Lewis's antiurban rants and esteem for the natural life. "Life is so fucked-up now, and so complicated," he tells Ed in the novel, "that I wouldn't mind if it came down, right quick, to the bare survival of who was ready to survive."[82] Lewis is the proverbial weekend warrior, whiling away at ill-defined white-collar work during the week before breaking free for two days of bow hunting, canoeing, and communing in the southern wilderness. The character serves, in scholar Steven Knepper's evaluation, as "Dickey's answer to [feminist and black nationalist] assaults on traditional masculinity."[83] Lewis sees nature as something to be conquered, not simply enjoyed. Ed regards his buddy's survivalism with awe, admiring the qualities in Lewis that he so obviously lacks. Predictably, Lewis sees urban life as the problem. "The city's got you where you live," he warns Ed in the book.[84] In an early version of the film script, Dickey (who also served as screenwriter) makes the character's antiurban critique even more unambiguous. "City life is killing you," Lewis insists. "It's *boring* you to death. You're rotting."[85] Although Ed is not completely sold on abandoning suburban comfort, Lewis is set up as a god-like individual in Ed's (and the reader's) mind.

Contemporary reviewers of the novel and film versions of *Deliverance* frequently assumed that Dickey used Lewis as a surrogate for his true feelings. Indeed, the author was an avid bow hunter and had canoed on southern rivers. Dickey claimed, though, that all of the characters reflected different parts of his personality, including the pitiful, blundering rape victim Bobby.[86] Furthermore, Dickey exposes Lewis's survivalist rhetoric to be nothing more than tough talk. The wannabe superman kills Bobby's rapist and orders his companions to bury the mountain man's body. But later, his apparent ironclad will falters. When the canoeists hit a rough section of rapids, Drew drowns and Lewis is injured. Lewis collapses physically and emotionally, forcing the ad man to unearth his manliness and transport the group to safety. In a climactic scene, Ed somehow summons the strength to climb the sheer face of a rock cliff to kill a mountain man who is hunting them.

"The film undercuts everything Lewis says," wrote the *New York Times*' Stephen Farber in a thoughtful analysis of the film's masculine themes. "Nature turns out to be threatening and destructive rather than regenerative."[87] Actually, Dickey does not totally discount all of Lewis's assertions. After all, it is manliness, not nature, that is restorative in *Deliverance*. Ed arrives at his "deliverance" by conquering his fears, resorting to violence, and surviving country wilds. "He knows what he's capable of, even though maybe only once," Dickey explained to Boorman during preproduction on the motion picture. "He knows it, and he knows he knows it."[88] This character development is born out in the novel by Ed's post-trip narration in which he reflects on his traumatic experience on the now dammed river: "The river and everything I remembered about it became a possession to me, a personal, private possession, as nothing else in my life ever had. . . . I could feel it—I can feel it—on different places on my body. It pleases me in some curious way that the river does not exist, and that I have it."[89] In other words, Ed carries the rapids and his triumph over a heartless environment—and his own former weakness—with him. The southern wilderness has reinstated his manhood. "In fact," scholar Pamela E. Barnett concludes, "Ed can safely return to the exact suburban, middle-class life that had threatened him in the beginning because he knows he has what it takes should it all come down to the man."[90]

Dickey thus lampoons Lewis's phony survivalism while leaving intact the character's critique of the city and his insistence that regeneration comes from the deployment of masculine power in the woods. By embracing violence, Ed, the personification of suburban America, faces the dangers of the wilderness and reaffirms his vitality. He has escaped the apparent traps of domesticity that come from living in suburbia and working in the city. The backwoods South in *Deliverance* is full of peril and claims three lives—those of Drew and the two mountain men. Still, it allows Ed to fulfill the unsatisfied feeling that hounds him in his regular life. In 1981 Dickey explained, "Ed Gentry's dilemma, as Lewis points out, is that he has everything the society promises." His emptiness "is to be dealt with not by the acquisition of goods but by something other, something inner."[91] Dickey's novel stresses this theme. It criticizes modernity by heralding the inner virtues waiting to be discovered while traversing a dangerous but revitalizing rural South.

Boorman's film somewhat tempers the regenerative aspect of Ed's encounter with the southern wilderness. The difference in Boorman's and Dickey's versions stems from the director's stylistic choice to begin the story with the suburban men's arrival at a small mountain community near the river without any background on Ed's life before the excursion. The viewer is not aware of the stakes involved in the character's masculine test; the film concentrates more narrowly on Ed and his friends' attempts to survive and therefore obscures the advertising executive's personal deliverance. On the issue of whether violence could help to bolster the slackening of modern American masculinity, the director outlined his departure from Dickey's point of view. "Dickey's beliefs," Boorman told an interviewer, "are not unlike Hemingway's, especially the idea that one attains manhood through some initiatory act of violence. For me, the contrary is true: violence doesn't make you a better person—instead, it degrades you."[92] The film itself is actually more ambiguous than Boorman's statement would suggest. Ed is haunted by his backwoods trials, yet the director also frames his resort to primitivism as necessary and courageous. Boorman's version shows that the recovery of Ed's masculinity enables him to save the lives of most of his friends even if the movie denies the ennobling savagery that Dickey promoted.

Boorman's and Dickey's enthusiasm for the utility of a violent rural South may have varied, but they offered nearly identical characterizations of the southern mountain men that populate *Deliverance*. The book and novel depart from Wallace's and *Walking Tall's* portrayal of salt-of-the-earth white southerners. *Deliverance's* mountain people are alien and unsettling, but Dickey, in particular, judges them as worthy of respect and emulation because they understand the value of force. Lewis is enthralled with them. He couples his antiurban/suburban critiques with an admiration for the anachronistic lifestyle of the mountain people (who are almost exclusively men) in both versions. These individuals, Lewis contends, live a more natural, robust existence than he and his suburban companions. Ed ponders that opinion during his car ride with Lewis to the river. Along the way, he mentally marks "the exact point where suburbia ended and the red-neck South began."[93] In this "red-neck South" lay considerable virtue, claims Lewis. Though "awfully clannish," the mountain people produce beautiful music and practice a natural lifestyle unfettered by modern intrusions.[94] They are the perfect models for withstanding the dystopian future of Lewis's fevered imagination, in which "the machines are going to fail, the political systems are going to fail, and a few men are going to take to the hills and start over."[95] These rural southerners already live in those hills, forging a hardscrabble existence that, in Lewis's estimation, guarantees them as real men, capable of thriving without the emasculating conveniences of contemporary life. "We're lesser men," Lewis tells Ed, but his overfed chum is unmoved at the time; he is content with his plum suburban life.[96]

The mountain people of *Deliverance* possess tantalizing traits of the rural South while also encapsulating the rough, unforgiving nature that Ed must brutally overcome to obliterate his suburban softness. This dual representation manifests itself most visibly early in the film and the novel. Before they can begin the canoe trip, the Atlantans must find two men who will transport their cars to Aintry, a town at the mouth of the Cahulawassee. There they can pick up their vehicles once their journey concludes. Ed and the others stop in a decrepit little community called Oree to fuel up and locate drivers.

Looking upon the elderly gas station attendant in these surroundings, Ed is flabbergasted, narrating, "He looked like a hillbilly in some badly cast movie, a character actor too much in character to be believed. I wondered where the excitement was that intrigued Lewis so much; everything in Oree was sleepy and hookwormy and ugly, and most of all, inconsequential. . . . It was nothing, like most places and people are nothing."[97]

With perhaps more than a hint of class superiority, Ed feels that this town and its residents can offer him little of value. They are too foreign. A seeming opportunity for rural-suburban unity occurs when the guitarist Drew encounters a mentally challenged banjo-playing boy who bests him in a frenzied, but good-natured, exercise in bluegrass showmanship. Afterward, Drew, who is the only member of his suburban cohort to treat the locals with respect, has a brief, friendly encounter with the gas station attendant. "He has made a true friendship," Steven Knepper writes, "an authentic connection with family."[98] The possibility of forging a permanent connection is lost, most notably in the film version, when the boy rebuffs Drew's enthusiastic offer of a handshake. As *Commonweal* stated in a review, contrary to the "affable dolt" in the book, "the boy in the film remains ominously hostile to every overture made by the canoers except the music."[99]

Deliverance furthers its unsettling portrait of distinctive white southern mountain people by delineating the ways in which their lifestyle has disfigured them. Early in the novel, Ed ponders why so many rural southerners are afflicted with missing fingers and other deformities. "There is always something wrong with people in the country," he reflects, and refers to the rural South as "the country of nine-fingered people."[100] He is confused by southern farmers who are far from the paradigm of health that their "fresh air and fresh food and plenty of exercise" should seemingly afford them.[101] And, yet, Ed's own compromised manhood makes his critical judgments suspect. Boorman extends Dickey's emphasis on the degradation of Oree's residents. The actor Billy Redden, who portrayed the banjo player, wore makeup that made him look inbred. "Talk about genetic deficiencies," Bobby says to Ed in the film. "Isn't that pitiful?"[102] At another point, the director's camera lingers on a woman holding a severely disabled child. In his *Life* review of the film, critic Richard Schickel noted the "malformed" mountaineers that the suburbanites encounter. He deduced that this artistic choice represented Dickey's belief that "there is . . . no social or psychological deliverance to be found in the currently fashionable belief in the retreat to primitivism."[103]

Schickel's analysis makes sense only if one ignores the symbolism of the film's mountain men (and the rural South) in general. In *Deliverance*, these squirrelly characters are not so much real people as sites upon which the suburbanites must prove their manhood. Boorman's recollections attest that the film version's treatment of rural white southerners, at least, aims more for symbolism than realism. The director said "that the journey of these urbanites is also a journey through time, through America's history, in search of its beauty, its power, its resources and its wealth."[104] The residents of *Deliverance*'s wild imagined South, Boorman continued, "live by the old frontier values, in an autonomous society in which they themselves build their houses, cultivate their land and defend themselves against outsiders."[105] The intrusion of modern life imperils that lifestyle, as Lewis notes at the beginning of the film—"We're [i.e., modern man] gonna rape this whole goddamn landscape"—and rather than willingly succumb to feminization, the mountain men rape back.[106]

Lewis errs in thinking that the guarded rustics he and his companions encounter are prime masculine specimens. Still, Ed swings too far to the other side by brushing them off as degenerates and nothing more. In his book, Dickey sees them as possessing untrammeled manliness that is lacking in the temperature-controlled, plastic lifestyle of the Atlanta suburbs. The unremitting savagery of their environment has debauched the mountain folk because it has not been tempered by the personal restraint typically associated with modern masculinity.[107] The weekend adventurers in the film and the novel already have that restraint in (ultra)abundance. By conquering the "nine-fingered people" and heroically saving his friends, except the (apparently) murdered Drew, he has avoided what Theodore Roosevelt and psychologist G. Stanley Hall, seventy-five years earlier, would have recognized as "overcivilization," injecting himself with a dose of violence and aggression to become a "real" man.[108] *Deliverance* glories in this reformed southern man, no longer impeded by his meaningless office job and suburban existence, as the American everyman. The rural white southerners that Ed encounters are as foreign as the residents of another planet. Their home is a place apart: distinctive, confusing, dangerous, and, in Boorman's hands, a territory of lingering terror. Most importantly, it is a place where "men can be men," simultaneously embodying and easing the masculine anxieties circulating through 1970s American culture.

Conclusion

George Wallace's presidential campaigns, *Walking Tall*, and *Deliverance* similarly represented manhood in crisis, which could be alleviated by the supposedly innate violence of the white South. The image of an ass-kicking, Masculine South owed much to the Vicious South narrative of the civil rights era even when the first narrative rejected the second discourse's racist aspects. The region's purported penchant for violent action over careful thinking, these cultural productions spelled out, was the perfect cure for what their creators perceived as masculine decline and the accompanying loss of order in late 1960s and early 1970s American society. It is the Masculine South's drumbeat refrain of the white South as savior that cemented its power and durability as a cultural and political tool in this era.

As a presidential candidate, George Wallace juxtaposed a hardy white South with a flaccid non-South, contending that the former was immune to the latter's urban and social ills. The Alabamian swore that the United States' problems arose in part from its squeamishness toward exerting control over criminals and antiwar and minority dissenters. By following the example of the South, he insisted, white American men could reclaim the potency necessary to combat disorder in the streets. *Walking Tall* excised the white supremacy of Wallace's message while holding true to his linkage of masculine regeneration and social order. The fictionalized Buford Pusser invited Americans to reflect upon the rural South to recover their inner vigilante and vigorously stifle lawbreakers. *Deliverance* doubled down on this spectacle of white southern savagery, arguing that suburban life feminized men and that only by conquering the southern wilderness could men reconstitute their strength.

All of these incarnations of the Masculine South were, at their core, reactionary. Their target was a soft American society set adrift from its traditions and in need of a severe lashing. This conservative depiction of the rural white South as a bastion of tradition and stability in the midst of a chaotic American society ironically paralleled countercultural fantasies of the region. Without ignoring the myriad differences in how they conceptualized the South, one can see how these two imaginings similarly underscored an intense dissatisfaction with the state of late 1960s and early 1970s American society. It is a testament to the power and flexibility of white southernness that individuals as oppositional as southern demagogues and dope-smoking hippies could exploit it.

Debates about the utility of the white South and the politics of kicking ass did not end here. Further incarnations of the Masculine South would inform the popularity and public reaction to southern rock, a genre born in the South that enjoyed huge national success in the 1970s. The contrasting styles of the two most popular southern rock bands, Lynyrd Skynyrd and the Allman Brothers Band, would offer, respectively, reactionary and progressive imaginings of the cultural potential of the white South: as traditional and often rural, largely defined in racial terms, and capable of teaching Americans how to live freer, less encumbered lives.

CHAPTER 4

A Tale of Two Souths

The Allman Brothers Band's Countercultural Southernness and Lynyrd Skynyrd's Rebel Macho

When Lester Bangs heard what he considered the embodiment of the white southern mind-set—"When in doubt, kick ass"—he was sitting in a bar in Macon, Georgia.[1] It was a logical place to be in the mid-1970s for a journalist writing for the rock-hungry readers of *Creem* magazine. Macon was the new nerve center of American music. There Capricorn Records president Phil Walden had amassed a musical empire of southern bands that had rather suddenly acquired massive commercial traction. The music press often grouped together such Capricorn artists as the Allman Brothers Band, Wet Willie, Elvin Bishop, and the Marshall Tucker Band with other native, long-haired, generally working-class white southern musicians, like Lynyrd Skynyrd, under the label "southern rock."

Southern rock was a sound—an amalgam of blues-rock, rhythm and blues, and country—but it was also a statement about the meaning of the white South. White southern pride was a major theme of the music, but like other positive imaginings of the South in the post–civil rights era, its purveyors (and, to some extent, fans and national commentators) also predicated the value of white southernness as a solution to national ills. The genre's two most popular artists were Lynyrd Skynyrd and the Allman Brothers Band, both of whom produced numerous gold records and hit singles during the 1970s. Despite their similar commercial trajectories, these two bands presented very different versions of the white South in their music and personas.

The Allman Brothers Band's countercultural southernness offered its members as hippie-like representatives of an integrated New South, one that had healed the old wounds of regional racial strife by excising the white supremacist element from white southern manhood and that provided a model for national emulation. Commentaries on the group inevitably upheld the supposed naturalness, spirituality, and authenticity of close-knit south-ern family life as a soothing tonic for feelings of sociocultural and political alienation in the 1970s. Lynyrd Skynyrd's persona, on the other hand, took the virile manliness at work in the Allmans' image to manufacture a ram-bunctious southernness that symbolized not only white male freedom but also white male rebellion. This "Rebel Macho," as *New Musical Express* de-scribed Skynyrd's image in 1977, was steeped in the tradition of W. J. Cash's "hell of a fellow."[2]

The southernness of the two bands calls to mind what the Georgia-based rock group Drive-By Truckers calls "the duality of the southern thing" on its 2001 release *Southern Rock Opera*. In DBT's hands, the phrase refers to the ability of white southerners to acknowledge their racist past while celebrating the more commendable aspects of their heritage.[3] The band's brilliance aside, songwriter Patterson Hood oversimplified white southern identity (and out-siders' concepts of it). When Americans imagined the South in the 1970s, they did not think in strictly binary terms. Sometimes these ideas were congruent, and at other times they contrasted sharply. No better example illustrates this point than numerous southern rock fans' embrace of both the Allman Broth-ers Band's *and* Lynyrd Skynyrd's southernness; the hypermasculine, defiant white southernness of Skynyrd, born of the Masculine South, coexisted com-fortably in many fans' consciences with the healing, interracial stance of the Allmans, which owed much to the Down-Home South and Changing South discourses. How could one embrace both? At their core, both bands spoke to the larger cultural desire to mitigate racial discord, exert a revitalized mas-culine prowess, and combat the all-encompassing dilemma of rootlessness. These musicians and the response to them demonstrate the malleability of white southernness (in both liberal and conservative forms), the frequently overlapping nature of its various traits' appeal, and, like the people who had previously dreamed about the South, a certain promiscuity on the part of rock fans when it came to choosing tools to respond to the troubling problems of 1970s America.[4] In the South of the Mind, redneck fists and hippie peace signs both had their places.

"A Brotherhood of Enlightened Rogues": The Allman Brothers Band's Countercultural Southernness

The six-piece Allman Brothers Band formed in March 1969 in Jacksonville, Florida. Between 1969 and 1976, they released five hit albums and a number-two pop single, "Ramblin' Man" (1973). Initially a regional phenomenon, the group rocketed to mainstream stardom with the release of 1971's *At Fillmore*

East. Writer Marley Brant calls the LP "one of the classic rock and roll live albums, if not *the* classic rock and roll live album."[5] By 1974, the Allmans' concert attendance rivaled that of such high-powered British acts as the Who and the Rolling Stones.[6]

The group was originally composed of brothers Duane Allman and Gregg Allman, along with Dickey Betts, Berry Oakley, Butch Trucks, and Jai Johanny ("Jaimoe") Johanson, the sole black member. Guitar virtuoso Duane had first gained notoriety as a session player for FAME (Florence Alabama Music Enterprises) Studios in Muscle Shoals, Alabama. FAME famously employed a white session band that recorded behind a variety of black R&B artists in the 1960s and 1970s, including Aretha Franklin, Wilson Pickett, and Otis Redding. Stax Records, a legendary Memphis R&B label, also utilized an integrated session band, but the Allman Brothers Band would assume the place of the first commercially viable, integrated southern-grown *rock* group.

After signing to Capricorn, Duane Allman recruited other band members and recalled his younger brother Gregg from Southern California, where he had been performing as a solo artist. To lay down tracks, the Allman Brothers Band moved to Macon. "On the surface, Macon seems like it could have leaped out of one of Faulkner's classier sketchbooks," wrote Ben Edmonds of *Creem* in 1972. "Its streets are sleepy and tree-lined; though she shows the signs of a contemporary face-lift, the spirit of Macon is old and dignified."[7] The group's countercultural ethos clashed with the city's conservative, religious values. "Those people thought we were from another planet," Gregg said. "It was a real culture shock."[8] The band's alternative style did, however, eventually garner it a large hippie and youth following throughout the country. To many observers, Allmans' countercultural southernness meant that they were six men grounded in a traditional southern culture of rural landscapes and close family life who carried out an integrated personal and musical lifestyle.

The "Brothers" presented themselves as liberated southerners and models of racial tolerance, as evidenced by their multiracial makeup. This put them squarely at odds with the Macon community. Gregg Allman talked of "the perennial redneck questions" they had to endure: "Who them hippie boys and who's the nigger in the band?"[9] On the road, it was not any better. Crew member Kim Payne remembered that "the long hair was enough to start shit in most places, but Jaimoe . . . that was enough to spark the gasoline."[10] Even so, its members played down the significance of having a black player. Butch Trucks claimed, "It wasn't part of our thinking. We weren't an interracial band. We were just six guys playing music."[11] Despite Trucks's assertion, the band (or at least its record company) made an effort to champion its integrated image from the outset. The photographs used on the group's debut, 1969's *The*

Allman Brothers Band, are telling. The cover shows the long-haired group dressed like hippies and standing on the front porch of a decaying southern mansion. The striking mixture of modern and old reappears on the LP's gate-fold sleeve photo. Each member is seen sitting together (save Trucks, who is standing) in a stream surrounded by thick foliage. All are nude. The contrast of Jaimoe's black skin against the others' white skin, as well as the intimacy of the shot, told potential consumers that the band promoted a sense of inter-racial harmony. The use of a rural setting suggested that the Allman Brothers were connected to the land and to each other in countercultural brotherhood. Reflecting ten years later on the meaning of the band's southernness, southern journalist David Jackson called it "a revelation to see them naked ... with their black 'brother.'"[12]

Outside of the South, the Allmans' racially egalitarian iconography encour-aged listeners to imagine the region in new ways, deflating northern liberal notions of moral superiority on the race issue. "They have to be credited with confounding the racist stereotype [of the white southerner]," uttered a fan from just outside of Boston, where racial tensions raged in the 1970s in re-sponse to legal efforts to integrate schools through court-mandated busing.[13] The Allman Brothers Band powerfully contrasted with the white southerners of the Vicious South, a discourse on which many rock fans and countercul-turists had been raised. "My thoughts of the South were of a backward, uned-ucated, and racist group of folks," admitted one Allmans fan from Ohio. This self-described McGovernite argued that the group's integrated lineup proved a powerful corrective to nonsouthern stereotypes of white southerners. "The Allman[s]," he went on, "did ... dismiss a lot of the thinking of the south being a hot bed for racist ideals as they had a black man ... on drums and after the death of Berry Oakley filled his shoes with another black man, Lamar Williams on bass. I thought it was a slap in the face of any idea folks from up north held about the south being racist when the most popular band in America was from the south and had two black men as members."[14]

For some young liberal white southerners, in particular, Duane Allman was an ideal ambassador of a new brand of white southern masculinity, one that exemplified both open-mindedness and freedom. Decades after the southern rock boom of the 1970s, Louisianan Patricia Goddard told music journalist Mark Kemp that Duane Allman had deeply influenced her. For Goddard, Kemp stated, Allman "personified the ideal southern man," not the Neil Young caricature of the region.[15] She thought, "He's going to bring people to the point that they are going to have to take a real look at us and delve more deeply into our history and our racial interaction, our roots and our music, and come out with a real sense of who we are."[16] Randy Stephens, from

Gadsden, Alabama, compared the positive image of the South engendered by southern rock to the football dynasty of the University of Alabama. "Southern rock was like Alabama football," he believed. "Duane Allman was like [legendary 'Bama football coach Paul 'Bear'] Bryant. It was our way of saying we're as good as anybody."[17]

The Allman Brothers Band's fans who came to imagine the South in new ways took particular notice of the band's grounding in southern black musical culture. Particularly on its first few albums, the Allmans played hard-driving blues-oriented songs. These included originals like "Whipping Post" and "Midnight Rider" and covers of postwar black artists. The blues was unquestionably the band's greatest musical influence. While growing up, Gregg and Duane Allman "listened . . . incessantly" to Muddy Waters, Bobby Bland, Blind Lemon Jefferson, and Blind Willie Johnson on the late-night R&B radio programs on WLAC-Nashville.[18] Dickey Betts drew on similar influences and idolized black rock 'n' roller Chuck Berry.[19] For a rock band emerging in the late 1960s, playing blues-derived rock music hardly made it innovative. What differentiated the Allmans, according to numerous commentators, was the *way* they played the blues. Their original take on the genre, with their chugging, but nimble, rhythms coupled with soulful lyrics, was, according to observers, central to their authenticity as representatives of the Deep South. In a review of their first album, Lester Bangs notified readers that the Allman Brothers were "the real article . . . a white group who've transcended their schooling to produce a volatile blues-rock sound of pure energy, inspiration and love."[20]

Most music followers, impressed by the group's blues influences, contended that it had constructed not so much a replica of black approaches but rather a white complement to the blues, one that might be termed "white soul." Listeners perceived the Allmans as tapping into black musical forms to invent a sound that was not a rip-off of black culture. Fans and journalists credited the band with utilizing blackness to fabricate a more liberated version of the white southern male. "It was *confident* music," emphasized southern-born music scribe Chet Flippo, "full of the South's rhythms and carrying a sense of freedom, a wide-open feeling of room to move around in."[21]

The folk revival of the late 1950s and 1960s had created the yardstick used to measure the authenticity of the group's blues. For Grace Hale, young white folk artists' attempts to imitate the sound and affect of poor, rural black artists—to conceive authenticity as an "external" quality—"became increasingly difficult to pull off after the mid-sixties."[22] As noted in chapter 2, white revivalists, accordingly, changed what it meant to be "authentic." Instead, they chose to stress "internal" authenticity, characterized by its "emphasis on feelings."[23]

Now one need not have been born the descendent of slaves or even "sound black" to be deemed legitimate. In other words, white bluesmen could be as "real" as southern black bluesmen as long as they achieved the attainable goal of a demonstrating an equivalent depth of feeling.

The Allman Brothers Band's enthusiasts might have labeled the group's supposed authenticity in similar ways. Some of the earliest proponents of the Allmans' music were Atlanta's hip youths and their cultural voice, the local underground newspaper the *Great Speckled Bird*. The biggest backer of the Allmans at the *Bird* was Miller Francis Jr. In 1972, journalist Laurence Leamer called him "the most articulate of the cultural radicals" at the paper.[24] In a profile of the group's performance at Piedmont Park in Atlanta in April 1969, during a time when the Allmans were beginning to build their audience, Francis focused on the band's purported authenticity. He described that genuineness as interwoven with the Allmans' connection to black blues. In Francis's estimation, their music, like the best rock, spoke to the unique concerns of fellow "young white tribesman" (i.e., counterculturists) and set the stage for liberation from the stifling temperament of modern American society. Francis raved that the Allmans mined black blues "without exploiting its source."[25] Reflecting a racially primitivist strain that ran through the counterculture, the music reviewer exalted the band through racial objectification. He was sure that linking themselves to black culture would help hippies to reach their desired liberation more effectively. "Since our generation is tribal, totally unlike our parents and grandparents and their parents," he averred, "it is only natural that we would turn to the black man, whose tribal roots go so much deeper and do not have thousands of years of bullshit 'civilization' to cut them off from these roots, for forms with which to relate to the new world."[26] But, espousing the outlook of white blues revivalists, this countercultural perspective held that simply aping black musicians' versions of the blues would not lead white youths toward transcendence. "Our music must develop its own power, its own forms, its own patterns of relationship with our tribal roots and our space-age technology in an unbroken line all the way down into our preliterate origins and all the way out into unknown galaxies."[27]

Behind the implicit racism and questionable hippie philosophizing lay Francis's belief that the Allman Brothers Band's sound made it a forceful manifestation of the counterculture's critique of U.S. culture and society. Just as counterculturists often praised country-rock artists for their ability to regain the "feel" of southern culture, Francis contended that the Allman Brothers Band's music was not something that one could—or should—"'listen' to"; rather, "you feel it, hear it, move with it, absorb it."[28] Their blues ultimately let hip audiences "catch a glimpse of the kind of world we are becoming," one free of "the horrendous load of bullshit" of, presumably, contemporary consumer- and technology-driven American culture.[29]

Writers outside of the counterculture would more unequivocally tie the Allman Brothers Band's realness to its treatment of the blues and the way it recouped the "feel" of southern culture. Like piles of other articles on the group, Lorraine O'Grady's 1973 piece in the *Village Voice* stressed the group's southernness and indicated that its authenticity—its representation of some- thing apart from the feared banalities of nonsouthern culture—lay in its abil- ity to play the blues in a manner that drew from the music's essence without "affecting blackness."[30] O'Grady focused on singer Gregg Allman's vocals, a major draw for fans, too. "It was Gregg Allman's voice that first captured my attention," recalled one fan from Atlanta. "I suppose it was the closest thing I had heard to blues music."[31] O'Grady more specifically admired Allman's ability to draw on the "black" vocal style without ripping it off. To her this talent expressed the earthiness of the Deep South. His singing "is rooted in the kind of self-confident, self-conscious sexuality that you most often hear connected with black voices."[32] Her ear also caught "an almost translucent in- telligence, a calm, mystical, oddly interiorized turn of mind" in Allman's vocal style.[33] These characteristics, in O'Grady's mind, were intrinsically southern: "I know that Gregg is from the Deep South, that the intonations aren't being forced, that they are coming naturally."[34]

In the minds of many fans and critics, the Allman Brothers Band's musi- cal authenticity—what Ben Edmonds called "pure music"—stemmed from the group's perceived embodiment of an alluring white southern culture.[35] As one critic wrote, "the world from which they sprang" was a place where "the solace of whiskey, drugs, music, religion, and superstition are inextrica- bly linked."[36] Depending on one's perspective, this South sounded dangerous or magical—maybe both. Doubtless, though, Allmans' listeners commonly saw the South as an alluring land of welcome traditionalism. Music writer Jon Landau was one of them. "As someone who came from the North," he said, "Duane Allman represented something that was going on in the South that most people where I lived didn't know anything about." He led a band, according to Landau, that "conveyed a sense of roots, a sense of stability, a sense of realism. . . . They were authentic."[37] Akin to other opinion makers, Landau extolled Duane Allman and his cohorts as ambassadors of a deeply implanted white South and as implicit critics of the North and its supposed anomie, unrest, and fakery.

Responses to the group's purportedly soothing model of southern culture often reflected critics' sense that the group had retrieved, among other things, the religiosity of this background. Texas fan Steve Schmidt revered his first encounter with *At Fillmore East*, the Brothers' electrifying hit third album, as "like a religious experience."[38] Similarly, for Duane Allman, playing this music was "like church," while Jaimoe claimed, "It was so spiritual, the music, I can remember several times when I was so at peace with what I was playing that my soul actually left my body, right on stage."[39] For themselves and for their devotees, the group's music promised not just authenticity but transcendence. As with counterculturists embracing country-rock, the Allmans' audience took sustenance from their combination of countercultural mysticism and the supposed unaffectedness of the South's Christian beliefs; they lavished in the music's promise of a celestial encounter. The group even coined a phrase for the moment onstage when they seemed to be communicating musically with each other on an instinctual, cosmic level: "hittin' the note."[40]

Rock 'n' roll, like most southern music, was partially rooted in the church. But whereas Elvis Presley drew inspiration from gospel and Ray Charles adapted secular lyrics to existing hymns, the Allman Brothers Band transferred the rapturous feeling of southern religion to a high-intensity, hard-rocking context. According to Mark Kemp, who grew up in North Carolina during the 1970s, one could hear "the mournful echo of a country church choir" deep in the group's sonic stew.[41] The Allmans preached inclusion, not condemnation, while rejecting the rigid judgments of the region's conservative Christian denominations. Their "church" fit with the image of the South as a hospitable, welcoming community.

Audience reactions to the "religious experience" of the Allman Brothers' performances occurred against the backdrop of what Tom Wolfe trumpeted as the "Third Great Awakening" in the 1970s.[42] This "religious revival," Bruce Schulman contends, was "an outpouring of enthusiasm and spiritual experimentation that ran the gamut of American religious life."[43] The search for a sublime experience that pushed Americans to pursue a variety of spiritual outlets, from evangelical Christianity to New Age, also informed listeners' passion for the Allman Brothers Band. And again they located that desired transcendence in the South. As rock critic Andrew Kershaw alleged, "There's a feeling in each of the songs that the band has really grasped and is living the strength and intensity of the roots music of the South to an almost cathartic degree."[44] Put differently, listeners could find in the southern "religion" of the Allman Brothers Band's music at least a partial fulfillment of the search for "authentic" spirituality and individual redemption common in 1970s popular culture.

The Allmans' religious dimension linked the group to a broader excavation of roots in the 1970s. So did the other components of its "traditional" southernness, which carried with it an element of rural living. Besides their infamous nude photo shoot and debut album cover featuring the band standing next to an old plantation house, other promotional images showed the group in outdoor locales. Rural retreats proved therapeutic for its members. Idlewild South, on a lake outside of Macon, was their practice space for a time. There Gregg Allman could "feel like I didn't have a care in the world."[45] In 1972, his colleagues bought a 432-acre tract of land ("The Farm") in Juliette, Georgia, which served as "a group hangout."[46] As if to document the association between communalism, family-centeredness, and the rural South, a picture gracing the inside cover of the notably titled *Brothers and Sisters* LP (1973) featured the band and its wives, girlfriends, children, and crew members, posing in front of a rustic farm homestead.

The group's doctrine of brotherhood (i.e., its communal and familial spirit) could not be separated from its southernness in the public imagination. The Allmans' Brotherhood drew on the idea that the South—especially the white South—was more family-oriented than the North. "Family life is very vital in the South," Phil Walden told *Creem* in 1974. "Maybe it relates from rural days, when you lived out in the country [and] you hoped you had a lot of brothers and sisters, because that's the only god-damn people you had to play with." Walden considered the Allman Brothers Band "the beginning of a Southern renaissance," a collective birth of creativity among black and white southerners, many of whom, he remarked, had decided to stay in the region and work for its benefit.[47] Meditating on the Allman Brothers after their 1976 breakup, the *Village Voice*'s Dave Hickey construed that the group's southernness—and much of its appeal—pertained to its iconoclastic, communal ethos: "They were a band of brothers against the world. Where they came from nobody came from, and what they played nobody played—not with that combination of passion and precision which marks all Southern avocations from football to stock-car racing to rock-and-roll."[48]

Its response to the deaths of two of its members just over a year apart reiterated the band's reputation as southerners intent on maintaining the bonds of family and community. The Brotherhood suffered a serious setback with Duane Allman's death in 1971. Yet there was little serious thought of quitting. After playing at Duane's funeral service, his bandmates stepped out back to share a joint and listen to a pep talk by Gregg, who urged them to "keep playing, like my brother would've wanted us to."[49] "Of course," the now-lone Allman in the band recalled, "they all felt the same way."[50] Duane was technically never replaced, though in 1972, the Allmans did hire keyboardist Chuck Leavell to fill out their sound. Rather than destroying it, Duane's demise drew the group closer together. As a friend of the southern rockers explained, "Most of the Brothers are from rural areas in the South, from tight, close-knit families. . . . When Duane died, the question of identity became paramount. They switched their total allegiance to the family: The constant mention of brothers and sisters isn't any sham. It's a necessity."[51] Bassist Berry Oakley's death in 1972 resulted in more turmoil. Again, the remaining members soldiered on, quickly hiring Lamar Williams to take Oakley's place. The British music weekly *Melody Maker* credited the Allmans' perseverance with helping gain "them the love and sympathy of America's youth."[52] If anything, the tragedies made "the warmth" generated by their concerts "that much more genuine."[53] How could this band bounce back from such crippling losses stronger than before? Writer Geoff Brown attributed it to their southern origins: "Well, that's good ole Southern boys for you."[54] In other words, the South's distinctive familial quality instilled its people with a strength that was missing in other parts of the United States. Only southern boys like the Allmans, raised in a communal culture, would respond to unrelenting misfortune by growing closer.

Fans and commentators' frequent highlighting of the Brotherhood exposed their view of the white South as a communal refuge from the seemingly atomistic pull of nonsouthern life. It also laid bare the attractiveness of a revised version of traditional white southern masculinity that disconnected itself from racism. This new model added platonic male affection while simultaneously maintaining toughness and virility in its list of traits. Historian Mike Butler has detailed the Allmans and other southern rock bands' disentanglement of white supremacy from traditional white southern manhood. Although this new version of masculinity did not completely replace its predecessor, Butler argues, in the 1970s, "Southern white males began to separate their regional and racial identities for the first time in Southern history."[55] The Allman Brothers' lineup and music reflected this change. The group members' masculinity could thus tantalize liberal nonsoutherners looking for representations of racial harmony, even as this masculinity addressed a more conservative cultural impulse by endorsing the widespread concerns over declining manhood that George Wallace verbalized in his presidential candidacies.

The band's performance of gender combined both countercultural and imagined southern perspectives. The Allmans blended a tough, manly impulse with a peacefulness born of their hippie ethos. Their grit would prompt *Down Beat* to describe the group as able "to succeed on nothing more than good music and good old Southern *macho*," even as a fan tagged their live performances as "full of friendship [and] love of the music" and a spirit of connection with fellow concertgoers.[56] The band's ability, in the minds of observers, to join traditional southern and countercultural aesthetics is well articulated in the term "enlightened rogues," a moniker that Duane Allman gave

the group. Allmans biographer Scott Freeman stresses the Brothers' simultaneously hell-raising and tranquil natures. "They were a group of guys from
the South playing brilliant, sophisticated music, who projected the image of
peaceful hippies totally devoted to their art," Freeman contends. "And yet they
also were throwbacks to the outlaw days of the Old West, like Butch Cassidy's
Hole-in-the Wall Gang—lovable yet dangerous as they roamed from town to
town, playing rock 'n' roll rather than robbing banks."[57]

Freeman's statement underscores that much of the lure of southern rock
lay in its artists' hard masculinity, which, although situated in earlier gender
representations, carried with it an implicit critique of the feminist revolution
of the late 1960s and 1970s. Chroniclers and followers of the band got the message. In 1973, Andrew Kershaw intuited what he regarded as the Brothers' conventional views of the sexes: "Here was a true Southern band that lived wild,
toured amid heaps of comic books, coke, booze and girls, rode Harley David-
sons and behaved like guys from the South—where men are men, and girls
are Southern Belles ripe for the pickin'—are supposed to."[58] Notably, Kershaw
concluded that "the band's image" "hooked" its fans.[59] In other words, the
group's machismo was part of its draw. Its masculine trappings, even as they
reverberated with the current effort to restore the preeminence of the family
in public life, were in line with the rebellion against traditional expectations
for men in the postwar era. After all, the Brothers' big hit "Ramblin' Man"
embodied a "don't-try-to-tie-me-down" ethos. "The guys believe a woman's
place is in the home," Donna Allman, Duane's wife, said early in the group's
career. Profiling their living arrangements at the Big House, the twelve-room
Macon abode where some band members lived together until 1972, reporter
Betsy Harris went further, writing, "The women spend most of their time in a
domestic routine that would put the Ladies Home Journal to shame and en-
rage any Women's Lib woman worth her burned bra."[60] It was almost enough
to make George Wallace proud. The more roguish, less enlightened aspects of
the Allmans' persona dovetailed perfectly with anxieties about the seeming
enfeeblement of masculinity in 1970s America.

Wallace lashed out at hippie types and assorted longhairs for sapping
the country's potency, even as the Allman Brothers Band's countercultural
identification actually reinforced the conservative element of its masculine
image. Feminist scholars have taught that rather than staging a revolutionary
challenge to male-female relations, hippies frequently treated women as do-
mesticated "goddesses." Male counterculturists spouted rhetoric about sexual
liberation that often privileged men's needs over those of women.[61] The historiography of countercultural manhood is limited, although Tim Hodgdon
has offered a good starting point. He draws a dichotomy between "outlaw"

masculinity, as practiced by the Diggers of San Francisco's Haight-Ashbury district, and the "tantric," chivalrous, mystical masculinity of the rural Tennessee transplants the Farmies. The aggressive, swaggering Diggers sought to live without limits, while the Farmies aimed for a more structured existence. Both groups, Hodgdon articulates, often forced women into subservient roles. The Diggers and the Farmies reckoned that society would reconstitute a "natural" gender order once it was loosened from modern interferences.[62] The masculinity of the Allman Brothers Band's members should in part be understood as a blending of the categorical extremes posed by Hodgdon. Duane Allman's conception of the Brothers as "enlightened rogues" is again instructive. Their peaceful, racially liberated views coexisted with brash attitudes about gender roles fostered by many counterculturists.

Audiences thus saw in the Allman Brothers Band a complicated rendering of white southernness, one that celebrated its ascribed traditions of family, communalism, and masculine dominance but that also rejected the racism typically associated with that culture. The group's unique southernness wedded culturally liberal, conservative, and countercultural ingredients. This wide net accounted for much of the Allmans' repute in the 1970s, when their combination of racially reformed white southernness, rural authenticity, manly togetherness, and religiosity spoke to larger national desires to mine the racial harmony, personal realness, and spiritual and familial unity of the imagined South. The Brothers' southernness spawned a seductive antidote to the era's feelings of political, cultural, and social dislocation. Southern rockers Lynyrd Skynyrd displayed an equally seductive southernness, albeit one centered on defiance and unremorseful white hypermasculinity. The popularity of its violent, reactionary image further advanced the Masculine South discourse and, in tandem with the Allman Brothers, illustrated the overlapping appeals of the region as a site of both healing and rebellion.

"The Most Joyously Unreconstructed of All Southern Bands": Lynyrd Skynyrd's Rebel Macho

When Robert Christgau dubbed Lynyrd Skynyrd "joyously unreconstructed," he was following them on a 1975 tour of the South. The *Village Voice*'s self-appointed "Dean of American Rock Critics" enjoyed the Jacksonville, Florida, group's simple, straightforward music. "I love Lynyrd Skynyrd," he confessed, "a band that makes music so unpretentious it tempts me to give up subordinate clauses."[63] Far from artless, the group's sound actually combined an intertwined, three-guitar attack with often complex arrangements and thoughtful lyrics. In reality, Christgau appeared to be referencing the band's cultural messaging, or what he considered the uncomplicated southernness that Skynyrd presented to the world. Its members' region of origin beckoned to Christgau. He suggested—somewhat condescendingly—that the South was freer and more laid-back than the rest of the country and that it possessed a sensibility that could soothe the anxious nonsouthern psyche. It was a place with roots. After watching Skynyrd's drummer care for an endangered bird, the critic mused, "We are cynical about such stuff up North, but in the South they like to believe. The comfort and tradition of the place is enough to make a person expect that freedom is just around some corner of time."[64]

Christgau implied, though, that Skynyrd's South was not all porch swings, church socials, and mama's lemonade. "If I love Lynyrd Skynyrd I'm obliged to come to terms with its Southernness," he stated ominously.[65] Speaking for many of his liberal colleagues, he saw in the band a violent, strangely alluring dark side of white southernness along the lines of the Vicious South narrative. While the Allman Brothers Band's lyrics, words, and imagery also spoke to concerns about declining manhood, for many observers, Skynyrd represented full-on masculine rebellion. The group rejected the peaceful vibe of the Allmans' South, proudly self-identifying as defenders of the white South (if not white supremacy) standing ready to tussle with anyone who looked askance of them. The words of music reporters and fans reveal the common perception that Skynyrd's southernness and reactionary masculinity functioned, more singularly than the Allman Brothers Band's, as a backlash against what millions of Americans beheld as an increasingly feminized 1970s U.S. culture.

Lynyrd Skynyrd's original lineup included Ronnie Van Zant, Ed King, Gary Rossington, Allen Collins, Billy Powell, Leon Wilkeson, and Bob Burns.[66] Van Zant, the lead singer and lyricist, "was father, founder, and leader of Lynyrd Skynyrd," Powell later said.[67] He came from a neighborhood named Shantytown, a rough-and-tumble spot on the west side of Jacksonville populated by working-class people. There, instructed by his father, Van Zant learned to fight.[68] The band intended its name as a tongue-in-cheek tribute to Leonard Skinner, the physical education teacher at Robert E. Lee High School. Skinner strictly enforced the school's regulation against male students having long hair, a definite problem for Van Zant and his future bandmates. Ironically, for a group often labeled rednecks by the press, they were "constantly getting beat up by the rednecks," in the words of music writer John Swenson.[69] After going through various names and lineups, Lynyrd Skynyrd congealed into a formidable musical unit. Van Zant drove the members hard and to good effect. Holing up in "Hell House," a rickety cabin outside of Jacksonville, the band practiced from morning until night during its early days, honing its heavy-sounding combination of bluesy rock and country music that also drew on British hard rock influences like Free. In 1973 the group secured a recording contract with musician and producer Al Kooper's Sounds of the South label, a subsidiary of MCA. Over the course of producing five top-selling albums and several radio staples, including "Free Bird," "Sweet Home Alabama," "Saturday Night Special," and "That Smell," Skynyrd became one of the most popular bands in America. A 1977 plane crash in a Mississippi swamp killed Ronnie Van Zant and replacement guitarist Steve Gaines and left the rest of the band and crew severely injured.[70] Prior to the accident, producer Ron O'Brien claimed in 2001, "All indications were that Skynyrd was about to break the Southern Rock genre wide open and become the American equivalent of the Rolling Stones."[71]

As with the Allman Brothers Band, Lynyrd Skynyrd's southern origins were central to its public persona. But whereas the Allmans' countercultural aspects seemed to cut against stereotypes of the white South's looming violence and terror, for many music journalists, Van Zant and company served as the projection of a macho ideal, much like George Wallace or the filmic Buford Pusser. Press items frequently held them up as authentic representations of white southern working-class culture. Stories of musicians' unruliness were not uncommon in 1970s rock journalism; however, reporters consistently stressed a band-as-brawlers narrative in articles about Skynyrd and melded that story line with discussions of the group's regional origins. Its members, in short, were W. J. Cash's "hell of a fellow" come to life.[72] The stock profile of Skynyrd chattered endlessly about its offstage antics. Guitarist Ed King confirmed "there was . . . violent incidents every day on the road," and journalists exploited this reality to construct an image of Skynyrd as violent redneck simpletons from a hardscrabble South.[73] They equated the band's powerful sound with its personalities and similarly classified its music as straight-ahead, brutal, and intense. As the *San Francisco Examiner* claimed, "They don't just play rough music, they are rough music."[74] Working from apparently the same script, industry trade publication *Cashbox* called Skynyrd's music "tight, mean and rough," adding with a dose of innuendo, "they're one of the few rock acts in the business that really get it on."[75]

Lynyrd Skynyrd's lyrics contributed to its reputation for busting heads and teeth and furthered the association between the band's supposedly violent tendencies and its southern masculinity. For example, the song "Mississippi Kid," from its 1973 debut (*Pronounced 'Lĕh-'nérd 'Skin-'nérd*) involves a pistol-packing narrator who warns would-be assailants to stay clear:

> 'Cause if you people cause me trouble,
> Lord, I got to put you in the ground.[76]

Women, like male opponents, fare poorly in numerous Skynyrd's songs, usually functioning as either sexual conquests or victims of violence. Van Zant sometimes wrote about women in respectful terms, as sources of tender and loving desire.[77] Still, steeped in the blues lyrical tradition, the band's music displays a pervasive misogyny. "What's Your Name" (1977) unapologetically tells of a one-night stand on the road in Boise, Idaho, while in "On the Hunt" (1975), Van Zant recalls his father's boorish comparison of "a horse and a woman." How are they similar? "Well, both of them you ride."[78] The front man went further in other tunes, charging that women refused to remain faithful, and therefore were fair game for violence. "There are many ladies here among us," Van Zant sings in "Trust" (1975), "that'll stab you in the back when you ain't around."[79] And in "Cheatin' Woman," he relates his plot to shoot his lover, who, in one of the vocalist's weaker turns of phrase, "loved every man with pants on."[80]

In a rather characteristic comment, music journalist Tony Parsons dismissed the art of the band and directed his attention to its tunes' violent overtones, remarking that "the lyrics are a celebration of perennial Rebel Macho — man as predator, provider and abuser of women, and the rock 'n' roll star as contemporary outlaw, and, yeah, the south shall rise."[81] In 1976, Lester Bangs disparaged Skynyrd's members as "crude thudstomper hillbillies whose market value rested primarily on the fact that they could play their instruments about like they could plant their fists in your teeth."[82] One only had to survey the titles of articles about the band to get a sense of its wild image: "Lynyrd Skynyrd: Fifths and Fists for the Common Man" and "Live Lynyrd Skynyrd: One Mo' Brawl from the Road" distilled this persona.[83] *New Musical Express* partially subtitled a February 1977 article on the group as "Rivers of blood . . . the crunch of bone against bone."[84] Frequently, as Bangs's quote makes obvious, journalists characterized Skynyrd as country folk, reflecting W. J. Cash's notion that rural southern living and violence went hand in hand. As with the Allman Brothers Band, Skynyrd's record company issued multiple photographs of its members in rustic settings. Al Kooper proposed that their good ole boy rural lifestyle lent the Floridians authenticity. "They're the real thing," he crowed to a music writer in 1974. "The Rolling Stones can carry on and dance around and have Southern accents, but these are the real thing. These boys have a shack in the middle of the Florida swamps, and in their spare time they chase alligators and go fishing for catfish."[85] Skynyrd had a hand in creating this image, too. On "I'm a Country Boy," from the band's third album, *Nuthin' Fancy* (1975), Van Zant sings as a cotton picker "down on the Dixie line" who abhors city life, with its "smoke chokin' up my air" and "cars buzzin' around." The narrator goes so far as to say, "I don't even want a piece of concrete in my town."[86] A year later the band released "All I Can Do Is Write about It," in which Van Zant praises the natural beauty of the South and bemoans the paving of the countryside. "You can take a boy a-out of ol' Dixieland," Van Zant proclaims, "Lord, but you'll never take ol' Dixie from a boy."[87] The link between Skynyrd, southernness, and rusticity was clear.

The South, as portrayed by the band's followers, became a rude, yet romantic, masculine refuge where violence was a way of life. Tony Parsons began his article on the group with a description of Ronnie Van Zant's father Lacy beating up his then seventeen-year-old son for cursing Ronnie's mother. The writer also related the singer's claim that he had recently bested his father in a scuffle for the first time.[88] Even the occasional reporter who sought to dispel that Skynyrd's members frittered away the hours curating alcohol-fueled beat-downs usually approached the band members with a sense of trepidation. Joanne Jeri Russo of 'Teen magazine assured her young readers that the musicians were not unruly peckerwoods, but were actually quite well behaved. Accompanying the band on a Los Angeles–St. Louis flight, and later to Jacksonville, though, she expressed apprehension at being locked in a plane with an outfit known "as the South's rowdiest rock 'n roll rednecks," who had rocketed into the public eye behind "sensational stories of torn-up dressing rooms, drunken brawls and lawless rabble-rousing."[89] These stories were based in truth, yet ultimately they said more about journalistic fantasies and the desire to sell copy than the complicated reality of the group itself.

Fans sometimes viewed Skynyrd in analogous ways, fascinated by what one listener pegged as "the rebel flag waving, hell raising, beer drinking, fist fighting, redneck band."[90] Other fans distilled its southern appeal more succinctly. One New York southern rock listener stated that "the [Allman Brothers Band] is more about loving your fellow man while Skynyrd is more about being a rebel."[91] For both Skynyrd's fan base and the music media, an important aspect of the band's star power was thus the supposed interconnectedness of its southernness and its manly, physically defiant spirit, which clashed with social constraints.

Even more than its fierce reputation, Lynyrd Skynyrd became known for its unapologetic celebration and defense of white southern masculinity. The group lacked the interracialism of the Allman Brothers Band and exerted its southern pride more vocally. Ed King contended that Skynyrd's members never associated with blacks—"I mean, none at all!"[92] Some commentators wondered if Skynyrd's riotous white southernness placed them in league with the region's racist tradition. Creem's Jaan Uhelszki, for instance, expected to hear "some juicy tales of nigger skinnings" when she interviewed the band in 1976.[93]

Skynyrd broadcast its white southern pride and rebellious masculinity, if not necessarily its racial attitudes, by incorporating the Confederate flag into its act. The group used this and other Confederate iconography in album art and onstage as much as—if not more than—other southern rock bands. Its logo, for instance, consisted of a cigar-smoking skull wearing a Stetson hat, motorcycle sunglasses, and a Confederate flag neckerchief.[94] An average Lynyrd Skynyrd concert in the South began with a tape of an orchestral version of "Dixie" playing as the musicians took the stage. The band frequently played entire shows against the backdrop of a massive Confederate flag.[95] At other times, roadies lowered the emblem dramatically during performances of "Sweet Home Alabama."[96] In a 1974 *Rolling Stone* profile, Tom Dupree stated incorrectly that Skynyrd did not fly the Confederate flag when it played outside the South.[97] Ed King denies that the band ever discussed whether the flag should not be displayed in certain locales, claiming "it wasn't a big deal."[98] Southern rock chronicler Scott B. Bomar deems that in an effort by Van Zant to distance Skynyrd from its confining "southern" image, by about 1975 "the band stopped blasting 'Dixie' from the loudspeakers before they took the stage, and didn't always use the Confederate flag in their live performances."[99] Whatever the case, coverage of the group's nonsouthern concerts throughout the 1970s mentioned the flag's presence onstage.[100] During a July 1977 show at the Oakland (California) Coliseum—a long way from the Deep South—Skynyrd played against the backdrop of a replica of Mount Rushmore. The stage, with a huge Confederate flag situated in the middle, separated Washington and Jefferson from Roosevelt and Lincoln.[101] At concerts inside and outside the South, some fans waved their own Confederate flags, betraying a deep identification with the band, particularly its rebellious southern attitude. Ronnie Van Zant stated that European crowds "like" the flag "because they think it's macho American."[102] It is a telling admission. These fans were loving the unrestrained masculinity that they thought the emblem represented.

Van Zant's comment makes sense when reviewing the place of the Confederate battle flag in 1970s American culture. A reporter decided in 1969 that it had come to stand for "simple rebellion, the degenerate form of any nameless revolt, indeed for any anomic nut with a generalized gripe."[103] Self-styled rednecks, whom Americans no longer figured as southern necessarily, expressed these "generalized gripe[s]." Whereas the redneck had once been a pariah in national culture, by the 1970s many conservative, non-working-class whites strived to emulate this icon of southern rural culture. Bruce Schulman argues that "these demi-rednecks" "adopted the term *redneck* as a badge of honor, a fashion statement, a gesture of resistance against high taxes, liberals, racial integration, women's liberation, and hippies."[104] This was the way in which George Wallace used the term when he proudly christened his southern and nonsouthern supporters rednecks. The Confederate flag was one key totem of this identity, a barometer of one's reactionary sociocultural, if not political, druthers. It is what historian David Goldfield called, in supporters' eyes, "a symbol of freedom against oppression and for individual rights and self-determination."[105] An Atlanta factory worker described it more pithily as meaning "get the hell off my back and leave me the hell alone."[106]

Both southern and nonsouthern fans similarly espoused Skynyrd's view that the flag exemplified defiance and defensive southern chauvinism rather than racism. Rick Whitney, a fan from the group's hometown of Jacksonville, Florida, delineated the emblem in masculine terms. He stated, "The rebel flag always meant bikers, rebels, or Southerners in general, not this anti-black symbol from the racist South and the Civil War era. . . . Skynyrd used it just to show southern pride."[107] "With Skynyrd," Patricia Goddard proposed, "I think it was the 'wild eyed southern boy' usage of the flag[.] I tend to believe that it was less about race and more about [the] cultural identity of the hard rockin, hard drinkin, rowdy southern boy identity that a good deal of their audience could relate to."[108] Along these lines, a suburban Philadelphia fan pointed to the Confederate flag as symbolic of Skynyrd's message of manly robustness. "We more saw Bands like Skynyrd and the Outlaws as Gallant and honorable," he maintained. "Still fighting the Civil War and taking over the North."[109]

As this last person's comment reveals, Skynyrd's Rebel Macho celebrated not only the South—and its seeming masculine spirit—but also a prickly male defensiveness about the "southern way of life" with which some fans identified more universally. This outlook was central to the band's biggest hit, "Sweet Home Alabama," a warm, country-inflected rock song with a rolling rhythm that reached number 8 on the *Billboard* Hot 100 in 1974. The second verse includes a pointed rebuke of Neil Young. The Canadian rock star's song "Southern Man" (1970) paints southern white manhood as racist, while his "Alabama" (1972) reprimands George Wallace's state as aberrational. Young sings that Alabama has "the rest of the union to help [it] along," and yet he still finds it a land of "ruin."[110]

Van Zant singles out Young by name in "Sweet Home Alabama," before singing "a southern man don't need him around anyhow."[111] In concerts around the South, the line drew an ecstatic response. "When Van Zant sneered out that final line," Tom Dupree wrote about a 1974 Atlanta show, "the electricity almost became visible and the entire coliseum exploded in a triumphant roar. *Our boys!* they screamed." The group, Dupree went on, was "vindicating the thousands of kids who were wondering why they didn't feel guilty about loving life in the Deep South."[112] The band's kiss-off to Young tickled northern crowds as well. According to *Creem*'s Richard Riegel, "Sweet Home Alabama" was the band's "most popular song with Northern audiences." Why? "Guilty masochism, perhaps?" Riegel guessed.[113] More likely, these fans identified with the macho spirit of the lyrics even if they happened to like Young's music.

The Young verse in "Sweet Home Alabama" does little to rebut northern criticisms of the South. Highlighting Van Zant's failure to address his fellow rocker's charges, Jim Cullen states, "It is crucial to note that the suggestion that Young get lost echoes a century of similar advice that those north of the Mason-Dixon line should mind their own business." Cullen draws a parallel between Skynyrd's rebuke of Young and those late nineteenth-century southerners who beseeched northerners to let the South deal with the "Negro Question" by itself.[114] This perspective, while valid, is not how most fans of the band interpreted the song. It was, instead, a tonic for many of Skynyrd's white southern enthusiasts, who still smarted years later from the barbs of northerners who looked down on white southerners as backward and racist. One fan from Alabama resented what he considered unfair criticism of his home region and his fellow white southerners. "It was us against the world," he insisted. "I had travelled in the north as a teenager, NYC, Pennsylvania, DC. I was mocked, hated, despised, demeaned, because of where I was born."[115] Even nonsouthern Skynyrd fans could relate to the band's defensive southernness and its idealization of tough white southern masculinity. In a comment that underscored the patriarchal appeal of Skynyrd's Rebel Macho, a nonsouthern fan claimed that the band's message was an extension of a southern Civil War heritage that "wasn't about slavery. It was about defending your way of life, your family[,] your town, your home state and doing your duty against great odds even if you didn't necessarily agree with everything."[116]

While fans locked in on the band's manliness as indispensable to its defense of the white South, critics made much of the third verse of "Sweet Home Alabama" and its references to George Wallace. Here Lynyrd Skynyrd appears to endorse the controversial race-baiter:

> In Birmingham they love the governor
> (Boo, Boo, Boo)
> Now we all did what we could do
> Now Watergate does not bother me
> Does your conscience bother you?
> (Tell the truth)[117]

Van Zant tried to tell Robert Christgau that the boos came from the band as an indictment of the governor.[118] The rock critic was unimpressed, writing that Van Zant's "explanation, which seemed to imply that the jeers were intended in some abstrusely satirical way, made no sense to me."[119] According to Ed King, the booing crowd in fact represents the voices of northerners. The Skynyrd guitarist would claim, "it's not US (Skynyrd) going 'boo' . . . it's what the Southern man hears the Northern man say every time the Southern man'd say 'In Birmingham we love the gov'nor.' Get it? 'We all did what WE could do!' to get Wallace elected. It's not a popular opinion but Wallace stood for the average white guy in the South."[120] Fellow guitarist Gary Rossington backed up King's view, concurring with his interpretation of the boos and adding, "Ronnie liked Wallace and was for him."[121] Continuing the song's theme of southern defensiveness, the tune's speaker ends the verse by referencing the (at the time of the song's June 1974 release) ongoing Watergate scandal. He insinuates that it is a nonsouthern crime for which the South deserves no blame. This remark furthers the sentiment of the Neil Young verse: northerners should stop moralizing and leave the southland alone. Overall, Skynyrd used the third verse of "Sweet Home Alabama" to augment its status as defenders of an allegedly blameless, beleaguered class: white southern men.

The band's support for Wallace becomes more explicit when one examines its members' public statements about him. Although the governor had tempered his public racism by the mid-1970s, he remained a divisive figure. In 1975, Wallace, recognizing his odd kinship with the group, made the Floridians honorary lieutenant colonels in the Alabama State Militia, a distinction Ed King said the band "took pride in."[122] Searching for signs of racism, music journalists grilled Skynyrd's members for their assessments of the governor. Their comments were rife with ambiguity. Their attempted balancing act sought to distance themselves from Wallace's racism while identifying with his masculine, southern image. Bassist Leon Wilkeson explained, "I support Wallace about as much as your average American supported Hitler," before adding, "I respect him, not as a politician—but as a man who hasn't given up what he was after. That's how we all feel."[123] Van Zant seemed to agree. He told Robert Christgau, "I don't like what he says about colored people."[124] Still, he informed reporter Lisa Robinson that Wallace was a "gentleman [who] has a lot of nerve." More than that, he had "balls. And I admire that."[125] In short, whatever reservations they may have had about his racial politics, the individuals in Skynyrd felt an affinity for Wallace's masculine prowess: he was a real man who stood up—figuratively at least—not only for the (white) South but also for the cause of masculine regeneration.

In spite of the press's interest in the band's Wallace connection, fans generally rejected charges of racism leveled against the musicians. In Skynyrd's catalog, Gary Nagle asserted, "There are no lyrics I know of, that speak to the proliferation of racial prejudice."[126] Other fans heard notes of racial progressivism in the group's music. One Pensacola, Florida, listener stated, "Ronnie Van Zant wrote lyrics which demonstrated inter-racial acceptance and friendship," pointing to the song "The Ballad of Curtis Loew" (1974), in which the white narrator describes his friendship with a socially disregarded elderly black bluesman.[127]

The disconnect between journalists' preoccupation with Skynyrd's racial ideology and fans' apparent lack of interest in the topic perhaps speaks to liberal reporters' Vicious South–style wariness of the white southern working-class culture that Lynyrd Skynyrd represented. But when they pushed aside racial issues or vowed that the band was actually racially enlightened, fans adopted what scholar David Stricklin has termed "a defiant southern perspective that avoided sinking into overt support for returning to the pre–civil rights days."[128] That defiance stemmed from the band's reputation as backwoods purveyors of violence, which in turn undergirded its message of masculine rebellion. The success of a rock group that preached this kind of message further demonstrates the powerful pull of the white South as a repository of male aggression and social control in the context of the 1970s, during which, according to many concerned Americans, the tradition of white masculine dominance was under assault.

Conclusion

The Allman Brothers Band's and Lynyrd Skynyrd's respective brands of southernness—Countercultural and Rebel Macho—drew, in part, varied audiences looking for different values in an imagined white South. The Allman Brothers further showcased one of the central components of country-rock's reception; that is, the alleged similarity in countercultural and so-called rural southern values. While the Brothers' southernness attracted listeners intrigued by the white South as an anachronistic alternative to modern America, they also seemed strikingly modern, with their example of whites and blacks living and working together toward a common goal. Lynyrd Skynyrd, in contrast, promoted white southern male defiance and violence as admirable traits central to the revalidation of white patriarchy.

Nevertheless, southern rock fans often embraced both Lynyrd Skynyrd and the Allman Brothers Band. That dual popularity was not just a product of good music or marketing. It also had to do with the ability of 1970s Americans to imagine the South in divergent ways without either recognizing or being troubled by the cognitive dissonance. After all, Ronnie Van Zant would once drunkenly proclaim himself "the Prince of Dixie" and Duane Allman "the king."[129] These bands were merely two sides of the same coin when it came to deploying white southernness as a counterweight to the unpleasant realities (and imaginings) of 1970s America. The Allman Brothers' and Skynyrd's southernness collectively addressed commentators' and fans' apprehensions of declining masculinity, racial strife, and social unrest. Whether the solutions to these problems lay closer to the ass-kicking, Rebel Macho (Masculine South) of Skynyrd or the brotherly countercultural southernness (a hybrid of the Changing and Down-Home Souths) of the Allmans was up for debate. But the groups' differing takes on white southernness at least offered audiences a chance to use the malleable imagery of the white South to express and calm some of their anxieties about race, family, and gender.

Despite their differing depictions of the region, both the Allman Brothers Band and Lynyrd Skynyrd united in their support of presidential candidate Jimmy Carter—himself a son of the South—during the 1976 campaign. The southern rockers' benefits concert helped to raise money for the former Georgia governor as he worked to establish himself as a feasible candidate. The Democrat's message, though similar to that of his beloved Allman Brothers, avoided any whiff of hippiedom or masculine chest thumping. Instead, he cast the region in a good light by playing up its supposed rural virtues and presenting the South at the forefront of racial progressivism in the post–civil rights era. Carter's enticing healing white southernness was a source of pride for white southerners like the members of Skynyrd and the Allmans, who were well acquainted with nonsouthern condescension. More importantly, though, Carter's persona also played well on the national level. It fit perfectly with the narrative of a nation searching to find itself politically, morally, and spiritually in the 1970s.

CHAPTER 5

"I Respect a Good Southern White Man"

Jimmy Carter's Healing Southernness and the 1976 Presidential Campaign

Sensing the American public's fascination with—and the cultural power of—Jimmy Carter's southernness during the 1976 presidential contest, Gerald Ford's Republican strategists turned to another southerner for advice. Their choice—Frances Kaye Pullen—perhaps revealed their desperation to combat a key part of the former Georgia governor's appeal. The Tennessee-born Pullen had written speeches for President Ford before she was transferred to Betty Ford's staff, where she performed the same duties for the First Lady; she was hardly a member of the GOP campaign's inner circle. Nonetheless, Pullen submitted a detailed and carefully crafted memo (more like "an essay," she jested).[1] In it, she concluded that Carter successfully merged different versions of a fantasied South, enabling him to attract fellow southerners hoping to gain nonsouthern respect for their oft-maligned region and to charm voters living outside of the southland. "Carter," Pullen observed, "is playing upon two essentially conflicting myths—the 'good ole boy' rural South and the 'black and white together' new South." And his "use of the southern mystique" was nothing more than "hoke," a false picture of the region that the news media were all too eager to internalize and disseminate.[2]

Folksy insults aside, Pullen captured one of the central strengths of Carter's campaign: his ability to deploy captivating southern symbols that connected with voters both regionally and nationally. Carter hailed from rural southern Georgia, where he oversaw a prosperous peanut business. His presidential run occurred during a key moment: just after the civil rights movement, when a racially progressive white southerner like himself could be seen as a mainstream figure well-suited to deal with the country's racial divides. He benefited from other accidents of circumstance, as well. For example, the Georgia constitution at the time prohibited the sitting governor from succeeding himself. This meant that when his single term as the state's chief executive ended in 1975, Carter was left with unlimited time to lobby for the presidency. This last factor, coupled with Democratic Party rule changes on fund-raising and delegate selection, made Carter's populist style of one-on-one campaigning incredibly effective. The *Atlanta Constitution* editor Reg Murphy had ridiculed him as a joke candidate when he first announced his presidential bid; by early 1976, he was a viable White House hopeful.[3]

In labeling Carter's southernness an asset, Pullen divulged that she had been paying attention to popular culture in addition to politics. By the mid-1970s, the white South had been, in some ways, rehabilitated on the screen and in print. Carter's drive to the White House drew on the Down-Home South of *The Andy Griffith Show* and *The Waltons* and exploited the increasing tendency of media outlets to see the South as free (or at least freeing itself) of its racial problems, with the news establishment mostly defining such issues as busing, discriminatory housing practices, and ghetto life as "new," predominantly nonsouthern problems. Carter's southernness even included a bit of the integrated, countercultural flair of the Allman Brothers Band, a personal favorite of Carter's, whose label head, Phil Walden, was one of the candidate's earliest and most active supporters and fund-raisers.

Carter invented no new narratives about the South. Instead, he innovated by fusing existing imaginings of the region and its people into an intoxicating combination of white southern cultural traditionalism and racial progressivism—an effort discerned by Pullen in her insightful memo—and presenting it as a worthy alternative to the problems of modern U.S. society. This approach had not previously been possible. Since the nineteenth century, Americans had often treated the South as a cultural and political Other, marred by racism, economic stagnation, and political demagoguery. But now, in the mid-1970s, the changing image of the region enabled Carter to combine powerful, formerly incongruent claims of both the South's post–civil rights racial transformation—what historian Charles Reagan Wilson has termed "the myth of the biracial South"—and the continuity of the seemingly timeless white southern rural virtues embodied by Carter's pastoral upbringing, farming background, and tight-knit family.[4] The candidate profited from widely circulated opinions like those underlying *Time*'s perspective in a special September 1976 issue on the South: "Could it be that in many ways [the region] can now teach the nation something about how to live?"[5] Despite cautioning that "the idea can be easily exaggerated," the magazine's answer was clearly yes. *Time* saw the South as "a place apart" and "a redoubt of old American tenets." It was "the last American arena with a special, nurtured identity, its own sometimes unfashionable regard for the soil, for family ties, for the authority of God and country."[6] These were potent ideas that when cooked down to their essence amounted to two things: authenticity and roots. When combined with assertions of racial harmony, they would serve as the basis not only for repairing a region's reputation in the national psyche but also, on a related note, for placing a white southerner hailing from the Deep South in the White House.

Carter made what is best termed his healing southernness applicable to the particular anxieties of the 1970s United States. Historians Beth Bailey and David Farber have called the decade a time of "incoherent impulses, contradictory desires, and even a fair amount of self-flagellation."[7] In this environment of uncertainty, Carter represented himself as the ultimate outsider, a man whose rural small-town southern origins served as a bulwark against the political and cultural tumult in Washington and the rest of the nation. While addressing persistent postwar apprehensions about alienating technologies and a dangerous and isolated existence in cities or a bland and unfulfilling life in the suburbs, Carter's healing southernness also spoke to more recent feelings of public helplessness in the face of government corruption, lies about Vietnam and Watergate, and the social turmoil of the late 1960s and early 1970s. His persona as a man with deep roots further responded to Americans' fears that the nation had drifted from its core beliefs in the durability of family, community, and political- and faith-based institutions. A May 1976 *Time* survey found that 61 percent of Americans "feel something is morally wrong in the nation." Among those voters, 54 percent supported Carter, versus 31 percent for Ford.[8]

What made Carter's embodiment of supposedly rural white southern values so important in the 1976 election was the perception—fueled by both the candidate and the press—of this southernness. Southern-born author Neal R. Peirce echoed the Georgian's argument that he was perfectly prepared to pull the country out of its deep angst. Carter's South, Peirce declared, involved an "honesty about race questions, direct and openly expressed religious faith, a deep sense of family and of place—all values so often lacking in the more acquisitive and devious North."[9] Indeed, Carter's roots as symbolized by his liberal racial views, rural hometown, inseparable family, and Southern Baptist religion addressed a bottomless American desire for healing in the 1970s. For citizens looking to revitalize the battered national spirit in the Bicentennial year, Carter's brilliant merging and wielding of imagined white southern culture promised a set of useful, albeit abstract, tools for cultural, social, and political rehabilitation. The Democrat exploited a powerful yearning for a redemptive, fantasied past as well as southerners' and nonsoutherners' desire to move past the troubling problem of race in America.

The Southern Issue

Although Carter's southernness nodded to voters' cultural trepidations and bolstered his post-Watergate, anti-Washington image, political pundits during the 1976 campaign questioned whether the Georgian's origins would ultimately prove a liability. They wondered if nonsoutherners, particularly northern liberals, would be able to put aside notions of benighted and buffoonish white southerners and elect the first Deep South president since 1848. (Most reporters agreed that the West Texan Lyndon Johnson did not count.)[10] Early in the primary season, Carter acknowledged this prejudice, but he told the *Washington Star* that perceptions of the white South had changed. "It's become of lesser significance," he said, "as people begin to realize more clearly that the South is no longer represented by people like George Wallace or [former Georgia governor] Lester Maddox."[11] Still, privately, Carter and his associates worried about a lingering anti-southern bias. In a letter to his wife and informal political advisor Rosalynn, Carter's daughter-in-law and campaign surrogate Judy cautioned that the candidate should be aware of the "prejudice against Southerners," however "subtle and ill-defined."[12] Carter's campaign director Hamilton Jordan claimed, "If there's something about Jimmy people don't like—his religion or he's from the South—it's easy to say he's fuzzy on the issues."[13]

The Carters and Jordan discovered plenty in the newspapers and magazines published during the election season to support their fears. Journalists gathered piecemeal evidence of this alleged anti-southern bias, which usually consisted of quotes from voters or Democratic Party officials. *Newsweek*'s Susan Fraker cited one Oregon voter who said, "I try to tell myself I don't care [that Carter is a southerner], but it's always in the back of my mind. I have to jump that hurdle everytime I listen to his accent."[14] Occasional letters to the editor in national publications indicated that part of the electorate was uncomfortable with a Deep South president. Shortly after the general election, one suburban Chicago reader told *Time* sarcastically, "Just what this country needs: a vague, big-spending, fast-talking hillbilly redneck in the White House. May God help us."[15]

Reporters themselves commonly engaged in unsupported speculation that anti-southern sentiment would substantially color voter response to Carter. For example, the *New Republic*'s Richard Strout (writing under the pseudonym TRB) recounted the following encounter: "I have a political activist friend in Washington who burst out against Carter with a vehemence that startled me: 'He's a two-faced louse!' he ejaculated or words to that effect. My friend thinks Carter's a hypocrite; maybe he is prejudiced; deep down perhaps, he is asking a variant of that old question, 'Can anything good come out of Georgia?'"[16] Conservative columnist George F. Will also diagnosed a tendency for white northern liberals to automatically label Carter a racist, suggesting that his southern origins were a definite factor in the opposition to his candidacy.[17]

Although most of the written coverage of candidate Carter and his family treated their southernness in positive terms, the same could not be said for political cartoons. These often portrayed the Carters as ignorant and backward and played on stereotypes of an unenlightened South.[18] After he clinched the Democratic nomination in New York, the cover of *Newsweek* showed Carter as a hayseed leading a march of donkeys through the big city.[19] One month earlier, the magazine published a piece by nationally syndicated cartoonist Pat Oliphant in which various segments of the Democratic Party establishment—George Wallace, Chicago mayor Richard J. Daley, and Washington senator Henry "Scoop" Jackson—arrive in Carter's hometown of Plains to pay their respects to the candidate, who sits on his front porch. Carter's famous smile is set into a cadaverous, sunken face. The Georgian looks like a barely animated corpse.[20] Scholar Alette Hill maintained that "Carter's clothing is that of a farmer, but his face is that of a grotesque opportunist."[21] A cartoon in the *Denver Post* managed to lampoon both Carter's southernness and his campaign promises to transcend petty partisan politics. In this drawing, the artist exaggerates his Georgia dialect. The Democrat proclaims to reporters, "Wahtuhgate? I don't intend to make Wahtuhgate an issue. . . . Let us fo'get Wahtuhgate . . . Wahtuhgate . . . Wahtuhgate!"[22]

The newspaper juxtaposed this cartoon with a satire piece titled "Love and Justice in the White House." Presenting the Carter clan as fish out of water at the president's residence, the column has the Carters planting peanuts in the Rose Garden, preparing to serve fried chicken to Mrs. Gandhi, and building a cotton gin on the White House lawn, which is brimming with encamped Carter relatives.[23] The family comes off, Alette Hill explains, as "presumably a southern version of the Beverly Hillbillies."[24] Elsewhere, cartoonists lampooned Carter's Southern Baptist faith, alternately drawing him as a grinning Jesus wrapped in the Confederate flag, a faith healer, and God's personal pick for president.[25] By reducing the governor to a hick, a misshapen corpse, or a deluded Baptist preacher, these caricatures leaned on pervasive stereotypes of white southerners as comical, fanatical, and aberrational.

Despite negative—or at least ambivalent—cartoon representations and conjecture about anti-southern bias, public opinion polls revealed scant evidence that Carter's southernness hurt his popularity among voters.[26] As noted, Americans possessed the ability to view the white South in antithetical ways simultaneously. And in an environment in which the Georgian's origins were constantly under a microscope, Carter and his surrogates did not shy away from his southernness. They positioned him as a transcendent figure who captured the best of the region's supposed traits while overcoming its racist baggage. An advisor alerted Carter and Hamilton Jordan early in the campaign to the potential benefit of a candidate who exceeded the expectations for a stereotypically demagogic southern politician. Were the candidate able to represent himself as "the 'good Southerner,'" the advisor theorized, "Carter should be able to turn this 'disadvantage' to his great advantage."[27]

Carter: The White Southerner as Racial Healer

If Carter was the "good southerner," then the "bad southerner" was George Wallace. Carter publicized himself as a living monument to southern racial reconciliation. He was a rural white southerner—seemingly the stereotype of the cracker—who had nevertheless risen above his bigoted surroundings. He used this identity to argue for his ability to move the nation forward in addressing and possibly resolving racial issues. In 1976 Carter challenged Wallace, now in the midst of his fourth try for the presidency, for the Democratic nomination. While the wheelchair-bound Alabamian now kept his overt racism in check, in the minds of many Americans, he remained the quintessential representation of the white South: angry, bigoted, and rabble-rousing. These characteristics, coupled with his reactionary politics, appealed to a considerable number of working- and middle-class nonsoutherners; yet for most moderates and liberals, Wallace embodied an old, bankrupt brand of southern—and indeed national—politics. As Marshall Frady wrote in 1975, "Only Gov. George Wallace remains now as a last vestige, a curious transitional urban mutant, of that long pageant of splendidly gargoylish, musky old demagogues during the South's age of tribal politics."[28] The "eminently inoffensive" (Frady's words) Carter told southerners that his primary battle with Wallace was "a matter of who best represents the South," although he just as easily could have been speaking to northerners.[29] After Carter beat Wallace in the early southern primaries (Florida and North Carolina), he laid claim to the mantle of the "good southerner."

Wallace understood the stakes involved in his contest with Carter. Based on the relative successes of his previous presidential runs, he knew that playing on voters' conflicting imaginings of the South was a crucial element for any white southerner seeking to make inroads into national politics. Wallace reacted testily to Carter's victories in the South and to the larger sense that the Georgian's southernness was now more relevant than the Alabamian's fiery, race-baiting methods. Journalist Elizabeth Drew remembered seeing a frustrated Wallace speaking before a North Carolina audience of supporters. He was clearly bitter at being out-southerned by Carter: "His face twisted in anger, his voice ringing with contempt, Wallace says, 'I'm not one who says, "I'm a Southerner but I'm a *different kind* of Southerner." What kind of Southerner does [Carter] *mean*? I think all Southerners are good.'"[30]

Media types identified in the "good southerner" versus "bad southerner" story line a symbolic passing of the torch from the Old South of Wallace to the New South of Carter.[31] The 1976 campaign marked the end of Wallace's pretenses to national power as well as his strong performance with white southern voters. Reg Murphy insisted that Wallace fell behind because he failed to adjust his outdated racial politics and to recognize the increasing influence of black southern voters.[32] Murphy and other journalists correctly deemed Carter more adept in his grasp of the shifting role of race in the new southern politics. In this revised state of affairs, white southern Democrats would need to attract both blacks and whites. They could no longer rely on racial demagoguery to sway voters, thus representing a break with the reactionary nature of the southern political scene before and during the civil rights era. The contest with Wallace, not surprisingly, allowed Carter to ground his southernness in racial healing rather than division. He repeatedly advertised the South's racial progress, describing passage of the 1964 Civil Rights Act and the 1965 Voting Rights Act as "the best thing that has happened in the South in my lifetime."[33] In speeches and promotional materials, he highlighted both his quiet attempts to oppose segregation in 1950s and 1960s south Georgia and his liberal racial record as governor.[34]

By referencing his racial egalitarianism, Carter was in part trying to allay nonsoutherners' assumption that his white southernness automatically made him a racist. The press often encouraged this reasoning by scrutinizing the Georgian's racial views. Reporters delved into Carter's conservative 1970 gubernatorial campaign in which he had courted the Wallace vote and declared himself "basically a redneck." They dwelled on his embarrassingly worded comment in April 1976 that urban Americans should be allowed to maintain the "ethnic purity" of their neighborhoods.[35] That these incidents did little to blunt the governor's success in the Democratic primaries suggests the power of Carter's persona as a white man who had risen above the racist culture of his homeland.

In accentuating his regional origins, Carter imparted that as a white southerner he was uniquely suited to actualize racial harmony in the nation. It seemed counterintuitive, but that claim could play to the desire of white Americans to address—or at least step beyond—the problem of race in the United States. This sentiment is apparent, for example, in the June 1976 Democratic survey responses of two white Wisconsinites. Asked about Carter's expected actions on racial issues, including busing, a middle-aged home contractor from Green Bay, Wisconsin, acknowledged the importance of the candidate's claim of knowing blacks. "Carter has lived and worked with coloreds," the anonymous pollster paraphrased the man. This self-disclosed Republican implied that the Georgian's integrated background would lead him to ease (or perhaps stifle) racial unrest by preventing forced busing and desegregation of white ethnic neighborhoods. Another voter interviewed by the Democratic team supported Carter's anti-busing position, despite her liberal affiliation. But this woman also claimed, according to the surveyor's notes, that "racism will be curtailed due to his great southern compassion."[36]

Regardless of their individual racial ideology, many whites could envision Carter's southernness as resulting in the alleviation of racial strife. This contention would have meant nothing without the support of black leaders, who often deemed southern white liberals particularly trustworthy on racial issues. Indeed, as Vernon Jordan, executive director of the Urban League said, in contrast to "basically paternalistic" northern liberals, "the Southern white man who gets converted to the cause—why, he would die for you."[37] Along the same lines, a Harlem resident told the *Washington Post* simply, "I respect a good Southern white man because he's not a hypocrite."[38] Much of the broader black electorate held this opinion, too. Polling information demonstrated that Carter's southernness was hardly a hindrance for blacks. He ultimately won 83 percent of their votes nationally, maintaining the Democratic Party's traditional dominance among this constituency.[39] Explaining such overwhelming support, Carter biographer Betty Glad averred,

> One might speculate that in their support for Carter, voting blacks, led by black pastors and politicians, were voting on the symbolic issue of the South more than on issues of substantive programs of social change. They were voting out of nostalgia, trust, and hope—nostalgia for the rhythms and religion of rural Christianity, trust in the leaders who told them Carter was all right on race issues, and hope that a man who grew up with and cared for blacks could make the transition into the new South of equality and justice more readily than a Northern stranger.[40]

Carter pushed beyond simply decreeing his southern racial progressivism. He also echoed the narratives of white southern moderates and liberals who insisted that the South had made great strides in overcoming its racial problems, and that in doing so, had something to teach the rest of the nation. As the *New York Times Magazine* reported in December 1975, "Carter thinks that other parts of the country—Boston, for example—are now passing through the period of trauma the South passed through a decade ago, and that they, too, will reach a point of racial understanding."[41] The Georgia Democrat thus exploited the about-face in national focus during the late 1960s from southern to northern racial conflict.

Carter's speech at the dedication ceremony for a new wing of the Martin Luther King Jr. Hospital of Los Angeles exemplified his efforts to present his racially progressive southernness as an asset outside of the South. On 1 June 1976, at a location not far from the Watts riot zones of 1965, where nonsoutherners had been faced with their own racial problems, the white southern Carter couched himself as an heir to the legacy of King's Dream. "I sometimes think that a southerner of my generation can most fully understand the meaning and the impact of Martin Luther King's life," Carter said. "He and I grew up in the same South, he the son of a clergyman, I the son of a farmer. We both knew, from opposite sides, the invisible wall of racial segregation."[42] The candidate went on to recount the experience of growing up in the Jim Crow South and the region's struggles to accommodate change. But because of that change, he now made a serious claim on the presidency—as a white southerner.[43] Carter's willingness to speak of the past wounds of the segregated South, in addition to his religious commitment, won him the support of many black leaders, including Georgia's Andrew Young and Martin Luther King Sr. These endorsements broadcast Carter's viability as a candidate to members of the black community and among northern liberals, many of whom looked to black leadership to determine if a candidate, especially a white southern candidate, was acceptable on civil rights issues.[44]

Carter's racial views did more than pass the liberal litmus test. Because these beliefs were those of a white southerner, one who had seemingly learned hard lessons during the civil rights movement, many voters perceived them as more authentic. On a national level, the governor's persona as a racial healer appealed to what historian Thomas Borstelmann has referred to as "the egalitarian, inclusive flavor of contemporary [1970s] America."[45] In addition to promising relief from the racial dilemma, Carter reflected most Americans' commitment to eradicating discrimination in public life.[46] Even as more insidious forms of inequality persisted, Americans longed to put the divisive racial fissures of the 1960s behind them. They hoped that this small-town Georgian who rose from a culture he claimed had gained wisdom from the movement for black equality might hold the solution for mollifying the country's continued racial anxieties.

Imagining Carter's Roots

In his southernness, Carter deftly combined the modern and progressive, in terms of racial views, with the traditional. Identifying southern values as "closeness to our places of worship," "a love of our land," and "a closeness in family," the Georgian encouraged voters to see in him the encapsulation of lost traits and traditions.[47] As Betty Glad has argued, "The rich and idealized description of Carter's roots during the campaign . . . tapped some broader national impulse to escape from the anomie of contemporary society and its social and political fragmentation by a return to the past." Moreover, "by looking to Plains and the values there, one could find the spiritual and social solace that seemed lacking throughout most of the nation."[48]

Plains was, unmistakably, an alluring location that seemed almost too good to be true. It was as if Hollywood, noted several journalists, had applied its magic to the town's appearance.[49] One could drive through the small, unassuming town in a couple of minutes, but it left a major impression on observers. The apparent incongruity—and yet perfectness—of a serious presidential candidate hailing from a place like Plains (population 683) drew the interest of the press and hundreds of daily visitors during the summer of 1976.[50] Helen Dudar wrote in *Esquire* that it was "a town so benign, so beguiling, so cute, so clearly the ideal site for the Home of an American President—and so superior to the vulgarity of, say, San Clemente [where Richard Nixon resided]—that you are ready to write campaign brochures for [Carter]."[51] When Norman Mailer ventured to Plains to interview the candidate after the primaries, he expected to see a gothic little town, marred by decay. Instead, he stumbled upon a welcoming, seemingly timeless locale: "It had the sweet deep green of an old-fashioned town that America has all but lost to the Interstates and the ranch houses" and other markers of the homogenized nation.[52]

Carter himself pushed voters to visualize his hometown as an antimodern bastion against the encroachment of unsettling postwar changes that threatened to destroy the bonds between Americans. His campaign autobiography *Why Not the Best?* stressed an idyllic upbringing. His descriptions addressed Americans' sense of nostalgia for a simpler time and the notion that rural places and small towns, particularly in the South, housed dormant traditions.

Such content sated the same wistfulness for "simpler" times exploited by *The Waltons* (CBS, 1972–1981), a nostalgia-tinged top-twenty television drama. According to Mike Chopra-Gant, the show achieved its "popularity . . . by reviving a set of positive emotional associations from a mythic America of the past, at a time when contemporary America was beset by a range of economic, social and political problems."[53] Viewers tuned in week after week to see the loving Walton family face down the challenges of the Depression while living among a colorful community of neighbors. In the 1976 campaign, the Waltons-Carters parallels were everywhere. "His family," writes Dominic Sandbrook, "was presented as a real-life equivalent of the Waltons."[54] TV critic Michael Kilian joked that under the influence of what he predicted would be a moralistic Carter presidency, CBS might air *Waltons* reruns in a solid three-hour block during prime time.[55] Despite such ribbing, readers of *Why Not the Best?* surely could not help but connect the dots between the admirable lives and rural southern locales of the fictional Waltons of Virginia and the real-life Carters of Georgia.

The book's longest chapter, "Farm," opens with a bit of hyperbole. Chronicling his early years on his 350-acre family tract in Archery, a predominantly black settlement near Plains, Carter reminisced, "My life on the farm during the Great Depression more nearly resembled farm life of fully 2,000 years ago than farm life today."[56] Despite some exaggeration, the candidate wove an enticing narrative of how his rural upbringing instilled in him traditional values. "We felt close to nature, close to the members of our family, and close to God," he stated.[57] During the campaign, Carter would describe his childhood as enriched by his family's love and devotion.[58] The Democrat also encouraged the public to see Plains as unchanging in its values—with the exception of racial segregation. "Plains, Georgia (1925)," read one photo caption in *Why Not the Best?*, "same in '75."[59]

His hometown, Carter maintained, was a place where people knew and could rely on each other. For Americans in the 1970s who were worried about the breakdown of the family structure, Carter's close kinship network lent credence to his pledge that his brand of moral leadership, drawing on tradition, would address this dilemma.[60] Speaking in Manchester, New Hampshire, in August 1976, Carter said, "I have campaigned all over America, and everywhere I go I find people deeply concerned about the loss of stability and the loss of values in our lives. The root of this problem is the steady erosion and weakening of our families."[61] This focus on family and values was typical of Carter, who, Betty Glad asserted, "implied that he could make the whole nation a caring people—he would make America like his family."[62]

Carter's rustic image was crucial in making this argument. Early television advertisements placed the Georgian on his farm, walking the fields or examining peanuts. The message was simple: here is a man untainted by Washington politics, whose values are as rich as the southern soil that grew them. Carter repeatedly discussed Plains in stump speeches, prompting reporters to probe its political and cultural significance. Kenneth Reich of the *Los Angeles Times* concluded, "The scenes of Plains go hand-in-hand with the central message in the speeches [Carter] has delivered throughout the country—that Americans and American government need to return to the old values, and that he is the man who represents them."[63] "Even in big cities," intimated the *Washington Post*'s Helen Dewar, "he talks about the smallness and intimacy of Plains and its people, appearing to evoke in his listeners a nostalgia for the old days and simple ways, in many cases a life they never knew."[64] Down-home descriptions of Plains thus benefited the outsider Carter, who associated his southernness with the unassuming town and held it aloft as a remedy for both Washington politics and sociocultural discontent.

The Carter team continued to wield the public fascination with Plains to its advantage, especially after the candidate clinched the Democratic nomination. Carter camped out in his hometown, met with policy advisors, and waited for the fall campaign against Gerald Ford to begin. He said that he wished to avoid the fate of marathon campaigners who "tend to lose stability and have their roots torn away."[65] For bored reporters, there was little to do in Plains. Democratic campaign officials, in turn, manufactured a series of local events for the press corps. Journalists watched and reported while Carter drained ponds, taught Sunday school classes, played softball, and inspected his peanut fields.[66] These events may have been mundane, but they served a real purpose. They plugged Carter's image as a disarming, humble, small-town southerner, one totally ensconced in his locale. Plus, they kept the media's and the public's attention fully directed to his promotion of southern rural and small-town traditions.

While in Plains, reporters took the opportunity to interview Carter's colorful family, a veritable collection of southern archetypes. There was the strong, sassy matriarch Lillian; the motorcycle-riding Charismatic Christian sister Gloria; the faith healer sister Ruth; and, most vivid, the hard-drinking, beer-bellied brother Billy. Carter's relatives furthered his "Plains-as-family-as-nation" concept with their local flair, reinforcing the candidate's southernness as a worthy, distinctive substitute for mainstream American politics and culture.

According to reporter Kandy Stroud, Carter's seventy-eight-year-old mother "Miz" Lillian was "spunky, determined, witty and a dominating influence on her sons."[67] Lillian was willing to speak her mind with humor about Jimmy and a variety of other issues, guaranteeing that her remarks would always make good copy. "I'm certainly in favor of doing things for old people," she once said at a press conference for the elderly rights organization the Gray Panthers. "I'm going to get old myself someday."[68] Visitors to Plains, whether members of the general public or the press corps, always found her accessible. She often manned her son's campaign headquarters and was willing to shake hands and talk with people about Jimmy. At other times she traveled, stumping in support of progressive causes and her son's candidacy. The press narrative frequently repeated Lillian's claims of instilling in young Jimmy his drive and determination and his racial open-mindedness, thus intensifying his appealing brand of healing southernness. As Helen Dudar wrote, "A lot of her has gone into her son: her appetite for learning, her feeling for black people, her grit."[69]

Lillian Carter's personification of "southern charm" made her a celebrity during the campaign. Nowhere was this more evident than at the festivities accompanying the Democratic National Convention in New York City in July 1976. Journalists sought her out for interviews; celebrities, Democratic politicos, even newsmen wanted to meet—and gush over—her. "I think I'm secretly in love with Miss Lillian," Walter Cronkite said at one event. Former radical Tom Hayden believed that "she could be another Eleanor Roosevelt."[70] Lillian hobnobbed with the well-known and the well-connected, including journalist Carl Bernstein and actress Shirley MacLaine.[71] Some of this fawning over Carter's mother was symptomatic of "peanut chic," or more broadly, "redneck (or southern) chic," a somewhat condescending fascination with all things south of the Mason-Dixon Line emerging in the mid-1970s that manifested itself in everything from the proliferation of country music stations outside of the South to northern urbanites pulling on cowboy boots and talking into their new CB radios.[72] Still, Jimmy could not have asked for a better ambassador for his southernness and his candidacy than Lillian.

Malcolm ("Mal") MacDougall, an advertising executive who served as the creative director for President Ford's onslaught against Carter, recollected one incident that epitomizes the boost Miz Lillian's southernness provided the Carter campaign. On the evening of 7 August 1976, MacDougall tuned his radio to the Boston call-in show *Sports Huddle*. The topic was the low-brow sport of wrestling. This was not the environment in which one might have expected to hear a presidential candidate's mother, but there she was, talking about her favorite wrestlers and discussing such intricacies as the merits of "midgets" in the sport (she did not like them). MacDougall marveled at the Carter campaign's imaginative use of Lillian, dispatching her to relate to the common folks in her down-home manner. This is how he set the scene: "One little phone call and 100,000 avid Boston sports fans had undoubtedly fallen in love with Jimmy Carter's mother. I pictured her hanging up the phone and dialing city after city, talk show after talk show, a smiling campaign worker at her shoulder, sliding type-written notes under her elbow. Her deep Southern accent, just slightly cracked with age, drawling into the telephone—and into a million homes a night."[73] As MacDougall understood, in her performance of rural white southernness, Lillian functioned as a surrogate for Jimmy, one who was able to exploit her cachet as a free-speaking southern matriarch into more generalized support for his folksy image. Jimmy's more buttoned-down personality—or his "official piety" as southern journalist Larry L. King called it—did not lend itself to this kind of outspokenness, nor would it have been appropriate for him to behave in this manner as he tried to represent himself as a serious presidential contender.[74] His mother not only loosened up his image; she fortified his allure as a representative of an enchanting rural South.

Carter's younger brother Billy fulfilled a similar function, but in more outlandish ways. He was, as one member of the media advanced, "the proverbial 'good ole boy,' as Southern as saw mill gravy and hominy grits."[75] Whereas Lillian was a sassy southern woman who simultaneously typified the best of Old South strong womanhood and New South racial tolerance, Jimmy's brother was what writer Roy Blount Jr. later called a "hero to beer drinkers and workingmen."[76] Billy's disarming style and willingness to speak to the bored press corps made him a media star. When visiting Plains, reporters and tourists stopped at Billy's gas station, where inevitably he would be guzzling beer, swapping stories, and telling a few off-color jokes with friends. "Yes, I'm a real Southern boy," he would tell journalists. "I got a red neck, white socks and Blue Ribbon beer."[77] When not wearing polyester leisure suits, brother Billy could be seen sporting blue jeans and T-shirts emblazoned with phrases like "Cast Iron," a reference to his astonishing gastrointestinal prowess.[78]

Billy's rube-like persona could have—and surely did—turn off some voters. He was unrefined and profane and had no qualms about drinking in front of (and sometimes with) reporters. But the delightfulness of the good ole boy was precisely this lack of sophistication. This stock character combined a hard masculinity with a seeming unaffectedness indicative of his southern environment. Bonnie Angela explained to *Time* readers in September 1976 that there was much to like about the good ole boy. To begin with, he knew how to have fun in an old-fashioned manner. He engaged in "comfortable, hyperhearty, all-male camaraderie" and his loose, casual social style focused on enjoying the company of friends. "Behind his devil-may-care lightheartedness, however," Angela surmised, "runs a strain of innate wisdom, an instinct about people and an unwavering loyalty."[79] Billy Carter was the incarnation of these ideas. *Boston Globe* journalist and fellow southerner Curtis Wilkie described him as "a fount of folk wisdom" eager to deflate pretentiousness and arrogance. One day in Plains, Wilkie and Billy observed a reporter on the street dressed in overalls and a straw hat chewing on a piece of straw. Recognizing this "act of ridiculous condescension," Wilkie later recalled, "Billy turned to me and said, 'Look at that asshole.'"[80]

Carter's campaign utilized Billy's "redneck power" to make the public see the worldlier candidate not as a real redneck, but as simply more accessible. In the midst of the Wisconsin primary, Hamilton Jordan hit on Billy's symbolic role. "Maybe that's what Jimmy needs to get rid of some of this churchy image he's got. Um'm, a brother whose standards are a little more relaxed, who boozes a little, that you can really relax with . . . the press won't have to be pushed to pick up on that."[81] Jordan was right. The Carter campaign's recognition that its candidate's southernness could attract national voters, Garry Wills suggested, caused Billy to go from "the family's closet redneck" to "something like the token redneck."[82]

With journalists anxious to cover the folksiness and apparent authenticity of mother Lillian, brother Billy, and the town of Plains itself, Carter gained a series of assets during the campaign. "Interesting in their own right," wrote Betty Glad, Lillian and Billy "provided relief from Jimmy's pieties, all the while reinforcing his basic claims of intelligence, morality, and dedication."[83] More importantly, his family served to highlight him as a man whose southernness was deeply grounded in domesticity, community, nature, and tradition.

These traits enhanced his persona as an untainted outsider and his more abstract promise to help Americans recover their moral bearings in the uncertain post-Vietnam, post-Watergate period. Carter exerted his southernness in populist terms as the antidote to the supposedly elitist, out-of-touch, and corrupt disposition of standard inside-the-Beltway politics. "His invocations of 'the people,'" Dominic Sandbrook asserts, "were perfectly calibrated to take advantage of the distrust of politicians after Watergate."[84] It was an appeal that stretched across political boundaries.

Along with his rural and family roots, Carter linked another traditional aspect of his southernness—his deep religious convictions—to broader, bipartisan trends in 1970s culture. His Southern Baptist, born-again faith and his reputation for speaking about it on the campaign trail certainly troubled some voters, who were dismayed by his devotion or wondered if, as president, he would blur the line separating church and state. According to historian Randall Balmer, the Georgian was one of the last in a long line of progressive evangelicals (notables have ranged from Charles Grandison Finney to William Jennings Bryan) who emphasized the role of performing good works—which sometimes necessitated entering into the world of politics—along with maintaining their deeply held faiths. Carter's approach to governance, as he would make clear during the 1976 campaign, was influenced by Reinhold Niebuhr. This theologian famously claimed, "The sad duty of politics is to establish justice in a sinful world." Carter took the maxim to heart; it was embodied in such liberal stances as upholding *Roe v. Wade* (despite his personal opposition to abortion), supporting environmental reform, and executing a foreign policy based on human rights, not Cold War anticommunism or *realpolitik*. The candidate benefited from the existence of an evangelical base that was not yet firmly aligned with conservative politics, let alone the Republican Party. A politician's position on abortion, for example, had yet to become a litmus test for many evangelical voters.[85] Carter's evangelical progressivism set him up perfectly to address the existential crisis, caused by both foreign and domestic factors, that beset Americans in the 1970s. Although critics would call the sometimes hard-to-pin-down Carter "fuzzy on the issues," they were not sure that policy solutions were necessarily the nation's needed prescription. The editors of *New York* magazine got it right when they heralded, "What liberals perceive as a political crisis may be in fact a crisis of spirit . . . and Jimmy Carter seems to have figured that out."[86]

While *New York* and other journalistic outlets speculated about the impact of the "God issue" on the Georgian's candidacy, they also reported that Southern Baptists were fully in the mainstream of U.S. religious thought.[87] They were part of what Catholic philosopher and writer Michael Novak referred to as "a hidden religious power base" of evangelical Christians.[88] According to internal Democratic polling in September 1976, 74 percent of respondents agreed with the statement "I respect Jimmy Carter for letting people see his religious side."[89] A national Gallup poll taken one month later confirmed that for voters who were swayed by Carter's religion, a two-to-one margin cited it as augmenting his appeal.[90]

Overall, Carter's religiosity attracted a variety of Americans, including those who did not identify themselves as evangelicals, because it fit with the cross-faith spiritual revival of the 1970s. The candidate's religious beliefs mostly benefited his candidacy because they supplemented his claim as a moral leader who hailed from a southern culture that offered lessons for the rest of the nation. Carter played up his religion as a refuge in an uncertain world. In a speech before the laymen of the Disciples of Christ on the campus of Purdue University, he referenced the dislocating events of Vietnam and Watergate. He also spoke to the gathering of his unwavering faith and of "our religious convictions [that] don't change."[91] The message did not go unheard. Commentators picked up on Carter's insinuation that his piety would spur him to restore badly needed moral guidance to a post-Watergate White House. Based on its own polling, *Time* concluded that "the Carter phenomenon" stemmed in large part from "the search for an indefinable quality of moral leadership."[92] Dean Francis B. Sayre of the Washington National Cathedral drew a connection between citizens' attraction to Carter's morality and their reaction to the turmoil of Vietnam and Watergate. For what *Time* called "wallowing" Americans, Sayre said, "he is the one who most looks like he has [the] spiritual quality" necessary to help the nation recover its bearings.[93] The man from Plains did not unequivocally claim that his religion would help to recharge the national spirit. But his professions of faith underlined the implications of his identity as a political outsider, one who through his hometown, family, and religion could offer the nation the healing balm of his southernness.

The Republican Attacks on Carter's Southernness

Gerald Ford's failed challenge to Jimmy Carter's southernness, especially among white southern voters, is a mostly forgotten factor in the GOP's loss of the White House that year. Even more importantly, it further underscores the magnetism of the Georgian's roots and the 1976 campaign's standing as a contest over the cultural meaning of the South in the post–civil rights era. The appeal of Carter's healing southernness placed Ford in an awkward position; nowhere was that truer than in the southern states. There, the president faced an uphill slog against Carter, who, exploiting his favorite son status, touted the possibility of becoming the first president from the Deep South in over a hundred years. This was bad news for Republicans, who had increasingly come to rely on the votes of white southerners in the presidential elections of the 1960s and early 1970s.

With much on the line—but virtually nothing to lose—Ford undertook a halting, intermittently bold, and ultimately ill-fated venture to undermine Carter's regional credentials. The GOP tried to bolster Ford's support among blacks by playing up his budget proposals that directly aided their communities. At the same time, Republicans contended that Carter had overstated his commitment to racial change in local and Georgia state politics in the 1960s and early 1970s.[94] It was a tough sell, though, because of Carter's kinship with black voters. Reflecting in early 1977 on the different reasons for the president's defeat, all of which lay outside of his control, Mal MacDougall, would muse, "if only the blacks."[95]

With the southern (and northern) black vote securely in Carter's column, the Ford campaign focused on the white electorate. It argued to white southerners that the Democrat's liberal policy positions clashed with their conservative political views on such issues as gun control, taxation, and the size of the federal government. Elsewhere, the Republicans struggled to counter the attractiveness of Carter's southern origins to nonsoutherners. It was especially frustrating for Ford because he had a good, all-American story: Grand Rapids, Michigan, upbringing. Eagle Scout. University of Michigan football star.

World War II veteran. More than two decades of public service in Congress. Still, the Upper Midwest lacked the exoticism of the rural South, and Ford could come across as bland and uncharismatic. His regional ties were no less deep than Carter's, but they somehow made for a less compelling narrative. What did Ford's Midwest offer the nation, after all? The promises of Carter's New South were clear, so the GOP stared in frustration as Ford's rival's simultaneously traditional and progressive brand of southernness enticed both southern and nonsouthern voters searching for alternatives to the political and cultural turmoil of the past decade.

Despite receiving the perceptive feedback of Kaye Pullen, the Ford campaign never outlined a systematic strategy for combating Carter's southernness outside of the South; that is, aside from trying to sow doubt in liberals' minds about his history on the race issue. Still, the Republicans recognized Carter's utilization of his southern background as a serious problem. Soon after Ford hired him in August 1976, Mal MacDougall met with Dick Cheney, the president's chief of staff, to discuss the upcoming fall contest. Cheney singled out Carter's well-articulated origins story and folksy kin as carrying a considerable advantage over Ford, who, in the staffer's eyes, voters saw as relatively rootless. "Everybody knows that Carter is a peanut farmer—even though he isn't a peanut farmer. He's a peanut wholesaler," Cheney complained. "Everybody knows about Plains, Georgia. And Lillian. Nobody really knows Ford. He never had a hometown. He never had a mother. He never had a childhood, as far as the American people are concerned."[96] At a strategy session weeks earlier, Cheney and others on the Ford team fretted that images of the president alongside his family would pale in comparison to the media depictions of Carter and his family in idyllic-seeming Plains.[97] Ford's tacticians had reason to worry. They could point to his solid midwestern upbringing and youthful athleticism. But that all seemed so generic next to Carter's out-of-time, real-life Mayberry.

A separate, but complementary issue, Carter's religiosity, proved especially tricky for the Ford campaign to navigate. It could hardly say outright, as it suspected, that Carter was exploiting his religion to score political points without opening itself to charges of hypocrisy. The Republicans generally refrained from direct personal attacks on Carter's mixture of religion and politics, while subtly promoting the president's own quieter expressions of faith. For instance, in undated meeting notes kept by Jerry Jones, staff secretary and deputy assistant to Ford, a quickly scrawled answer to the question of "how [to] handle [Carter's] religiosity" was simply "do nothing."[98] Instead, Ford relied on Rev. Billy Graham and other surrogates in the evangelical community to discredit his opponent. Such figures agonized publicly that Carter's vocalizing about his religion involved too much bluster. In contrast, Ford, although less showy in his claims of faith, "wears it in his heart," as one set of unidentified evangelicals claimed, and "Jimmy Carter wears his religion on his sleeve."[99]

On this issue, Carter handed his opponents an opening when he accepted an interview request from *Playboy*. Public figures giving interviews to the men's magazine was nothing new; both George Wallace and Martin Luther King Jr. had answered Hugh Hefner's call. Most controversial, however, were Carter's off-the-cuff comments, delivered after the interview was basically over, but as reporter Robert Scheer's tape recorder was still running. At this moment, Carter tried to allay concerns that his Southern Baptist faith would make him a judgmental moralizer-in-chief. "I've looked on a lot of women with lust," he volunteered. "I've committed adultery in my heart many times," he continued, before explaining, "Christ says, Don't consider yourself better than someone else because one guy screws a whole bunch of women while the other guy is loyal to his wife."[100] Carter would soon regret what he later termed the "ill-advised interview," as evangelical ministers pounced on both his choice of language (particularly his use of the word "screw") and his decision to provide *Playboy* with an interview in the first place. Within days, his sizable lead over Ford had shrunk by nearly fifteen points.[101] Many of those lost voters were evangelicals, who, as a result of their defections, would slightly favor the president on election day.

For the Ford campaign, the *Playboy* gaffe unveiled the unique opportunity to exploit both anti-southern bias against Carter and apprehensions among white southern evangelicals that the Democrat's social values were too liberal. One soon-released Ford television ad featured W. A. Criswell, ultraconservative minister and former president of the Southern Baptist Convention, sermonizing before his Dallas congregation on 10 October, with reaction shots from Ford, who was in attendance that day. The Criswell spot seemed like an effort on the part of the GOP to present a more "upright" image of the Southern Baptist faith without having to face accusations of attacking Carter's regional background. Never mentioning the president's opponent, the preacher applauds Ford for turning down a *Playboy* interview request ("And I like that!"). A voiceover then intones, "President Ford. He's the kind of man we should keep in the White House."[102] In purchasing radio and television airtime in major evangelical areas throughout the country to broadcast ads featuring Criswell, Ford made a serious drive to whittle down Carter's poll numbers.[103] In this case, it may have worked. But such concerted national attacks on issues enmeshed with the Democrat's southernness were rare. In general, the search for spiritual, cultural, and political rebirth at the heart of idealizations of Carter, his kin, his home, and his "southern" values proved a vexing issue for the Ford campaign on a national level, one for which it never devised an effective solution.

Not surprisingly, in its quest to neutralize the influence of Carter's southern persona, Ford's operation faced its biggest challenge in the South, where regional pride for the Georgian was destined to return many recently minted Republican whites—at least temporarily—to the Democratic fold. Carter's television advertisements often directly addressed or at least alluded to his rural and peanut-farming background and emphasized apparent links among southernness, family, land, and hard work.[104] His October spots pushed the issue further. Carter pollster Patrick Caddell stated, "They were blatant—waving the bloody rebel flag."[105] He was not exaggerating. In one television commercial, the announcer insinuates that a Carter victory would represent revenge for "years of coarse, anti-southern jokes and unfair comparison" and the region's status as "a political whipping boy." "The South has always been the conscience of America," the voiceover declaims, and "maybe they'll start listening to us now."[106] For southerners, namely white southerners, Carter alleged that regional identity was much bigger than policy positions: it comprised a shared history and a longing for national respectability and vindication that trumped a candidate's position on any single issue.

To unravel Carter's bond with his fellow white southerners, Republicans might have exploited the race issue. That was the path forged by Ronald Reagan four years later. And it might have worked in 1976, but Ford and his advisors rejected such gutter tactics. Moral considerations may have been involved in their decision; there was also the perception that using coded racism could hurt the GOP with nonsouthern voters. In a late September memo to the president, Jerry Jones and fellow White House staffer David Gergen warned, "You do not want to appear to be kowtowing to the South and especially to perceived Southern prejudices. If your supporters in Philadelphia find you stressing very conservative Southern themes, they could easily be alienated."[107] Anyone who had followed George Wallace's national rise over the past dozen years could tell that Gergen and Jones underestimated the extent to which race-baiting could lure nonsouthern whites. Still, especially in light of the subsequent resignation of Secretary of Agriculture Earl Butz in October for making bigoted remarks about blacks, it was a politically astute decision. With racist appeals off the table and Ford unable to compete with Carter's imaginative (and imagined) handling of rural southern culture, the Republicans had to try something else to reach white southern voters.

One option was to broadcast white southern voices that questioned the logic of voting for the Democratic candidate simply because of his regional affiliation. A pro-Ford "man-on-the-street"-style television spot features only Georgians, all of whom express anti-Carter sentiments. "I'd like to have someone from Georgia become president," one woman says, "but not Carter."[108] A second and more substantive approach employed by the Ford campaign was to construct southernness more narrowly—and self-servingly—as the equivalent of political conservatism. In other words, birthplace, family, and rural surroundings did not make one southern; rather, it was one's advocacy of conservative political perspectives that actually defined what it meant to be southern. While Carter flew the "bloody rebel flag" at full staff with white southern voters, Republicans told them that he had forsaken his region with his liberal politics and dependence on labor unions and other elements of the Democratic establishment. Ford's spokespeople hoped that with time they would be able to convince enough white southerners that a vote for Carter might boost regional pride, but only at the expense of the conservative agenda Fordites insisted was central to the white southern mind-set.

The Republicans recognized that this tactic could have perturbed white southerners and driven more of them toward Carter. The Ford staff's lengthy strategy memo to the president vowed, "The attack in the south must be on the issues. We should not attack [Carter] *personally* there since this would cause a backlash of regional pride."[109] Indeed, the midwestern Ford would have looked suspect criticizing his adversary as a far-left liberal lacking in true southernness. So he called on other white southern politicians to wage this attempted deconstruction of Carter's regional legitimacy for him.

For a quintessential representative of white southern conservatism, the Ford campaign chose Strom Thurmond, a clear nod to both the South's Democratic past and its Republican present and future. The South Carolina senator ran as the segregationist States' Rights Democratic (or Dixiecrat) presidential candidate in 1948. Increasingly disenchanted with the national Democrats' commitment to racial justice, he switched his allegiance to the GOP in 1964. Now he agreed to star in two pro-Ford television ads that both ran for one week during the fall campaign throughout the South.[110] Thurmond, in a straightforward, unpolished style, blasted Carter's southern credentials. In one spot he told viewers, "In a presidential election, it doesn't matter who's from the South. What matters is who is for the South. . . . When President Ford talks about the issues—defense, gun control, taxes, big government, inflation—he sounds more like a southerner than Jimmy Carter."[111] Thurmond's sentiments assuredly found support among an immense bloc of white southerners for whom policy overrode Carter's brand of southernness. For example, in a letter to *Time*, Tommy Thompson of Stone Mountain, Georgia, a "typical

Southerner, moderate to conservative," stated that "when Jimmy Carter starts talking issues, it will be revealed that the only thing Southern about Jimmy Carter is that he is from Georgia and has a Southern accent."[112]

Ford nevertheless strained to concoct effective imagery in his arduous quest to siphon away southern votes from the Democrat. In late September, the president embarked on a much-publicized seven-hour cruise down the Mississippi River through the Deep South aboard the steamboat *Natchez*. The trip was designed, a *Washington Post* report read, to demonstrate that "the GOP ticket has not abandoned the South."[113] A Dixieland band and women wearing antebellum garb accompanied the president. This jamboree of Old and New South clichés shared nothing in common with Carter's traditionally rooted but forward-thinking southernness of peanut farms and interracial unity. At various stops, Ford held his fire on Carter, assailing instead the Democrat's running mate Walter Mondale and his supposedly un-southern liberalism.[114]

After the river voyage was over, Ford continued his southern tour on land with carefully calibrated rhetoric. Current governor George Wallace joined him as a guest on the speaking platform at a campaign stop at Bates Field Municipal Airport in Mobile, Alabama. Obviously concerned about alienating nonsoutherners horrified by Wallace's racist history but wanting to reach pro-Wallace voters who supported many Republican programs, Ford talked vaguely of his and the governor's good working relationship and remarked on Wallace's strong showing in the 1972 Michigan Democratic primary. As a former college football player, the president was on safer ground lavishing praise on another guest, coach Bear Bryant. Ford mentioned "my opponent" (Carter) just once, jabbing him on the issue of defense spending—sacrosanct to many white southerners—which the Democrat had pledged to cut and Ford assured the audience he would expand.[115] Dick Cheney hit Carter harder on the subsequent flight from Mobile to Miami, classifying him as out of touch politically with his native region. The chief of staff implied to reporters that the Georgian's cultural magnetism for southerners would not override political considerations. "A man of [C]arter's liberal philosoph[y] has never carried the [S]outh," Cheney concluded.[116]

In its outreach to white southerners, Ford's team fumbled to find the right language to counter Carter's cultural allure. Bob Dole had encountered that predicament when, prior to agreeing to serve as Ford's running mate, he prodded Carter as "Southern-fried McGovern" in an awkward attempt to cast him as a left-winger.[117] The president's campaign staff realized that such language might strike numerous white southerners as demeaning, not only to Carter but also to the South; as a result, Dole changed his zinger: "I used to call [Carter] Southern-fried McGovern . . . but I have a lot of respect for McGovern."[118] Ford and his surrogates normally avoided public references to the governor that denigrated his home region or his popularity among its residents. A month after the Mississippi River trip, the president addressed the North Carolina State Fair in Raleigh. An early, unused draft of the speech filed in the papers of Ford's speechwriter and special assistant (and professional comedy scribe) Robert Orben contains a passage that bears the mark of Orben's background in working for the likes of Jack Paar and Red Skelton. It roasts the Democrat à la Strom Thurmond, for not sounding enough like a (white) southerner: Carter "has been fuzzy as a Georgia peach on a lot of issues, but he has made it clear that his proposals have anything but a southern accent."[119] Coming from Ford's mouth, White House advisors probably guessed, the passage would sound trite at best; at worst, listeners might construe it as an insult to Carter and other southerners. The final draft of the unrendered speech employs much less colorful—and far less awkward—language, with Ford slated to say that he "admire[d]" southerners' inclination to vote for a native son. "But it is also important that you look beyond the birthplace," the revised version reads, "and listen to what Governor Carter has been saying during his campaign for the presidency," followed by lines that lambast his liberal policy positions as being wrong for southerners.[120] Apparently, Republican staffers deemed even that too confrontational for the president to say, as Ford delivered an entirely different address at the state fair, one that voiced his conservative policy positions without attacking Carter before a southern audience.[121]

In covering the Ford-Carter matchup in the South, journalists often framed the contest, like the undelivered drafts of Ford's North Carolina State Fair speech, as a battle between an almost instinctive southern pride and steadfast conservative principles. Reporting from Louisiana, a *Baltimore Sun* correspondent conjectured that "the result here will depend on whether regional pride will outweigh the going perception of Mr. Carter as a liberal unacceptable to his Southern neighbors."[122] One campaign event, in particular, illustrated the Republicans' failure to define southernness in terms of political issues and to detach Carter from his large (for a modern-day Democrat) white southern base. On Labor Day weekend, the annual Southern 500 NASCAR race roared around the Darlington Raceway in South Carolina. Both Democrats and Republicans saw the event, a beloved southern tradition, as an opportunity to reach out to white Deep South voters. Carter made a personal appearance; Ford did not, sending Bob Dole in his place. With a crowd of seventy thousand looking on, Carter and Dole entered the egg-shaped racetrack riding in separate cars. Cheers and applause greeted Carter, who had propped himself on the back of a Cadillac convertible, while Dole endured relative indifference and a few boos. Once their cars stopped, both candidates stepped off. Ford's running mate headed immediately for the VIP box, but the southerner shook hands with mechanics before greeting the crowd in the grandstand. Dole watched as the Democrat soaked up the fans' adulation.[123] Media coverage of the event counted it as a public relations windfall for Carter. Among Republicans, a former U.S. representative from North Carolina summed up the general feeling that Dole's visit "was a complete disaster."[124] It was no wonder, then, that nothing seemed to come of Ford's brief notation on a memo the day after the Darlington race that showed he wanted his running mate to go after Carter for implying he had experienced a *Waltons*-esque childhood during the Depression, full of hardship, when in truth his family was relatively well-off compared to its neighbors.[125]

Journalists conceived the Southern 500 event as exhibitive of Carter's ability to tap into white southern chauvinism. The Darlington racing fans may have agreed with Dole's politics more, *Newsweek*'s Pete Axthelm declared, but Carter knew these people's culture. "As a group they saw Dole as an outsider," the reporter wrote. "It was Carter who could understand their weeks of sweaty work and endless weekends of fondly polishing and tuning the cars that are their escapes and their joys. It was Carter who could say that race drivers have always been his heroes—and make the fans believe it."[126] For many people at the race, journalist Martin Schram advanced, the fact that Carter hailed from the South and represented it with pride was enough. One of those fans, Billy Johnston, complained to Schram about everything from Carter's liberalism to his pledge to offer "amnesty" to Vietnam War draft dodgers (Carter actually called for a "pardon") and his sizable spending proposals. Despite these views, when the reporter asked him why he still cheered the candidate, Johnston responded, "He's a southerner, isn't he?"[127]

Such commentary, which posited mindless white southern egotism as the key to Carter's support in the region, essentially amounted to an argument that his white backers in the South suffered from false consciousness.[128] Purveyors of this view failed to recognize the depth of thought that lay behind the pride. Many of Carter's white southern supporters were focused, like non-southern voters, on his enthralling portrayal of his southern roots. Political scientist and native Georgian Margaret Law Callcott, for instance, admitted to a journalist the role of regional "pride" in her fondness for Carter while also admiring how "he stands for those Southern values of family, community, religion and public service that have not been emphasized in recent years."[129] The Democratic nominee himself also pointed to the importance of his progressiveness on the race issue as key to his popularity in the South. "There was a disinclination [before the civil rights movement]," he said in the language of the Changing (or was it Changed?) South, "to admit that we had ever made a mistake. There was later a feeling of pride that we had made progress. And, recently, I think there was even a feeling of superiority in the Southern consciousness that we had handled the rights issue better than other parts of the country."[130] Whatever the reason many white southerners fell in behind Carter, the fact that he made them feel good about their region and its place within the nation should not be dismissed as mere chauvinism. His unique blend of racial tolerance and possibly revitalizing rural southern values influenced legions of voters in the South, just as in the North, to punch their ballot for the man from Plains.

Ultimately, Carter's fortune in attracting minority, rural, and lower- and middle-income voters across the nation allowed him to stave off a late-stage Ford surge and win the election by fewer than two million votes. He lost the white southern vote to Ford, but his 46 percent among that group was a notable accomplishment.[131] The *Harvard Crimson* informed readers the day after the election that Carter "was more successful in courting Southern votes than any Democrat since Franklin D. Roosevelt." George McGovern had not cracked even 30 percent in 1972.[132] Carter was also more adept than recent Democrats in capturing the votes of white southern Protestants.[133] Strom Thurmond and other Ford supporters were correct, in a sense, when they claimed that the president better represented the South, or, rather, the white South. Ford and white southerners were better aligned on most political issues. And yet, setting policy aside, Republicans could not negate the cultural power of a white southerner who stood up for his region and accomplished the impressive feat of celebrating southern rural life while rising above the white South's racist image.

Conclusion

Ford did not lose, of course, simply because of Jimmy Carter's southernness. His controversial pardon of Nixon surely was a factor. He did have advantages, though, that partially offset his negatives. For example, Ford edged out his opponent among voters on the question of which candidate could better handle foreign affairs and most policy issues. But one postelection poll showed Americans favoring Carter as the candidate whom they felt "more comfortable with . . . as a person . . . more at ease."[134] The country may have had reservations about the Georgian as someone who was "fuzzy on the issues" or who tried to be all things to all people. Nevertheless, as Erica J. Seifert has stated, "voters preferred Carter to Ford on personal qualities," many of which indisputably derived from his southernness.[135] The Democrat proved that even as the South's political and economic distinctiveness declined, the region's power, utility, and malleability as a cultural construct in the post–civil rights era remained as strong and volatile as ever. Carter wove an irresistible tapestry of healing and nostalgia constructed from the fibers of rural traditions and interregional and interracial healing. In 1976, his personality and message found a receptive audience of Americans worn down by the political and cultural tumult of the 1960s era.

The good feelings would not last long. Four years later, with soaring inflation and the Iran Hostage Crisis plaguing him, and a mobilized conservative evangelical outreach effort bent on stymieing his reelection chances, Carter's southernness no longer seemed so refreshing—or consequential. In his 1980 reelection bid, he fell hard to a former screen actor and governor, Ronald Reagan, a candidate who also knew a thing or two about how to construct a bewitching, folksy image, and who offered America a new way to feel good about itself.

Playing That Dead Band's Song

In the years after Jimmy Carter's presidential victory, many of the issues that had fueled imaginings of the South in the 1960s and early 1970s—the civil rights movement, the Vietnam War, and presidential misconduct, for instance—were no longer pressing concerns for most Americans. Regardless, white southernness, in its various forms, remained available for cultural and political exploitation by those who were skillful enough to wield it. The Changing South, with its strong linkage to the civil rights era, faded in visibility, but the Down-Home South and the Vicious South (along with the related Masculine South) still resonated in southern chic-soaked popular culture and politics as the 1970s ended and the 1980s dawned.

As president, Jimmy Carter's southernness earned him the expected antisouthern barbs. His administrative style relied more on his technocratic side than on his down-to-earth persona, sometimes to his micromanaging detriment, and he left the down-home charisma to his kin. Brother Billy did what Billy did best, endorsing products like a beer that bore his name, urinating on an airport runway, and engaging in questionable dealings with the Libyan government. Mother Miz Lillian, on the other hand, avoided her youngest son's public lows; during Jimmy's presidency, she traveled abroad, won humanitarian awards, and was selected as an honorary chair of the Peace Corps National Advisory Council in 1980. She even held her own with Johnny Carson on a 1979 episode of the *Tonight Show*, carrying herself with her trademark genteel feistiness.

What should have been a trivial private fishing trip in April 1979 served as a strong indication that Jimmy Carter, who had been the master of southern imagery during the 1976 campaign, had lost his touch. He looked on helplessly as the press used his southernness against him to confirm allegations about his flailing, "passionless" presidency. The triggering event happened as the nation encountered rising oil prices, and in the aftermath of the Three Mile Island nuclear plant disaster of the previous month. With the pressures of his office mounting, the president returned to Georgia for a break. On 20 April, he ventured out by himself on a rowboat to go fishing near his home. The trip was uneventful, other than Carter being "attacked," reporters would later claim, by a hostile-looking swamp rabbit that some dogs had chased into the water. He used his paddle to splash water at the critter, foiling its effort to reach the president's boat. Later, thanks to the loose talk of Press Secretary Jody Powell, perhaps fueled by some freely flowing alcohol, reporters ran with the story of Carter's clash with, depending on the writer, "Peter Rabbit," "Banzai Bunny," or the homicidal rabbit from *Monty Python and the Holy Grail*, constructing a momentous affair out of a nonevent.[1]

Nancy Isenberg explains that the incident "became a metaphor for a wimpy presidential leadership style, feeding the legend of the country boy who turned coward in what should have been familiar terrain—the marshy wilds of the Georgia backcountry."[2] That's why the "killer rabbit" episode was particularly ominous for Carter: not only did it showcase the negative public perception of his presidential abilities; it also revealed his tenuous hold on his southern image. This was a man who had once shrewdly engineered photo ops of baseball games and pond drainings in Plains for his political benefit. Now, he more closely resembled Bobby in *Deliverance*—with clear differences—than a true son of the southern soil (or waterways, for that matter). The imagined South could be a fickle friend.

As Carter lost his handle on the Down-Home South narrative, conservative Republican Ronald Reagan successfully took up the mantle of the Vicious South as he began his 1980 presidential campaign. In early August, the former actor and California governor spoke at the Neshoba County Fair in Philadelphia, Mississippi. Sixteen years earlier, Ku Klux Klan members had murdered civil rights organizers Chaney, Goodman, and Schwerner near the town, an event that made national headlines and sparked a heavily publicized FBI investigation. Reagan made no reference to the killings in his address to the crowd. At one point, he advocated for "states' rights," a favorite term deployed by segregationists, like Wallace in 1968, when making more subtle racial appeals to white voters. Reagan's choice of language in a place that symbolized the Vicious South at its most fiendish was purposeful. Michael Retzer, a member of the Mississippi GOP leadership, had told the Republican National Committee in late 1979 that Reagan should visit the fair if he wanted to find an audience of "George Wallace inclined voters."[3] Of course, such people lived outside of the South, too, and Reagan's speech in Mississippi signaled that he would also be amenable to the views of nonsouthern whites who rejected a robust civil rights agenda. Republicans avowed that there was nothing racist about plans to shrink the size of the federal government and cut social programs, but these proposals indeed carried racial undercurrents. As Reagan advisor Lee Atwater explained in 1981, "Obviously, sitting around saying, 'We want to cut this,' is much more abstract than even the busing thing and a hell of a lot more abstract than 'Nigger, nigger.'"[4] The soon-to-be-president caught plenty of press criticism for the Neshoba County Fair speech. Still, his sentiments were red meat for white voters throughout the country who had deemed Wallace's retrograde racial politics a positive characteristic inextricably welded to his southernness. Just as Carter's Down-Home south-ernness had charmed a national audience, one did not have to be southern to answer the call of Reagan's dog-whistle version of the Vicious South.

Away from the cutthroat world of presidential political campaigns, in the landscapes of television and film, the Masculine and Down-Home Souths fused. Rather than offering an explicit and pointed critique of the urban or suburban existence like *The Andy Griffith Show* or *The Beverly Hillbillies*, the television show *The Dukes of Hazzard* (CBS, 1979–1985) presented a "family-friendly" world of unapologetic, if unthreatening, masculinity, female eye candy, and souped-up cars. The series centers on the antics of two male cous-ins and their family: the impulsive, low-level troublemaker Bo and the cooler, more responsible Luke, along with their sexy, resourceful cousin Daisy (Elly May meets 1970s Jiggle TV) and the rough-around-the-edges, folksy patri-arch Uncle Jesse. Taking place in fictional Hazzard County, Georgia, the show replicates Down-Home South tenets like the power and importance of family and the ennobling nature of rural living.

The series echoed current popular culture trends by reversing the typical "good guys" versus "bad guys" scenario. Bo and Luke are the heroes, or as the Waylon Jennings–sung theme song explains, "just-a good ol' boys" steadfast in their values ("Wouldn't change if they could"), and committed to righting wrongs even if it forces them to live outside of the law ("Fightin' the system like-a two modern-day Robin Hoods").[5]

On probation for running moonshine, Bo and Luke often run afoul of the corrupt county commissioner Boss Hogg and his lackey, Sheriff Rosco P. Coltrane. From week to week, viewers could count on stories that pitted the Duke clan against Hogg and Coltrane or a parade of other criminals. If all the boys-will-be-boys hijinks did not offer enough excitement, the audience could always turn to Daisy in her nearly ever-present painted-on short-shorts and impractically high heels for another sort of amusement. *The Dukes of Hazzard* scored high ratings and made nearly $200 million annually, even if its "success perplexed the critics, annoyed the snobs, and infuriated the manners police," according to show star Ben Jones.[6]

What was the program's allure? Certainly, the ubiquitous car chases punctuated by Bo's "yee-haw!" helped. (Augmenting the Dukes' rebellious charisma, they cruise around in—and frequently slide across the hood of—a 1969 Dodge Charger called the General Lee that features a Confederate flag emblazoned on the roof, though the show has nothing much to say about race or politics.) There was something else, too. While *The Dukes of Hazzard* lacks much of the sharp social commentary of 1960s Down-Home South comedies, it shares those programs' evocation of a place that seems somehow beyond time. As David Hofstede writes in his book about *Dukes*, "The outside world might change, but there was a timeless quality to the mythical land of Hazzard that will forever be immune from the uncertainties of life beyond its borders."[7] As the 1970s came to a close and imaginings of the South shifted, if television audiences wanted a show that managed a toned-down version of the Rebel Macho of Lynyrd Skynyrd combined with the cornpone elements of the *Beverly Hillbillies*, *Dukes* was it.

Car chases and a freewheeling southern masculine vigor, albeit without *The Dukes of Hazzard*'s celebration of southern rural values, also infused the silly and extremely popular *Smokey and the Bandit* films (1977, 1980, 1983), starring Burt Reynolds in full-on charm mode as Bandit. "I wanted to play a Southern hero," Reynolds later wrote, "a guy who was proud of being from the South. *Smokey* gave me the chance to do that."[8] Not unlike *The Dukes of Hazzard*, specific plot details are relatively unimportant to the movie's revved-up testosterone levels and even more revved-up car action. The first, arguably best, and most profitable entry in the franchise centers on Bandit in his supercharged Pontiac Trans Am running interference for his buddy's illegal shipment of Coors beer while evading the eternally exasperated Sheriff Buford T. Justice ("Smokey"), played with comedic aplomb by Jackie Gleason. If Paul Henning was wrong to say the message of *The Beverly Hillbillies* was simply "have fun," this directive could have easily been applied to the *Bandit* movies; even the most generous of critics thought so. Gary Arnold of the *Washington Post* called the original *Smokey* "*all-American* escapist entertainment" and "the first consistent, sustained screwball comedy about macho Good Ole Boys on the open road."[9] Granted, the films traffics in clichés about the South, but in Bandit, Reynolds created an icon of a lovable Masculine South (far from the kind he encountered as Lewis Medlock in *Deliverance*), a symbol of white southern male rebellion—and, yes, a "southern hero"—that sucked in southerners and nonsoutherners alike.

The massive viewership for the *Bandit* movies and *The Dukes of Hazzard* reveals that in the wake of Jimmy Carter's capture of the White House, there emerged in popular culture, in the words of James C. Cobb, "a South that was not just acceptable but actually appealing to other Americans, one they could admire and celebrate rather than fear and despise, a South that, at long last, seemed to represent something of the best their nation could offer rather than the worst."[10] Of course, Americans had been finding much to admire in the South for some time. But Cobb is right in his suggestion that southern chic was more than just an empty fad.

Nevertheless, negative, or at least deeply conflicted, visions of the white South existed alongside these mostly positive imaginings. The quintessential take on 1980s greed, the hit prime-time soap opera *Dallas* (CBS, 1978–1991), aired weekly on television. It features J. R. Ewing, a ruthless oil baron, who engages repeatedly in nefarious schemes to stay on top of the Texas oil indus-try. Peter Applebome called J. R. "thoroughly despicable" and described the show's premise this way: "Every week . . . [the Ewings] and various relatives, friends and enemies lie, cheat and connive their way into America's heart in a sordid spectacle that is a cross between [the 1956 James Dean film] 'Giant' and [long-running TV soap opera] 'The Secret Storm.'"[11] *Dallas* is most commonly read as a critique of rapacious American capitalism and Reagan-era extrava-gance, with the Sunbelt South serving as ground zero for the evils of the sys-tem. Using the South as a stand-in for the worst aspects of American society had recent precedent: both Howard Zinn in *The Southern Mystique* (1964) and director Robert Altman in his film *Nashville*, released eleven years later, had made the same claim. However, Applebome indicated that viewers could be simultaneously captivated and repelled by *Dallas*, a program that combined terrible behavior with glamorous high living. Audiences could therefore watch the series as an aspirational exercise.

More traditional notions of white southern backwardness reminiscent of the old Vicious South and other condescending narratives still wielded power as the "decade of excess" began. In his darkly tragicomical 1980 song "Play It All Night Long," the iconoclastic singer-songwriter Warren Zevon offers one bleak, near parodic example. The song profiles a rural white southern family more deprived (and depraved) than any characters Erskine Caldwell, William Faulkner, or Flannery O'Connor ever dreamed up. Zevon details, among other things, the family's struggles with elderly incontinence, posttraumatic stress disorder, incest, cancer, bovine disease, and alcoholism. Zevon biographer George Plasketes undersells the song, if anything, in calling "Play It All Night Long" "a lurid descent into dysfunction and rural degeneration."[12] The song's horrors are punctuated by a chorus that namechecks Lynyrd Skynyrd's "Sweet Home Alabama ("that dead band's song") and urges the family members to "turn those speakers up full blast" and "play it all night long."[13]

Zevon's swipe at Lynyrd Skynyrd as the salve of choice for the most benighted of white southerners was the icing on the cake. This was "the country of nine-fingered people," as James Dickey would have put it. The portrait of these freakish southerners was far from positive, and yet Zevon's sketch of the white South fit into the Masculine South's conception of rurally derived toughness and authenticity. In the second half of the song's final stanza, the artist sums up "country living" as "sweat, piss, jizz, and blood."[14] For Zevon, life in the rural white South may have been crude, tragic, and overly associated with bodily fluids, but it was *real*. Like the disadvantaged mountaineers of *Deliverance*, there was something oddly admirable about Zevon's southern family trying to persevere in the face of ridiculous challenges, self-inflicted or otherwise.

Many Americans, in fact, were "play[ing] that dead band's song" and absorbing and utilizing various other perspectives on the white South at the start of the 1980s, and they typically did so without Zevon's apparent irony. It had been an active twenty years of fantasizing about the southland. When voters cast their presidential ballots for George Wallace or Jimmy Carter, when hippies and straight Americans dug the rustic sounds of the Band, and when viewers sat down to be reassured by small-town southern life on *The Andy Griffith Show*, they were taking part in an ongoing national conversation that was less about white southerners, or even the South itself, than it was about Americans attempting to come to terms with the real and perceived problems of their nation, from racism to suburban insipidness, governmental deceit, and masculine and familial decline. During one of the most contentious eras in American history, white southernness, filtered through the lens of popular media, functioned as an unlikely force of both healing and division, love and rancor, traditionalism and progressivism.

The South of the Mind still survives, long after 1980, of course; Americans continue to deploy its malleable narratives, so rich, and yet so unstable, in meaning (even within an individual conscience) to address concerns about their own identities and that of their country. When Americans are in the mood for some heavy soul searching, or need to wrestle with the most troubling issues of their times, the white South is always there to guide them, in all of its attractive, troubling, and fascinating manifestations. In the South of the Mind, we are all like Robbie Robertson, looking in on a distant country shack, fantasizing about the lives of its inhabitants, but really all the while thinking only about ourselves.

ACKNOWLEDGMENTS

The South of the Mind began as a paper on country-rock and the counterculture in Randy Roberts's Twentieth-Century Popular Culture History research seminar at Purdue University in the spring of 2005. At the time, I had no idea that I would spend more than a decade parsing the meaning of the imagined South. Expectedly, I have racked up debts to numerous individuals and institutions in the process.

First, I would like to thank the members of the editorial and production staffs of the University of Georgia Press for seeing merit in my project and for facilitating its publication. Without them, this book would have remained a dissertation. The two anonymous reviewers of the manuscript provided indispensable assistance; they volunteered clear and constructive critiques that improved the finished version immeasurably.

Thanks to Mark Hanley at Truman State University, my undergraduate alma mater, for encouraging my work, serving as a model for teaching excellence, and letting me spend time in the oldies diner he has constructed in his home.

Mark thought it was a good idea that I went to Purdue to pursue my MA, and it was. There, Robert May was an early mentor, who graciously deferred to my decision to move my research focus from the nineteenth-century "real" South to the twentieth-century fantasied version of the region. Nancy Gabin and the late Michael Morrison were instrumental in encouraging me to follow my interests in music, which led me down the wider avenues contained in this book.

At Temple University, where I earned my PhD, I benefited from a veritable dream team of experts in recent American history. Bryant Simon was (and still is) always full of ideas and questions, and he helped me stay focused on my goals. Beth Bailey encouraged me to think harder about the issues in my work and to always consider historical context and why my argument matters. David Farber's example has made me both a better scholar and a better teacher. When this project was in the dissertation stage, Brian Ward served as my outside reader and asked probing questions of my work. Bryant, Beth, David, and Brian have also provided counterexamples to the claim that academics cannot write.

Having completed much of this book outside of a traditional community of scholars, I relied heavily on the input of historians and other academics whom I joined on various conference panels. Maurice Wallace, Matthew Barbee, Grace Hale, Ted Ownby, Bruce Schulman, Joe Crespino, Allison Graham, Mark Huddle, John McMillian, and Josh Davis made comments and offered suggestions that frequently challenged my thinking and made the finished product appreciably better.

I am incredibly indebted to Kay Culhane, former Access Services Manager at Phillips Library, Aurora (Illinois) University. She heroically tracked down obscure articles that informed every chapter of this book. In the process, she probably learned by accident more about Lynyrd Skynyrd and the Allman Brothers Band than she could have anticipated or wanted.

Thanks also to the Interlibrary Loan staffs at Indian Prairie Public Library in Darien, Illinois, and at Thomas Nelson Community College in Hampton, Virginia, for securing me access to materials in a timely fashion. The folks in the microfilm room at the Harold Washington Library Center in Chicago granted invaluable access to a host of newspapers and magazines.

The search for the imagined South granted me the privilege of stepping into two presidential archives. The Gerald R. Ford Presidential Foundation generously awarded me a travel grant that enabled me to spend a week in Ann Arbor, Michigan, conducting research at the Ford Presidential Library. Archivists William McNitt and Stacy Davis acted as wonderful guides through a dizzying variety of resources. Likewise, the staff of the Jimmy Carter Presidential Library in Atlanta, especially Albert Nason, assisted me in locating the material I needed, despite the nonexistence of "southernness" as a records search term.

One of the joys of this project has been interviewing and corresponding with musicians and music fans. Ed King (Lynyrd Skynyrd) and Chris Hillman (the Byrds and the Flying Burrito Brothers) kindly agreed to speak with me about their memories of southern rock and country-rock, respectively, and revealed valuable insights. I offer my appreciation as well to the numerous

1970s southern rock fans who granted me their time and recollections. Their perspectives were essential.

My fellow graduate students at Temple made my time thinking through this project in its early stages more enjoyable and intellectually enriching. They include Abby Perkiss, Jay Wyatt, Dolores Pfeuffer-Scherer, Matt Johnson, Ryan Edgington, and Kate Scott. Drew McKevitt created the template for my southern rock questionnaire and gave me advice on how to best use this type of research tool.

Thanks also to my Purdue colleagues, including Andrew Busch, Renee Searfoss, Erin Kempker, Amy Rogers Dean, Sara Morris, Carla Fisher, and Ryan Anderson. Scott Randolph, in particular, is a gentleman and a scholar.

At the North Carolina School of Science and Mathematics in Durham, where I worked for three years, I had the pleasure of teaching an energetic, enthusiastic, and talented student body. I found supportive and committed colleagues there in the Humanities Department, especially John Woodmansee, my co-instructor in American Studies, and Michael Mulvey.

Thanks to my dean, Patrick Tompkins, and my History Department colleague Hannah Powers at Thomas Nelson Community College, who have patiently and supportively listened to me go on about my research.

To the list of people who have sustained me as I have worked on this project, I add my family, who have always taken an interest in and encouraged my scholarship. Years ago, my parents built entire vacations around my historical interests (thanks to my brother Matt for hanging in there and being—I hope—somewhat appeased by the occasional ballpark visit). My apologies to my dad for excluding any reference in the preceding chapters to what I like to believe is his favorite song (even if it is not), Mountain's "Mississippi Queen." I thank my brother Marshall, the professional musician of the family, for lending me a greater appreciation of music, which surely influences several sections of this book.

The Young family have been a further source of aid. They gave me support (and for a time, a home) while I researched and wrote this book. Becky Young helped me in the earliest stages of research by graciously allowing me to use her college library privileges. (I assume the statute of limitations for her transgression has passed.)

I think that the spouses of academics deserve some kind of auxiliary PhD for all of their patience, sacrifice, and assistance. Sarah Young is no exception. She has been my partner on this project from the beginning. Drawing on her impressive skills as a writer and editor, she did an incredible amount of work, smoothing over clunky prose, formatting drafts, transcribing interviews, and acting as a sounding board when I became stuck. Without her, this book would not exist. I can never repay her support and dedication through all these years.

And, finally, thank you to my younger self, the proud owner of a *Dukes of Hazzard* T-shirt, lunchbox, and wallet, who perhaps sparked my current interest in this topic. I hope I have done justice to his (unconscious) fascination with white southernness.

Southern Rock in the 1970s

Survey Questions

1. A few easy questions to begin: When and where were you born? Where did you live during the 1970s? How would you describe your social and economic environment?

2. When and where did you hear southern rock for the first time? How old were you? Who introduced you to the music? What were your initial impressions?

3. What southern rock concerts did you attend (include city, venue, and dates, if possible)? Please describe your remembrances of these events: the band's performance, the crowd's reaction, the way people dressed, the overall atmosphere, and so on.

4. What southern rock fan literature did you read, if any (fanzines, fan club publications, national music magazines—*Rolling Stone*, *Creem*, *Crawdaddy*, etc.)?

5. What most attracted you to southern rock? In other words, why did you become a fan?

6. At the time, can you describe your impressions of the South? What kinds of traits/values did you associate with the South? How did southern rock help to influence and/or reinforce these impressions?

7. List and discuss any bands that you considered yourself a fan of. What made these bands "southern rock"? Please comment specifically on how they represented the South and contributed to your thinking about the South.

8. What types of audiences were attracted to the various bands in the genre? Did certain bands appeal to a particular audience? (example: Allman Brothers v. Lynyrd Skynyrd)

9. What did you think about some southern rock bands' use of the Confederate flag and/or Confederate iconography? For what purpose did you think they were using the flag?
10. How would you characterize your political orientation, if you had any, in the 1970s?
11. What were your other interests besides music?
12. If there is anything else you wish to add, I encourage you to do so below. Also, if you have any suggestions for other questions I could ask to help me better understand the experiences of southern rock fans in the 1970s, please don't hesitate to make suggestions.

Adapted from a questionnaire created by Andrew C. McKevitt.

NOTES

Introduction. Raising the White South

1. Richard N. Goodwin, "The End of Reconstruction," in *You Can't Eat Magnolias*, ed. H. Brandt Ayers and Thomas H. Naylor (New York: McGraw-Hill, 1972), 57–58.

2. Ibid., 65.

3. Ibid., 66.

4. Jack Temple Kirby, *Media-Made Dixie: The South in the American Imagination*, rev. ed. (Athens: University of Georgia Press, 1986), 144.

5. John Egerton, *The Americanization of Dixie: The Southernization of America* (New York: Harper's, 1974), 216.

6. Ibid., 22.

7. Quoted in David Farber, *The Age of Great Dreams: America in the 1960s* (New York: Hill & Wang, 1994), 55.

8. Farber, *Age of Great Dreams*, 55.

9. Malvina Reynolds, "Little Boxes," Schroder Music 420119071, 1962; renewed 1990.

10. Gerry Goffin and Carole King, "Pleasant Valley Sunday," The Monkees, Colgems 66-1007, 1967, 7-inch single.

11. "Port Huron Statement," *The Sixties Project*, http://www2.iath.virginia.edu/sixties/HTML_docs/Resources/Primary/Manifestos/SDS_Port_Huron.html (accessed 5 March 2017).

12. Norman Mailer, *The Armies of the Night: History as a Novel, the Novel as History* (New York: New American Library, 1968), 86–87.

13. Ibid., 87.

14. Vance Packard, *A Nation of Strangers* (New York: David McKay, 1972), 10.

15. Dominic Sandbrook, *Mad as Hell: The Crisis of the 1970s and the Rise of the Populist Right* (New York: Knopf, 2011), 69.

16. Ibid., 62.

17. Rick Perlstein, *The Invisible Bridge: The Fall of Nixon and the Rise of Reagan* (New York: Simon & Schuster, 2014), 166.

18. Ibid.

19. Michael Sean Winters, *God's Right Hand: How Jerry Falwell Made God a Republican and Baptized the American Right* (New York: HarperOne, 2012), 124.

20. Jim Cullen, "Reconstructing Dixie: Confederate Mythology in Rock 'n' Roll," in *The Civil War in Popular Culture: A Reusable Past* (Washington, D.C.: Smithsonian, 1995), 117.

21. Colin Escott, *The Grand Ole Opry: The Making of an American Icon* (New York: Center Street, 2006), unpaginated e-book, Google Books (accessed 6 August 2017).

22. Robbie Robertson, radio interview by Redbeard, *In the Studio with Redbeard* (1988), quoted in Peter Viney, "The Night They Drove Old Dixie Down (Revisited)," *The Band*, http://theband.hiof.no/articles/dixie_viney.html (accessed 5 March 2017).

23. Cullen, "Reconstructing Dixie," 117.

24. Eric Hobsbawm, "Introduction: Inventing Traditions," in *The Invention of Tradition*, ed. Eric Hobsbawm and Terence Ranger (Cambridge: Cambridge University Press, 1983), 2.

25. Twelve Southerners, *I'll Take My Stand: The South and the Agrarian Tradition* (1930; repr., New York: Harper, 1962), xxviii.

26. Ibid., xxix.

27. Louis D. Rubin, "Introduction to Torchbook Edition," in *I'll Take My Stand*, xiv.

28. Alan Lomax, *The Land Where the Blues Began* (New York: Pantheon, 1993), ix.

29. W. J. Cash, *The Mind of the South* (New York: Knopf, 1941), 58.

30. Ibid., 97.

31. Ibid., 428–429.

32. "Psychoanalysis of a Nation," *Time*, 24 February 1941, 98.

33. See C. Vann Woodward, "White Man, White Mind," *New Republic*, 9 December 1967, 28–30; David Hackett Fischer, *Historians' Fallacies: Toward a Logic of Historical Thought* (New York: Harper Perennial, 1970), 219–220. For an example of the persistence of Cash's book in influencing those writing about the South and white southerners decades after its author's death, see William Lee Miller's invocation of *The Mind of the South* in his discussion of President Jimmy Carter's southernness. *Yankee from Georgia: The Emergence of Jimmy Carter* (New York: Times Books, 1978), 35, 173.

34. Bruce J. Schulman, *From Cotton Belt to Sun Belt: Federal Policy, Economic Development, and the Transformation of the South, 1938–1980* (New York: Oxford University Press, 1991); James C. Cobb, *The Selling of the South: The Southern Crusade for Industrial Development, 1936–1990*, 2nd ed. (Urbana: University of Illinois Press, 1993); Numan V. Bartley, *The New South, 1945–1980* (Baton Rouge: Louisiana State University Press, 1995); Gavin Wright, *Old South, New South: Revolutions in the Southern Economy since the Civil War* (Baton Rouge: Louisiana State University Press, 1996).

35. Jon Smith, *Finding Purple America: The South and the Future of American Cultural Studies* (Athens: University of Georgia Press, 2013), 30.

36. Benedict Anderson, *Imagined Communities: Reflections on the Origin and Spread of Nationalism* (London: Verso, 1983).

37. Tara McPherson, *Reconstructing Dixie: Race, Gender, and Nostalgia in the Imagined South* (Durham, N.C.: Duke University Press, 2003), 3. For other works that explore this dichotomy or treat the South as an imagined space, including some published in the University of Georgia Press's New Southern Studies Series edited by Jon Smith and Riché Richardson, see Susan-Mary Grant, *North over South: Northern*

Nationalism and American Identity in the Antebellum Era (Lawrence: University Press of Kansas, 2000); Erich Nunn, *Sounding the Color Line: Music and Race in the Southern Imagination* (Athens: University of Georgia Press, 2015); Houston A. Baker Jr., *Turned South Again: Re-thinking Modernism/Re-reading Booker T* (Durham, N.C.: Duke University Press, 2001); Allison Graham, *Framing the South: Hollywood, Television, and Race during the Civil Rights Struggle* (Baltimore: Johns Hopkins University Press, 2001); Leigh Anne Duck, *The Nation's Region: Southern Modernism, Segregation, and U.S. Nationalism* (Athens: University of Georgia Press, 2006); Deborah E. Barker and Kathryn McKee, eds., *American Cinema and the Southern Imaginary* (Athens: University of Georgia Press, 2011); Scott Romine, *The Real South: Southern Narrative in the Age of Cultural Reproduction* (Baton Rouge: Louisiana State University Press, 2008); Riché Richardson, *Black Masculinity and the U.S. South: From Uncle Tom to Gangsta* (Athens: University of Georgia Press, 2007); Jennifer Rae Greeson, *Our South: Geographic Fantasy and the Rise of National Literature* (Cambridge, Mass.: Harvard University Press, 2010); Mary Beth Swetnam Mathews, *Rethinking Zion: How the Print Media Placed Fundamentalism in the South* (Knoxville: University of Tennessee Press, 2006); and Smith, *Finding Purple America*. For global perspectives, see Jon Smith and Deborah Cohn, eds., *Look Away! The U.S. South in New World Studies* (Durham, N.C.: Duke University Press, 2004); and Helen Taylor, *Circling Dixie: Contemporary Southern Culture through a Transatlantic Lens* (New Brunswick, N.J.: Rutgers University Press, 2001).

Although the work of historians, other pieces of scholarship in this realm are Edward L. Ayers, "What We Talk about When We Talk about the South," in *All over the Map: Rethinking American Regions*, ed. Edward L. Ayers, Patricia Nelson Limerick, Stephen Nissenbaum, and Peter S. Onuf (Baltimore: Johns Hopkins University Press, 1996), 62–82; Brian Ward, "'By Elvis and All the Saints': Images of the American South in the World of 1950s British Popular Music," in *Britain and the American South: From Colonialism to Rock and Roll*, ed. Joseph P. Ward (Jackson: University Press of Mississippi, 2001), 187–213; and Brian Ward, "Music, Musical Theater, and the Imagined South in Interwar Britain," *Journal of Southern History* 80, no. 1 (February 2014): 39–72.

38. Peter Applebome, *Dixie Rising: How the South Is Shaping American Values, Politics, and Culture* (New York: Times Books, 1996), 10.

39. For an illuminating introduction, see Joel Cooper, *Cognitive Dissonance: Fifty Years of a Classic Theory* (Thousand Oaks, Calif.: Sage, 2007).

40. Mike Chopra-Gant, *The Waltons: Nostalgia and Myth in Seventies America* (London: I.B. Tauris, 2013), 79.

41. Howard Zinn, *The Southern Mystique* (New York: Knopf, 1964), 262.

42. Ibid.

43. C. Vann Woodward, "The Search for Southern Identity," in *The Burden of Southern History*, rev. ed. (Baton Rouge: Louisiana State University Press, 1968), 3–25.

44. John Shelton Reed, *The Enduring South: Subcultural Persistence in Mass Society* (Chapel Hill: University of North Carolina Press, 1972), 83.

45. C. Vann Woodward, "A Second Look at the Theme of Irony," in *Burden of Southern History*, 213–233.

46. James C. Cobb, "'We Ain't White Trash No More': Southern Whites and the Reconstruction of Southern Identity," in *The Southern State of Mind*, ed. Jan Nordby

Gretlund (Columbia: University of South Carolina Press, 1999), 144–145. For other works on southern identity, see James C. Cobb, *Away Down South: A History of Southern Identity* (New York: Oxford, 2005); and Trent Watts, ed., *White Masculinity in the Recent South* (Baton Rouge: Louisiana State University Press, 2008).

47. Dan T. Carter, *The Politics of Rage: George Wallace, the Origins of the New Conservatism, and the Transformation of American Politics* (New York: Simon & Schuster, 1995; repr., Baton Rouge: Louisiana State University Press, 1996).

48. For challenges to the political "southernization" thesis, see Matthew D. Lassiter, *The Silent Majority: Suburban Politics in the Sunbelt South* (Princeton, N.J.: Princeton University Press, 2006); and Byron E. Shafer and Richard Johnston, *The End of Southern Exceptionalism: Class, Race, and Partisan Change in the Postwar South* (Cambridge, Mass.: Harvard University Press, 2006).

49. Applebome, *Dixie Rising*, 22.

50. Bruce J. Schulman, "The Reddening of America," chap. 4 of *The Seventies: The Great Shift in American Culture, Society, and Politics* (New York: Free Press, 2001).

51. James N. Gregory, *The Southern Diaspora: How the Great Migrations of Black and White Southerners Transformed America* (Chapel Hill: University of North Carolina Press, 2005).

52. James C. Cobb, "From Muskogee to Luckenbach: Country Music and the 'Southernization' of America," in *Redefining Southern Culture: Mind and Identity in the Modern South* (Athens: University of Georgia Press, 1999), 90. This essay originally appeared in the winter 1982 issue of the *Journal of Popular Culture*.

53. Kirby, *Media-Made Dixie*.

54. Karen L. Cox, *Dreaming of Dixie: How the South Was Created in American Popular Culture* (Chapel Hill: University of North Carolina Press, 2011).

55. Anthony Harkins, *Hillbilly: A Cultural History of an American Icon* (New York: Oxford University Press, 2004), 4.

56. Nancy Isenberg, *White Trash: The 400-Year Untold History of Class in America* (New York: Viking, 2016).

57. Matthew D. Lassiter and Joseph Crespino, eds., *The Myth of Southern Exceptionalism* (New York: Oxford University Press, 2010).

Chapter 1. The Many Faces of the South

1. "The Thaw in the South," *Nation*, 28 March 1966, 348.

2. Ibid.

3. William G. Carleton, "The South's Many Moods," *Yale Review* 55, no. 4 (1966): 623–640.

4. The historiography of the 1960s civil-rights-era South typically details the ways in which something akin to the Vicious South, as utilized by civil rights protesters and the media, roused Americans to the evils of Jim Crow and lent considerable opposition to white southerners' efforts to preserve their segregated way of life. For an example of this literature, see Gene Roberts and Hank Klibanoff, *The Race Beat: The Press, the Civil Rights Struggle, and the Awakening of a Nation* (New York: Random House, 2006). Recent scholars, though, have begun to acknowledge that while what I call the Vicious South discourse was indeed powerful and pervasive in the American consciousness during the 1960s, Americans simultaneously imagined the

South in contradictory ways. See, for instance, Karen L. Cox, *Dreaming of Dixie: How the South Was Created in American Popular Culture* (Chapel Hill: University of North Carolina Press, 2011), 166; Allison Graham, *Framing the South: Hollywood, Television, and Race during the Civil Rights Struggle* (Baltimore: Johns Hopkins University Press, 2001); and Joseph Crespino, "Mississippi as Metaphor: Civil Rights, the South, and the Nation in the Historical Imagination," in *The Myth of Southern Exceptionalism*, ed. Matthew D. Lassiter and Joseph Crespino (New York: Oxford University Press, 2010), 99–120.

5. John Howard Griffin, *Black Like Me* (New York: Houghton Mifflin, 1961; repr., New York: New American Library, 2003), 51.

6. Ibid., 86.

7. Ibid., 90.

8. "Black Like Me," *Time*, 28 March 1960, Academic Search Complete (54200538).

9. Robert Bonazzi, *Man in the Mirror: John Howard Griffin and the Story of* Black Like Me (Maryknoll, N.Y.: Orbis, 1997), 131–133, 136.

10. See, for example, Frank London Brown, "What It's Like to Live as a Negro in the South," *Chicago Tribune*, 22 October 1961, D4; Dan Wakefield, "Traveling Second Class," *New York Times Book Review*, 22 October 1961, 45; and Earl Banner, "White Man Lived as Negro," *Boston Globe*, 26 November 1961, B16.

11. John Steinbeck, *Travels with Charley: In Search of America* (New York: Viking, 1962; repr., New York: Penguin, 2002), 186.

12. Ibid., 189.

13. Ibid., 195.

14. Ibid., 196.

15. Ibid., 195.

16. Ibid., 197.

17. Ibid., 201.

18. Ibid., 205.

19. Eric F. Goldman, "Steinbeck's America, Twenty Years After," *New York Times Book Review*, 29 July 1962, 5.

20. Kenneth Weiss, "Steinbeck Covers the U.S.," *Washington Post*, 29 July 1962, G6.

21. Sasha Torres, *Black, White, and in Color: Television and Black Civil Rights* (Princeton, N.J.: Princeton University Press, 2003), 17.

22. Ibid., 17–18.

23. Ibid., 19.

24. Graham, *Framing the South*, 2.

25. Dan Wakefield, "Intrusions in the Dust," in *Between the Lines* (New York: New American Library, 1966), quoted in Graham, *Framing the South*, 2.

26. John Herbers, "The Reporter in the Deep South," *Niemen Reports*, April 1962, in *Reporting Civil Rights: Part One: American Journalism, 1941–1963*, ed. Clayborne Carson et al. (New York: Library of America, 2003), 639.

27. David Farber, *The Age of Great Dreams: America in the 1960s* (New York: Hill & Wang, 1994), 94.

28. David Nevin, "A Strange, Tight Little Town, Loath to Admit Complicity," *Life*, 18 December 1964, in *Reporting Civil Rights: Part Two: American Journalism, 1963–1973*, ed. Clayborne Carson et al. (New York: Library of America, 2003), 280.

29. Stuart H. Loory, "Reporter Tails 'Freedom' Bus Caught in Riot," *New York Herald-Tribune*, 21 May 1961, in Carson et al., *Reporting Civil Rights: Part One*, 573; "Mississippi versus the United States," *Newsweek*, 8 October 1962, 32.

30. "Case History of a Sick City," *Newsweek*, 30 September 1963, 27.

31. "Personal Letter from Muriel and Art Lewis to Her Mother, Selma, Alabama, March 19, 1965," in *The Eyes on the Prize Civil Rights Reader: Documents, Speeches, and Firsthand Accounts from the Black Freedom Struggle, 1954–1990*, ed. Clayborne Carson et al. (New York: Penguin, 1991), 222.

32. "The Central Points," *Time*, 19 March 1965, Academic Search Complete (54030283).

33. Elizabeth Hardwick, "Selma, Alabama: The Charms of Goodness," *New York Review of Books*, 22 April 1965, in Carson et al., *Reporting Civil Rights: Part Two*, 356.

34. Ibid., 357.

35. Ibid., 358.

36. Ibid., 359.

37. Ibid., 360.

38. Roy Reed, "Alabama Police Use Gas and Clubs to Rout Negroes," *New York Times*, 8 March 1965, in Carson et al., *Reporting Civil Rights: Part Two*, 327.

39. George B. Leonard, "Midnight Plane to Alabama," *Nation*, 10 May 1965, in Carson et al., *Reporting Civil Rights: Part Two*, 328, 331, 338.

40. "Indignation in the North," *Time*, 19 March 1965, Academic Search Complete (54030320).

41. Crespino, "Mississippi as Metaphor," 101.

42. "Tale of Two Cities," *Washington Post*, 3 February 1964, A14.

43. "The South: Into a New Century," *Newsweek*, 3 May 1965, 26.

44. "The Other South," *Time*, 7 May 1965, Academic Search Complete (54030726).

45. Ibid.

46. Ibid.

47. Ibid.

48. Ibid.

49. Ibid.

50. Willie Morris, "Foreword," *Harper's*, April 1965, 126.

51. Louis E. Lomax, "Georgia Boy Goes Home," *Harper's*, April 1965, 159.

52. Walker Percy, "Mississippi: The Fallen Paradise," *Harper's*, April 1965, 168.

53. Ibid., 172.

54. Harper Lee, *To Kill a Mockingbird* (Philadelphia: Lippincott, 1960; repr., New York: Harper, 2010), 5.

55. Ibid., 6.

56. Charles J. Shields, *Mockingbird: A Portrait of Harper Lee* (New York: Owl Books, 2007), 21.

57. Harper Lee, interview by WQXR-FM, Newark, N.J., March 1964, in *Hey, Boo: Harper Lee and* To Kill a Mockingbird, dir. Mary Murphy, First Run Features DVD, 2011.

58. Shields, *Mockingbird*, 183.

59. Eric Sundquist, "Blues for Atticus Finch," in *The South as an American Problem*, ed. Larry J. Griffin and Don H. Doyle (Athens: University of Georgia Press, 1995), 186, quoted in Graham, *Framing the South*, 160.

60. Lee, *To Kill a Mockingbird*, 233.

61. Ibid., 86.

62. Philip T. Hartung, "The Child Is Father of the Man," *Commonweal*, 22 February 1963, 572.

63. Lee, *To Kill a Mockingbird*, 194.

64. Graham, *Framing the South*, 17.

65. Joseph Crespino, "The Strange Career of Atticus Finch," *Southern Cultures* 6, no. 2 (Summer 2000): 15.

66. Lee, *To Kill a Mockingbird*, 87.

67. On Lee's paternalism, see Crespino, "Strange Career of Atticus Finch," 15.

68. Lee, *To Kill a Mockingbird*, 247.

69. Ibid., 101, 247.

70. Thomas F. Haddox, "Elizabeth Spencer, the White Civil Rights Novel, and the Postsouthern," *Modern Language Quarterly* 65, no. 4 (December 2004): 563.

71. John Ball, *In the Heat of the Night* (New York: Harper & Row, 1965; repr., New York: Carroll & Graf, 2001), 1.

72. Ibid., 5.

73. Ibid., 87.

74. Stuart Henderson, review of *In the Heat of the Night*, 21 January 2008, *PopMatters*, http://www.popmatters.com/review/in-the-heat-of-the-night/ (accessed 5 August 2017).

75. Anthony Boucher, "Criminals at Large," *New York Times Book Review*, 2 May 1965, 32.

76. *In the Heat of the Night*, dir. Norman Jewison, Mirisch Corporation, 1967.

77. Graham, *Framing the South*, 179.

78. Ball, *In the Heat of the Night*, 161.

79. Ibid., 172–173.

80. Jack Temple Kirby, *Media-Made Dixie: The South in the American Imagination*, rev. ed. (Athens: University of Georgia Press, 1986), 142.

81. "A Kind of Love," *Time*, 11 August 1967, 72.

82. Richard Schickel, "Two Pros in a Super Sleeper," *Life*, 28 July 1967, 10, quoted in Aram Goudsouzian, *Sidney Poitier: Man, Actor, Icon* (Chapel Hill: University of North Carolina Press, 2004), 267.

83. Kirby, *Media-Made Dixie*, 142.

84. Joseph Morgenstern, "Red-Neck and Scapegoat," *Newsweek*, 14 August 1967, 83; Norman Jewison, dir., commentary, *In the Heat of the Night*, MGM DVD, 2001.

85. Goudsouzian, *Sidney Poitier*, 267.

86. Marian Dern, "A Southern Sheriff Faces Some Problems," *TV Guide*, 24 April 1965, 5–8; "TV Ratings: 1964–1965," *ClassicTVHits.com*, www.classictvhits.com/tvratings/1964.htm (accessed 28 January 2017).

87. "Case History of a Sick City," 24.

88. Donald Freeman, "I Think I'm Gaining on Myself," *Saturday Evening Post*, 25 January 1964, 69.

89. Phoebe M. Bronstein, "Televising the South: Race, Gender, and Region in Primetime, 1955–1980" (PhD diss., University of Oregon, 2013), 97.

90. "The Show That Has H.A.Q.," *TV Guide*, 11 May 1963, 25.

91. Graham, *Framing the South*, 158.

92. James Flanagan, "Deconstructing Mayberry: Utopia and Racial Diversity in the *Andy Griffith Show*," *Continuum: Journal of Media & Cultural Studies* 23, no. 3 (June 2009): 308.

93. Graham, *Framing the South*, 158.

94. Erik Barnouw, *Tube of Plenty: The Evolution of American Television*, 2nd rev. ed. (New York: Oxford University Press, 1990), 326–327.

95. Joseph A. St. Amant, "Mrs. Peterson Tells NAACP How the Poor Are Victimized," *Washington Post*, 8 July 1966, A6.

96. Gustavo Pérez Firmat, *A Cuban in Mayberry: Looking Back at America's Hometown* (Austin: University of Texas Press, 2014), 62.

97. Walter Burrell, "Hollywood Happenings: Why Dark Faces Scarce on 'Andy Griffith Show,'" *New Journal and Guide*, 11 March 1967, 18, quoted in Pérez Firmat, *Cuban in Mayberry*, 61.

98. "TV Mailbag," *Chicago Daily Tribune*, 28 January 1961, F2.

99. Freeman, "I Think I'm Gaining on Myself," 70.

100. *Variety Television Reviews*, vol. 8, ed. Harold Prouty (New York: Garland, 1989), 2 October 1963, quoted in Pérez Firmat, *Cuban in Mayberry*, 110–111.

101. Donald Kirkley, "Look and Listen with Donald Kirkley," *Baltimore Sun*, 14 October 1960, 4F.

102. Richard Kelly, *The Andy Griffith Show*, rev. ed. (Winston-Salem, N.C.: John F. Blair, 1988), 41.

103. Pérez Firmat, *Cuban in Mayberry*, 35–46.

104. "Opie's Hobo Friend," dir. Bob Sweeney, *The Andy Griffith Show*, CBS Television, 13 November 1961; Pérez Firmat, *Cuban in Mayberry*, 43. Pérez Firmat includes this dialogue to highlight his argument about Mayberry's resistance to change. I've corrected his transcription slightly based on my own viewing of the scene.

105. "Man in a Hurry," dir. Bob Sweeney, *The Andy Griffith Show*, CBS Television, 14 January 1963.

106. Don Rodney Vaughan, "Why *The Andy Griffith Show* Is Important to Popular Cultural Studies," *Journal of Popular Culture* 38, no. 2 (November 2004): 409.

107. "Man in a Hurry."

108. Kelly, *Andy Griffith Show*, 89.

109. Ibid., 12.

110. "The South Rises Again," dir. Joseph Depew, *The Beverly Hillbillies*, CBS Television, 29 November 1967.

111. "Simon Legree Drysdale," dir. Bob Leeds, *The Beverly Hillbillies*, CBS Television, 4 March 1970.

112. Aaron K. Ketchell, "Hillbilly Heaven: Branson Tourism and the Hillbilly of the Missouri Ozarks," in *Dixie Emporium: Tourism, Foodways, and Consumer Culture in the American South*, ed. Anthony J. Stanonis (Athens: University of Georgia Press, 2008), 137.

113. Farber, *Age of Great Dreams*, 54.

114. Lawrence Laurent, "Ignorance IS Bliss with the 'Hillbillies,'" *Washington Post*, 7 June 1963, B10.

115. Richard Warren Lewis, "The Golden Hillbillies," *Saturday Evening Post*, 2 February 1963, 32, 33.

116. "The Corn Is Green," *Newsweek*, 3 December 1962, 70.

117. Farber, *Age of Great Dreams*, 54.

118. "Robin Hood and the Sheriff," dir. Joseph Depew, *The Beverly Hillbillies*, CBS Television, 4 October 1967.

119. Anthony Harkins, *Hillbilly: A Cultural History of an American Icon* (New York: Oxford University Press, 2004), 196.

120. Both UPI and the *New York Times* quoted in Lewis, "Golden Hillbillies," 30.

121. Hal Humphrey, "Hillbilly Series Divides Classes," *Los Angeles Times*, 9 January 1963, D11.

122. "Letters" ("TV's Golden Corn"), *Saturday Evening Post*, 2 March 1963, 4.

123. "The Show That Has H.A.Q.," 25.

124. "Letters" ("TV's Golden Corn"), *Saturday Evening Post*, 2 March 1963, 4; "On the Cob," *Time*, 30 November 1962, Academic Search Complete (54210158).

125. Both Hano and Shayon quoted in Harkins, *Hillbilly*, 196.

126. Quoted in Harkins, *Hillbilly*, 203.

127. Harkins, *Hillbilly*, 202.

128. Ibid.

129. Stuart Hall, "The Whites of Their Eyes: Racist Ideologies and the Media," in *Gender, Race, and Class in Media: A Text-Reader*, 2nd ed., ed. Gail Dines and Jean M. Humez (Thousand Oaks, Calif.: Sage, 2003), 91, emphasis in original, quoted in Phoebe Bronstein, "Comic Relief: *The Andy Griffith Show*, White Southern Sheriffs, and Regional Rehabilitation," *Camera Obscura: Feminism, Culture, and Media Studies* 30, no. 2 (2015): 137.

130. Bronstein, "Comic Relief," 145.

131. See Sharon Monteith, "Exploitation Movies and the Freedom Struggle of the 1960s," in *American Cinema and the Southern Imaginary*, ed. Deborah Barker and Kathryn McKee (Athens: University of Georgia Press, 2011), 194–216.

Chapter 2. "This World from the Standpoint of a Rocking Chair"

1. Chris Hillman, interview by author, 14 December 2009.

2. Ben Fong-Torres, *Hickory Wind: The Life and Times of Gram Parsons* (New York: Pocket Books, 1991), 89.

3. Ibid., 90.

4. Jerry Hopkins, "McGuinn's Role with New Byrds Container for the 'Old' Sound," *Rolling Stone*, 11 May 1968, 6. Like Timothy Miller in his study of hippies, I use *Rolling Stone* as a "countercultural" source. For a dissenting view, see John McMillian, *Smoking Typewriters: The Sixties Underground Press and the Rise of Alternative Media in America* (Oxford: Oxford University Press, 2011), 122.

5. David Farber, "Building the Counterculture, Creating Right Livelihoods: The Counterculture at Work," *The Sixties: A Journal of History, Politics, and Culture* 6, no. 1 (2013): 2.

6. For an argument that the underground press should be considered largely as a product of the New Left, see McMillian, *Smoking Typewriters*, 11–12.

7. Doug Rossinow, "The New Left in the Counterculture: Hypotheses and Evidence," *Radical History Review* 67 (Winter 1997): 79–120.

8. See, for example, Laurence Leamer, *The Paper Revolutionaries: The Rise of the Underground Press* (New York: Simon & Schuster, 1972), 61; and John Leo, "Politics Now the Focus of Underground Press," *New York Times*, 4 September 1968, 49.

9. In regard to music, studies of the counterculture generally have focused on the place of rock 'n' roll in the movement. See Theodore Roszak, *The Making of a Counter Culture: Reflections on the Technocratic Society and Its Youthful Opposition* (Garden City, N.Y.: Doubleday, 1969; repr., Berkeley: University of California Press, 1995), 291; Timothy Miller, *The Hippies and American Values* (Knoxville: University of Tennessee Press, 2011), 71–84; George Lipsitz, "Who'll Stop the Rain? Youth, Culture, Rock 'n' Roll, and Social Crises," in *The Sixties: From Memory to History*, ed. David Farber (Chapel Hill: University of North Carolina Press, 1994), 206–234; and Robert C. Cottrell, *Sex, Drugs, & Rock 'n' Roll: The Rise of America's 1960s Counterculture* (Lanham, Md.: Rowman & Littlefield, 2015), 123–136, 276–277, 282–283. Scholarly work on the counterculture and country-rock is sparse. See Michael Allen, "'I Just Want to Be a Cosmic Cowboy': Hippies, Cowboy Code, and the Culture of a Counterculture," *Western Historical Quarterly* 36, no. 3 (Autumn 2005): 275–299; and Xiang Xu, "When the Counterculture Picked Up a Southern Twang: A Cultural Analysis of Late Sixties and Early Seventies Country Rock Movement" (MA thesis, University of Mississippi, 2014). Another useful academic work on country-rock is Olivia Carter Mather, "'Cosmic American Music': Place and the Country-Rock Movement, 1965–1974" (PhD diss., University of California, Los Angeles, 2006).

Popular works that address country-rock vary in analytical quality and typically offer limited cultural context on the rise of the genre. They include Peter Doggett, *Are You Ready for the Country: Elvis, Dylan, Parsons and the Roots of Country Rock* (London: Viking, 2000; repr., New York: Penguin, 2001); John Einarson, *Desperados: The Roots of Country Rock* (New York: Cooper Square, 2000); Barney Hoskyns, *Waiting for the Sun: Strange Days, Weird Scenes, and the Sound of Los Angeles* (New York: St. Martin's, 1996; repr., 1999), 165–172; Ed Ward, Geoffrey Stokes, and Ken Tucker, *Rock of Ages: The* Rolling Stone *History of Rock & Roll* (New York: Rolling Stone/Summit, 1986), 389–394; and Ritchie Unterberger, *Eight Miles High: Folk-Rock's Flight from Haight-Ashbury to Woodstock* (San Francisco: Backbeat Books, 2003), 171–202.

10. A. J. Mayer, "Shucking It!" *First Issue* (Ithaca, N.Y.), 11 November 1968, 32.

11. Mike Bourne, "Skull Tones," *Spectator* (Bloomington, Ind.), 23 September 1969, 20.

12. Rossinow, "New Left in the Counterculture," 98.

13. Lizabeth Cohen, *A Consumer's Republic: The Politics of Mass Consumption in Postwar America* (New York: Knopf, 2003).

14. James N. Gregory, *The Southern Diaspora: How the Great Migrations of Black and White Southerners Transformed America* (Chapel Hill: University of North Carolina Press, 2005), 180.

15. Gerald W. Haslam with Alexandra Haslam Russell and Richard Chon, *Workin' Man Blues: Country Music in California* (Berkeley: University of California Press, 1999), 16.

16. Ibid., 199, 201.

17. Mather, "Cosmic American Music," 65.

18. Quoted in Haslam, *Workin' Man Blues*, 205.

19. Hillman, interview by author.

20. Michael Nesmith, *Magnetic South*, liner notes, RCA Victor LSP 4371, 1970; BMG F:BM720, 1999, CD.

21. Pamela Des Barres, untitled essay, in *Gram Parsons with the Flying Burrito Brothers Live at the Avalon Ballroom 1969: Archives, Volume One*, Amoeba Records, no pressing number, 2007, 6.

22. Haslam, *Workin' Man Blues*, 14.

23. Bill C. Malone, *Country Music, U.S.A.: A Fifty-Year History* (Austin: University of Texas Press, 1968), viii.

24. Bill C. Malone, *Don't Get above Your Raisin': Country Music and the Southern Working Class* (Urbana: University of Illinois Press, 2002), 15.

25. Paul Hemphill, *The Nashville Sound: Bright Lights and Country Music* (New York: Simon & Schuster, 1970), 13.

26. Ibid., 31.

27. John D. McCarthy, Richard A. Peterson, and William L. Yancey, "Singing Along with the Silent Majority," in *Side-Saddle on the Golden Calf: Social Structure and Popular Culture in America*, ed. George H. Lewis (Pacific Palisades, Calif.: Goodyear, 1972), 61.

28. Tari, "The Politics of Country Rock," *Berkeley Barb*, 2–8 May 1969, 12.

29. Ira Allen, "We Don't Take Our Trips on LSD," *Harry* (Baltimore), 8 January 1971, 14.

30. Farber, "Building the Counterculture," 3.

31. Malone, *Don't Get above Your Raisin'*, vii.

32. Ibid.

33. Michael J. Kramer, *The Republic of Rock: Music and Citizenship in the Sixties Counterculture* (New York: Oxford University Press, 2013), 64.

34. Ibid., 50–51.

35. John Wolfe, "Positively Queen Jane Approximately," *Distant Drummer* (Philadelphia), November 1967, 9.

36. The Blimp, "All the Flattop Cats & the Dungaree Dolls Are Really Gonna Rock It at the Sock Hop Ball," *First Issue* (Ithaca, N.Y.), September 1969, 34.

37. Jon Sabin, "Here, There, and Down on the Ground," *First Issue* (Ithaca, N.Y.), February 1969, 46.

38. A. J., "Country Pie," *Berkeley Barb*, 18–24 April 1969, 12.

39. Jake Fury, "Real Country Rock," *Berkeley Barb*, 22–28 August 1969, 4.

40. Quoted in Bob Proehl, *The Gilded Palace of Sin* (New York: Continuum, 2008), 7.

41. Linda Ronstadt, *Simple Dreams: A Musical Memoir* (New York: Simon & Schuster, 2013), 50.

42. For Peterson's comparison of "hard-core" versus "soft-shell" country music, whose differences hinge on categories of speech, singing style, lyrics, songwriting, instruments, instrumental style, singer's origin, stage presentation, personal life, clothes/hair style, and career longevity, see Richard A. Peterson, *Creating Country Music: Fabricating Authenticity* (Chicago: University of Chicago Press, 1997), 150–154.

43. Rupert Fike, "The Flying Burrito Brothers," *Great Speckled Bird* (Atlanta), 2 June 1969, 9.

44. Mike Hansen, "A Spoonful of Byrd Droppings & Buffalo Chips," *Rag* (Austin), 25 November 1968, 11.

45. Steve Rosen, "Dillard and Clark," *Spectator* (Bloomington, Ind.), 4 March 1970, 21.

46. Jon Landau, "Country & Rock," *Rolling Stone*, 28 September 1968, 24.

47. Mike Bourne, "Skull Tones," *Spectator* (Bloomington, Ind.), 29 April 1969, 19.

48. Jonathan Takiff, "Cryptic Commentaries," *Distant Drummer* (Philadelphia), 18 June 1970, 14.

49. Bud Scoppa, *The Byrds* (New York: Scholastic, 1971), 85. For countercultural praise of Buck Owens, see Mike Bourne, "The Long Country Road," *Spectator* (Bloomington, Ind.), 1 July 1969, 13.

50. Hemphill, *Nashville Sound*, 60. For discussions of the performance of authenticity across various eras of country music, see Pamela Fox, *Natural Acts: Gender, Race, and Rusticity in Country Music* (Ann Arbor: University of Michigan Press, 2009); Joli Jensen, *The Nashville Sound: Authenticity, Commercialization, and Country Music* (Nashville: Country Music Foundation and Vanderbilt University Press, 1998); Peterson, *Creating Country Music*; and Dianne Pecknold, *The Selling Sound: The Rise of the Country Music Industry* (Durham, N.C.: Duke University Press, 2007).

51. Grace Elizabeth Hale, *A Nation of Outsiders: How the White Middle Class Fell in Love with Rebellion in Postwar America* (New York: Oxford University Press, 2011), 98.

52. Ibid.

53. David Satterfield, "Country Music in America," *Spectator* (Bloomington, Ind.), 19 November 1969, 23.

54. Alec Dubro, review of *Silk Purse* by Linda Ronstadt, *Rolling Stone*, 25 June 1970, 56.

55. See, for example, Nicholas G. Meriwether, "The Counterculture as Local Culture in Columbia, South Carolina," in *Rebellion in Black and White: Southern Student Activism in the 1960s*, ed. Robert Cohen and David J. Snyder (Baltimore: Johns Hopkins University Press, 2013), 218–234.

56. A good starting point for learning about the Back to the Land movement is Timothy Miller, *The 60s Communes: Hippies and Beyond* (Syracuse, N.Y.: Syracuse University Press, 1999).

57. For a discussion of The Farm, see Timothy Hodgdon, *Manhood in the Age of Aquarius: Masculinity in Two Countercultural Communities* (New York: Columbia University Press, 2008), 136–197.

58. Jinny A. Turman-Deal, "'We Were an Oddity': A Look at the Back-to-the-Land Movement in Appalachia," *West Virginia History* 4, no. 1 (Spring 2010): 12. See also Carter Taylor Seaton, *Hippie Homesteaders: Arts, Crafts, Music, and Living on the Land in West Virginia* (Morgantown: West Virginia University Press, 2014).

59. Joseph Crespino, "Mississippi as Metaphor: Civil Rights, the South, and the Nation in the Historical Imagination," in *The Myth of Southern Exceptionalism*, ed. Matthew D. Lassiter and Joseph Crespino (New York: Oxford University Press, 2010), 105–106.

60. Frank Gruber, "The Burritos: 'Dinja Ever Hear Country Music Before?'" *Distant Drummer* (Philadelphia), 13–19 March 1969, 13.

61. Jim Cullen, "Reconstructing Dixie: Confederate Mythology in Rock 'n' Roll," in *The Civil War in Popular Culture: A Reusable Past* (Washington, D.C.: Smithsonian, 1995), 125.

62. Neil Young, "Southern Man," *After the Gold Rush*, Reprise Records RS 6383, 1970.

63. Jimmy McDonough, *Shakey: Neil Young's Biography* (New York: Random House, 2002), 338.

64. See, for example, Allison Graham, *Framing the South: Hollywood, Television, and Race during the Civil Rights Struggle* (Baltimore: Johns Hopkins University Press, 2001).

65. Bob Dylan, "Only a Pawn in Their Game," *The Times They Are A-Changin'*, Columbia Records 8905, 1963.

66. Edwin T. Arnold, "What the Movies Told Us," *Southern Quarterly* 34, no. 3 (Spring 1996): 64.

67. Dennis Fitzgerald, "Easy Rider Too Easy," *Spectator* (Bloomington, Ind.), 28 October 1969, 22. This review originally appeared in *Space City News* (Houston).

68. Dan, "Easy Rider," *Extra* (Providence, R.I.), 12 August 1969, 12.

69. Robert A. Henning, "Easy Hater," letter to the editor, *Distant Drummer* (Philadelphia), 12–18 March 1970, 4.

70. Howard Zinn, "The South as a Mirror," in *The Southern Mystique* (New York: Knopf, 1964), 217–263.

71. Raymond Mungo, *Total Loss Farm: A Year in the Life* (New York: Dutton, 1970), 82.

72. Ibid., 84.

73. Ibid., 83.

74. Ibid.

75. Ibid., 87.

76. Ibid., 82.

77. Gram Parsons and Bob Buchanan, "Hickory Wind," *Sweetheart of the Rodeo*, The Byrds, Columbia Records CS 9670, 1968.

78. Roger McGuinn and Gram Parsons, "Drug Store Truck Drivin' Man," *Dr. Byrds and Mr. Hyde*, The Byrds, Columbia Records CS 9755, 1969.

79. Proehl, *Gilded Palace of Sin*, 25.

80. For more on the counterculture's fascination with western imagery and the "cowboy code," see Allen, "I Just Want to Be a Cosmic Cowboy." Richard A. Peterson traces the rise of cowboy imagery in country in *Creating Country Music*, 81–94.

81. Proehl, *Gilded Palace of Sin*, 20–30.

82. Terry Slater and Jacqueline Erte, "Bowling Green," *The Everly Brothers Sing*, The Everly Brothers, Warner Bros. Records W/WS 1708, 1967.

83. Ibid.

84. "The Introduction: The Everly Family (1952)," *Roots*, The Everly Brothers, Warner Bros. Records WS 1752, 1968; Doggett, *Are You Ready for the Country*, 108.

85. Gram Parsons and Bob Buchanan, "Hickory Wind," *Sweetheart of the Rodeo*, The Byrds, Columbia Records CS 9670, 1968.

86. Ira Louvin and Charles Louvin, "The Christian Life," *Sweetheart of the Rodeo*, The Byrds, Columbia Records CS 9670, 1968; Hillman, interview by author.

87. Jon Landau, review of the Byrds and Flying Burrito Brothers concerts, *Rolling Stone*, 4 April 1969, 16. The review referred to a series of shows performed on 20–23 February 1969 in Boston.

88. Allen, "I Just Want to Be a Cosmic Cowboy," 280.

89. Jack Egan and Arthur Schmidt, review of *Hand Sown . . . Home Grown* by Linda Ronstadt, *Rolling Stone*, 3 May 1969, 29.

90. Jerry Rubin, "Rubin Raps: Money's to Burn," *Berkeley Barb*, 19–26 January 1968, quoted in Miller, *Hippies and American Values*, 120.

91. Quoted in Miller, *Hippies and American Values*, 120.

92. A. J., "Country Pie," 12.

93. Chris Hillman and Gram Parsons, "Hippie Boy," *The Gilded Palace of Sin*, The Flying Burrito Brothers, A&M Records SP 3122, 1969.

94. John Einarson with Chris Hillman, *Hot Burritos: The True Story of the Flying Burrito Brothers* (London: Jawbone Press, 2008), 131.

95. Stanley Booth, review of *The Gilded Palace of Sin* by the Flying Burrito Brothers, *Rolling Stone*, 17 May 1969, 15.

96. Rob Holton, "'Real Country and Real People': The Countercultural Pastoral 1948–1971," in *Beat Culture: The 1950s and Beyond*, ed. Cornelis A. van Minnen, Jaap van der Bent, and Mel van Elteren (Amsterdam: VU University Press, 1999), 103.

97. Ibid., 104.

98. Tom Smucker, "Bob Dylan Meets the Revolution," *Fusion*, 31 October 1969, in *Bob Dylan: A Retrospective*, ed. Craig McGregor (New York: William Morrow, 1972), 303, 305.

99. John Burks, "The Underground Press," *Rolling Stone*, 4 October 1969, 13.

100. Tari, "Politics of Country Rock," 12.

101. Ibid.

102. Gene Guerrero Jr., "Cash," *Great Speckled Bird* (Atlanta), 24 March 1969, 11.

103. Joseph Ferrandino, "Rock Culture and the Development of Social Consciousness," *Radical America*, November 1969, in *Power to the People! New Left Writings*, ed. William Slate (New York: Tower, 1970), 195.

104. Ibid., 194.

105. Doug Rossinow, "'The Revolution Is about Our Lives': The New Left's Counterculture," in *Imagine Nation: The American Counterculture of the 1960s and '70s*, ed. Peter Braunstein and Michael William Doyle (New York: Routledge, 2002), 101.

106. Stephen Bloomfield and Robin Shaikun, "Looking Back at 'Easy Rider,'" *New City Free Press* (New York), 30 November 1970, 16.

107. This history is chronicled in a number of works on the progressive country (aka redneck rock) scene. See Jan Reid, *The Improbable Rise of Redneck Rock*, new ed. (Austin: University of Texas Press, 2004); Jason Mellard, *Progressive Country: How the 1970s Transformed the Texan in Popular Culture* (Austin: University of Texas Press, 2013); Barry Shank, *Dissonant Identities: The Rock 'n' Roll Scene in Austin, Texas* (Middletown, Conn.: Wesleyan University Press, 1994); and Travis D. Stimeling, *Cosmic Cowboys and New Hicks: The Countercultural Sounds of Austin's Progressive Country Music Scene* (New York: Oxford University Press, 2011).

108. Reid, *Improbable Rise of Redneck Rock*, 78.

109. Mellard, *Progressive Country*, 74.

110. Ibid., 57.

111. Jeff Nightbyrd, "Cosmo Cowboys: Too Much Cowboy and Not Enough Cosmic," *Austin Sun*, 3 April 1975, 13, quoted in Stimeling, *Cosmic Cowboys and New Hicks*, 74–75.

112. Nightbyrd, "Cosmo Cowboys," 14, opinion cited in Stimeling, *Cosmic Cowboys and New Hicks*, 75.

113. For a class-based examination of country-rock, see Jefferson Cowie, *Stayin' Alive: The 1970s and the Last Days of the Working Class* (New York: New Press, 2010), 179–187. The quote is found on page 179.

114. Barney Hoskyns, *Across the Great Divide: The Band and America*, rev. ed. (Milwaukee: Hal Leonard, 2006), 55.

115. Robert Palmer, "A Portrait of the Band as Young Hawks: Rolling Stone's 1978 Feature on 'The Last Waltz,'" *Rolling Stone*, 29 March 2011, http://www.rollingstone .com/music/news/a-portrait-of-the-band-as-young-hawks-rolling-stones-1978-feature -on-the-last-waltz-20110329 (accessed 7 August 2017), originally published as "A Portrait of the Band as Young Hawks," *Rolling Stone*, 1 June 1978.

116. Alfred G. Aronowitz, "Friends and Neighbors Just Call Us the Band," *Rolling Stone*, 24 August 1968, 8.

117. Greil Marcus, *Mystery Train: Images of America in Rock 'n' Roll Music*, 5th rev. ed. (New York: Plume, 2008), 46.

118. Hoskyns, *Across the Great Divide*, 168.

119. See, for instance, Miller Francis Jr., review of *The Band* by the Band, *Great Speckled Bird* (Atlanta), 8 December 1969, 5; and "Reviews," *Dallas News*, 9–22 December 1970, 15.

120. Jay Cocks, "Down to Old Dixie and Back," *Time*, 12 January 1970, Academic Search Complete (53801792).

121. Howard Gladstone, "The Robbie Robertson Interview," *Rolling Stone*, 27 December 1969, *The Band*, http://theband.hiof.no/articles/rr_intreview_rs1969.html (accessed 1 November 2009). This is a reprint of the *Egg* interview.

122. Levon Helm with Stephen Davis, *This Wheel's on Fire: Levon Helm and the Story of the Band* (New York: William Morrow, 1993), 173.

123. John Poppy, "The Band: Music from Home," *Look*, 25 August 1970, 26.

124. Mike Jahn, "'The Band' Rocks with Hillbilly Ease," *New York Times*, 29 December 1969, 34.

125. Jack Lyne, "The Band Ain't Hype!," *Space City News* (Houston), 5 December 1969, 17.

126. Hoskyns, *Across the Great Divide*, 185–186.

127. Ibid., 186.

128. Ibid.

129. Ibid.

130. Xu, "When the Counterculture Picked Up a Southern Twang," 27; Jaime R. Robertson, "King Harvest (Has Surely Come)," *The Band*, The Band, Capitol Records STAO-132, 1969.

131. Jaime R. Robertson, "Rockin' Chair," *The Band*, The Band, Capitol Records STAO-132, 1969.

132. See Peter Viney, "Up on Cripple Creek," *The Band*, http://theband.hiof.no /articles/up_on_cripple_creek_viney.html (accessed 7 August 2017).

133. Jaime R. Robertson, "Up on Cripple Creek," *The Band*, The Band, Capitol Records STAO-132, 1969.

134. Greil Marcus, "Epilogue: Treasure Island," in *Stranded: Rock and Roll for a Desert Island*, ed. Greil Marcus (New York: Random House, 1979; repr., New York: Da Capo, 1996), 256.

135. David Emblidge, "Down Home with the Band: Country-Western Music and Rock," *Ethnomusicology* 20, no. 3 (September 1976): 550.

136. "Marcel Proust," review of *Stage Fright* by the Band, *Harry* (Baltimore), 16 October 1970, 14.

137. Robbie Robertson, *Testimony* (New York: Crown, 2016), 333.

138. Helm, *This Wheel's on Fire*, 188.

139. Jaime R. Robertson, "The Night They Drove Old Dixie Down," *The Band*, The Band, Capitol Records STAO-132, 1969.

140. Cullen, "Reconstructing Dixie," 122.

141. Quoted in Rob Bowman, "The Band," in *The Band: A Musical History* box set, The Band, Capitol Records, CCAP77409-6, 2005, 42.

142. Hoskyns, *Across the Great Divide*, 192.

143. Ralph J. Gleason, review of *The Band* by the Band, *Rolling Stone*, 18 October 1969, http://www.rollingstone.com/music/albumreviews/the-band-19691018 (accessed 5 March 2017).

144. Don Buday, "The Band Was Awfully Good . . . ," *Los Angeles Free Press*, 30 January 1970, 35.

145. Ed Ward, "The Band," in *The Rolling Stone Illustrated History of Rock & Roll*, rev. ed., ed. Jim Miller (New York: Random House/Rolling Stone, 1980), 311.

146. Poppy, "The Band," 26.

147. Ibid.

148. Cocks, "Down to Old Dixie and Back."

149. Ibid.

150. Ibid.

151. Quoted in ibid.

152. Helm, *This Wheel's on Fire*, 177.

153. Barney Hoskyns, "*A Musical History*: A Review and an Interview with Robbie Robertson (2005)," in Hoskyns, *Across the Great Divide*, 418.

154. Mather, "Cosmic American Music," 239.

Chapter 3. "When in Doubt, Kick Ass"

1. Lester Bangs, "When in Doubt, Kick Ass," *Creem*, November 1974, 24.

2. Ibid.

3. W. J. Cash, *The Mind of the South* (New York: Knopf, 1941), 50.

4. For a useful discussion of sixties-era social and cultural movements as based on "liberation," see Andrew Hartman, *A War for the Soul of America: A History of the Culture Wars* (Chicago: University of Chicago Press, 2015), chap. 1.

5. Trent Watts, "Introduction: Telling White Men's Stories," in *White Masculinity in the Recent South*, ed. Trent Watts (Baton Rouge: Louisiana State University Press, 2008), 2.

6. Port Huron Statement, quoted in Michael Kimmel, *Manhood in America: A Cultural History*, 3rd ed. (New York: Oxford University Press, 2012), 193.

7. Barbara Ehrenreich, *The Hearts of Men: American Dreams and the Flight from Commitment* (Garden City, N.Y.: Anchor Press, 1983), 143.

8. Herb Goldberg, *The Hazards of Being Male: Surviving the Myth of Masculine Privilege* (New York: Signet, 1976; repr., Gretna, La.: Wellness Institute, 2000), 15–16.

9. Natasha Zaretsky, *No Direction Home: The American Family and the Fear of National Decline, 1968–1980* (Chapel Hill: University of North Carolina Press, 2007), 110.

10. Quoted in Sally Robinson, *Marked Men: White Masculinity in Crisis* (New York: Columbia University Press, 2000), 23–24.

11. Dominic Sandbrook, *Mad as Hell: The Crisis of the 1970s and the Rise of the Populist Right* (New York: Knopf, 2011), 93.

12. Quoted in Kimmel, *Manhood in America*, 199.

13. Jerry Rubin, *DO IT! Scenarios of the Revolution* (New York: Simon & Schuster, 1970), 144.

14. David English and the staff of the London *Daily Express*, *Divided They Stand* (Englewood Cliffs, N.J.: Prentice Hall, 1969), 171.

15. Ray Jenkins, "Mr. and Mrs. Wallace Run for Governor of Alabama," *New York Times Magazine*, 24 April 1966, 92.

16. "Stand Up for America," George Wallace 1968 presidential campaign brochure, *4President.org*, http://www.4president.org/brochures/wallace68.pdf (accessed 30 November 2015).

17. Quoted in Robert Sherrill, *Gothic Politics in the Deep South: Stars of the New Confederacy* (New York: Grossman, 1968), 297.

18. Dan T. Carter, "The Politics of Anger, 1963–1968," in *A History of Our Time: Readings on Postwar America*, 8th ed., ed. William H. Chafe, Harvard Sitkoff, and Beth Bailey (New York: Oxford University Press, 2012), 315.

19. "Why They Want Him," *Time*, 18 October 1968, Academic Search Complete (54041960).

20. Lewis Chester, Godfrey Hodgson, and Bruce Page, *An American Melodrama: The Presidential Campaign of 1968* (New York: Viking, 1969), 283.

21. George C. Wallace, "The Inaugural Address of Governor George C. Wallace," 14 January 1963, Alabama Department of Archives and History, http://www.archives.state.al.us/govs_list/inauguralspeech.html (accessed 8 March 2017).

22. Joseph E. Lowndes, *From the New Deal to the New Right: Race and the Southern Origins of Modern Conservatism* (New Haven, Conn.: Yale University Press, 2008), 79.

23. Theodore White, *The Making of the President, 1968* (New York: Atheneum, 1969), 346; "Wallace's Army: The Coalition of Frustration," *Time*, 18 October 1968, Academic Search Complete (54041959).

24. "Wallace's Army."

25. English and the staff of the London *Daily Express*, *Divided They Stand*, 357.

26. James Jackson Kilpatrick, "What Makes Wallace Run?," *National Review*, 18 April 1967, 400, 402.

27. Ibid., 400.

28. See, for example, Jody Carlson, *George C. Wallace and the Politics of Powerlessness: The Wallace Campaigns for the Presidency, 1964–1976* (New Brunswick, N.J.: Transaction, 1981).

29. George Lardner Jr. and Jules Loh, "The Wonderful World of George Wallace," *Esquire*, May 1969, 118.

30. Tom Wicker, "In the Nation: Wallace's Powerful Medicine," *New York Times*, 12 December 1967, 46.

31. Tony Parsons, "The Skynyrds: An Everyday Story of Country Folk," *New Musical Express*, 26 February 1977, 7–8.

32. "Promises, Promises," *Newsweek*, 21 October 1968, 31.

33. Lowndes, *From the New Deal to the New Right*, 88.

34. Roy Reed, "Wallace Loses Some Momentum," *New York Times*, 20 October 1968, E2.

35. White, *Making of the President, 1968*, 349–350.

36. Douglas Kiker, "Red Neck New York: Is This Wallace Country?," *New York*, 7 October 1968, 25.

37. Marshall Frady, *Wallace* (New York: World, 1968), 6–7.

38. "Wallace and His Folks," *Newsweek*, 16 September 1968, 26.

39. Ibid., 27.

40. Rowland Evans and Robert Novak, "Auto Workers' Support for Wallace May Foretell a Political Revolution," *Washington Post*, 30 September 1968, A21.

41. Dan T. Carter, *The Politics of Rage: George Wallace, the Origins of the New Conservatism, and the Transformation of American Politics* (New York: Simon & Schuster, 1995; repr., Baton Rouge: Louisiana State University Press, 1996), 367.

42. Sherrill, *Gothic Politics in the Deep South*, 265–266.

43. Ibid., 265.

44. Frady, *Wallace*, 11.

45. Ibid., 2.

46. Quoted in Sherrill, *Gothic Politics in the Deep South*, 265–266.

47. Ibid., 266.

48. "Wallace's Army."

49. George Lardner, "Wallace: Steadily Growing Response Convinces Him He Can Win," *Washington Post*, 15 September 1968, A8.

50. Chester, Hodgson, and Page, *American Melodrama*, 283.

51. Samuel Lubell, *The Hidden Crisis in American Politics* (New York: Norton, 1970), 76.

52. Michael W. Flamm, *Law and Order: Street Crime, Civil Unrest, and the Crisis of Liberalism in the 1960s* (New York: Columbia University Press, 2005), 165.

53. Frady, *Wallace*, 13.

54. Ibid., 10–11, 224.

55. Hunter S. Thompson, *Fear and Loathing: On the Campaign Trail '72* (San Francisco: Straight Arrow, 1973; repr., New York: Warner, 1983), 127.

56. Ibid., 156.

57. Robert Reinhold, "Surge by Carter on National Basis Indicated in Poll," *New York Times*, 29 March 1976, 1.

58. "Walking Tall," *Internet Movie Database*, http://www.imdb.com/title/tt0070895/business?ref_=tt_dt_bus (accessed 23 October 2017). The film's gross amounts to more than $126 million in 2016 dollars.

59. Jack Temple Kirby, *Media-Made Dixie: The South in the American Imagination*, rev. ed. (Athens: University of Georgia Press, 1986), 151.

60. Judith Crist, "Hick, Hack, Hokum, Ho-Hum," *New York*, 18 February 1974, 74.

61. Gareth Jones, review of *Walking Tall*, *Monthly Film Bulletin*, January 1974, 16.

62. Michael Robbin, review of *Walking Tall*, *New Times*, 27 March 1974, 4.

63. "Keeping It," *Washington Post*, 3 March 1974, *Potomac Magazine*, 11, 41.

64. Ibid., 41.

65. Allison Graham, *Framing the South: Hollywood, Television, and Race during the Civil Rights Struggle* (Baltimore: Johns Hopkins University Press, 2001), 184.

66. Jim Higgins and Shirley Rose Higgins, "'Walking Tall' in McNairy County," *Chicago Tribune*, 25 March 1973, sec. 4, 11.

67. Gene Siskel, "'Tis the Season to Be Dirty, Tough, Etc.," *Chicago Tribune*, 16 March 1973, sec. 2, 3.

68. Pauline Kael, "The Street Western," *New Yorker*, 25 February 1974, 102.

69. Kirby, *Media-Made Dixie*, 151.

70. Frady, *Wallace*, 11.

71. *Walking Tall*, dir. Phil Karlson, Bing Crosby Productions, 1973; Paramount Home Entertainment, 2007, DVD.

72. Ibid.

73. Ibid.

74. Harvey Sax, "Tall Walking," *Great Speckled Bird* (Atlanta), 7 May 1973, 9.

75. Peter Biskind, "Vigilantes, Power and Domesticity: Images of the 50's in *Walking Tall*," *Journal of Popular Film* 3, no. 3 (Summer 1974): 227.

76. Ibid., 226.

77. Ed Madden, "The Buggering Hillbilly and the Buddy Movie: Male Sexuality in *Deliverance*," in *The Way We Read James Dickey: Critical Approaches for the Twenty-first Century*, ed. William B. Thesing and Theda Wrede (Columbia: University of South Carolina Press, 2009), 205.

78. "Deliverance," *Internet Movie Database*, http://www.imdb.com/title/tt0068473/business?ref_=tt_dt_bus (accessed 23 October 2017). This amounts to approximately $268 million in 2016 dollars. According to IMDB, the film's budget in 1972 was approximately $2,000,000.

79. Edmund Fuller, "Football Star, Fighter Pilot, Poet—Now a Novelist," *Wall Street Journal*, 25 March 1970, 14.

80. *Deliverance* theatrical trailer, *Deliverance* (special ed.), dir. John Boorman, Warner Bros., 1972; Warner Home Video, 2007, DVD.

81. James Dickey, *Deliverance* (New York: Houghton Mifflin, 1970; repr., New York: Dell, 1975), 15.

82. Ibid., 41.

83. Steven Knepper, "'Do You Know What the *Hail* You're Talkin' About?': *Deliverance*, Stereotypes, and the Lost Voice of the Rural Poor," *James Dickey Newsletter* 15, no. 1 (Fall 2008): 20.

84. Dickey, *Deliverance*, 46.

85. Quoted in J. W. Williamson, *Hillbillyland: What the Movies Did to the Mountains and What the Mountains Did to the Movies* (Chapel Hill: University of North Carolina Press, 1995), 161.

86. James Dickey, letter to Dr. John Foster West, 20 October 1972, in *The One Voice of James Dickey: His Letters and Life, 1970–1997*, ed. Gordon Van Ness (Columbia: University of Missouri Press, 2005), 172.

87. Stephen Farber, "'Deliverance'—How It Delivers," *New York Times*, 20 August 1972, D9.

88. James Dickey, letter to John Boorman, 5 September 1971, in Van Ness, *One Voice of James Dickey*, 149.

89. Dickey, *Deliverance*, 233–234.

90. Pamela E. Barnett, "James Dickey's *Deliverance*: Southern, White, Suburban Male Nightmare or Dream Come True?," *Forum for Modern Language Studies* 40, no. 2 (2004): 157.

91. James Dickey, letter to Richard Finholt, 14 January 1981, in Van Ness, *One Voice of James Dickey*, 323.

92. Michel Ciment, *John Boorman*, trans. Gilbert Adair (London: Faber and Faber, 1986), 129.

93. Dickey, *Deliverance*, 37.

94. Ibid., 43.

95. Ibid., 40.

96. Ibid., 45–46.

97. Ibid., 51.

98. Knepper, "Do You Know?," 24.

99. Colin L. Westerbeck Jr., "Down a Lazy River," *Commonweal*, 29 September 1972, 526.

100. Dickey, *Deliverance*, 51–52.

101. Ibid., 52.

102. *Deliverance* (special ed.), dir. Boorman.

103. Richard Schickel, "White Water, Black Doings," *Life*, 18 August 1972, 8.

104. Ciment, *John Boorman*, 129.

105. Ibid.

106. *Deliverance* (special ed.), dir. Boorman.

107. See, for example, Timothy Shuker-Haines, "Home Is the Hunter: Representations of Returning World War II Veterans and the Reconstruction of Masculinity, 1944–1951" (PhD diss., University of Michigan, 1994), 374.

108. See Gail Bederman, *Manliness and Civilization: A Cultural History of Race and Gender in the United States, 1880–1917* (Chicago: University of Chicago Press, 1995).

Chapter 4. A Tale of Two Souths

1. Lester Bangs, "When in Doubt, Kick Ass," *Creem*, November 1974, 24.

2. Tony Parsons, "The Skynyrds: An Everyday Story of Country Folk," *New Musical Express*, 26 February 1977, 7.

3. Patterson Hood and Drive-By Truckers, "The Southern Thing," *Southern Rock Opera*, Drive-By Truckers, Soul Dump Records, 2001; Lost Highway 088 170 308-2, 2002.

4. For a survey of scholarship on southern rock, which often ignores the larger national trends and sometimes conflicting messages that drove the popularity of the genre's artists, see Ted Ownby, "Freedom, Manhood, and White Male Tradition in 1970s Southern Rock Music," in *Haunted Bodies: Gender and Southern Texts*, ed. Anne Goodwyn Jones and Susan V. Donaldson (Charlottesville: University Press of Virginia, 1997), 369–388; Mike Butler, "'Luther King Was a Good Ole Boy': The Southern Rock Movement and White Male Identity in the Post–Civil Rights South," *Popular Music and Society* 23, no. 2 (Summer 1999): 41–61; J. Michael Butler, "'Lord, Have Mercy on My Soul': Sin, Salvation, and Southern Rock," *Southern Cultures* 9, no. 4 (Winter 2003): 73–87; Barbara Ching, "Where Has the Free Bird Flown?: Lynyrd Skynyrd and White Southern Manhood," in *White Masculinity in the Recent South*, ed. Trent Watts (Baton Rouge: Louisiana State University Press, 2008), 251–265; Bartow J. Elmore, "Growing Roots in Rocky Soil: An Environmental History of Southern Rock," *Southern Cultures* 16, no. 3 (Fall 2010): 102–128; Cecil K. Hutson, "The Darker Side of Dixie: Southern Music and the Seamier Side of the Rural South" (PhD diss., Iowa State University,

1995); and Maarten Zwiers, "Rebel Rock: Lynyrd Skynyrd, Normaal, and Regional Identity," *Southern Cultures* 21, no. 3 (Fall 2015): 85–102.

5. Marley Brant, *Southern Rockers: The Roots and Legacy of Southern Rock* (New York: Billboard Books, 1999), 76.

6. Scott Cain, "Allmans Sound a Lucrative Note," *Atlanta Journal and Constitution*, 2 June 1974, 13-A.

7. Ben Edmonds, "Snapshots of the South," *Creem*, November 1972, 39.

8. Scott Freeman, *Midnight Riders: The Story of the Allman Brothers Band* (Boston: Little, Brown, 1995), 47.

9. Gregg Allman with Alan Light, *My Cross to Bear* (New York: William Morrow, 2012), 128.

10. Alan Paul, *One Way Out: The Inside History of the Allman Brothers Band* (New York: St. Martin's, 2014), 34.

11. Taylor Hill, "Wanee and Warcraft: A Conversation with Butch Trucks," *Jambands.com*, 11 April 2006, http://www.jambands.com/features/2006/4/11/wanee-and -warcraft-a-conversation-with-butch-trucks (accessed 6 August 2017).

12. David Jackson, "Voices from the Silent South," *Village Voice*, 30 April 1979, 62.

13. Gary Nagle, email communication to author, 23 May 2009. This email was a follow-up response to my southern rock questionnaire. In spring 2009, I posted messages on specific southern rock band Internet message boards and contacted individuals who had signed guest books of various bands' websites. I sent interested people a questionnaire that asked them to reflect on their experiences as southern rock fans from 1969 to 1980. I received thirty responses. Several respondents asked to remain anonymous. For the questions, see the appendix.

14. Anonymous 1, author's southern rock questionnaire, 23 May 2009.

15. Mark Kemp, *Dixie Lullaby: A Story of Music, Race, and New Beginnings in a New South* (New York: Free Press, 2004), 45.

16. Ibid.

17. Randy Stephens, author's southern rock questionnaire, 26 May 2009.

18. Richard Albero, "Duane Allman: 'Just Rock On, and Have You a Good Time,'" *Guitar Player*, June 1973, 22.

19. Michael Brooks, "Meet Dick Betts," *Guitar Player*, October 1972, 26.

20. Lester Bangs, review of *The Allman Brothers Band* by the Allman Brothers Band, *Rolling Stone*, 21 February 1970, http://www.rollingstone.com/music/albumreviews/the -allman-brothers-band-19700221 (accessed 10 March 2017).

21. Chet Flippo, "Getting By without the Allmans," *Creem*, November 1974, 36.

22. Grace Elizabeth Hale, *A Nation of Outsiders: How the White Middle Class Fell in Love with Rebellion in Postwar America* (New York: Oxford University Press, 2011), 97.

23. Ibid., 98.

24. Laurence Leamer, *The Paper Revolutionaries: The Rise of the Underground Press* (New York: Simon & Schuster, 1972), 102.

25. Miller Francis Jr., "The Allman Brothers Band Play Piedmont Park," *Great Speckled Bird* (Atlanta), 19 April 1969, 10.

26. Ibid. For more on such views, see Timothy Hodgdon, *Manhood in the Age of Aquarius: Masculinity in Two Countercultural Communities* (New York: Columbia University Press, 2008), 44–47.

27. Francis, "Allman Brothers Band Play Piedmont Park," 11.

28. Ibid., 10.

29. Ibid.

30. Lorraine O'Grady, "First There Is a Mountain, Then There Is No Mountain, Then . . . ?," *Village Voice*, 2 August 1973, 42.

31. Danny Nix, author's southern rock questionnaire, 28 June 2009.

32. O'Grady, "First There Is a Mountain," 42.

33. Ibid.

34. Ibid.

35. Edmonds, "Snapshots of the South," 40.

36. Dave Hickey, "Why the Allman Brothers Died Young," *Village Voice*, 11 October 1976, 12.

37. Quoted in Freeman, *Midnight Riders*, 69.

38. Steve Schmidt, author's southern rock questionnaire, 22 May 2009.

39. Both quotes are in Hickey, "Why the Allman Brothers Died Young," 13.

40. Grover Lewis, "Hitting the Note with the Allman Brothers Band," *Rolling Stone*, 25 November 1971, 53.

41. Kemp, *Dixie Lullaby*, 29.

42. Tom Wolfe, "The 'Me' Decade and the Third Great Awakening," *New York*, 23 August 1976, 26–40.

43. Bruce J. Schulman, *The Seventies: The Great Shift in American Culture, Society, and Politics* (New York: Free Press, 2001), 92.

44. Andrew Kershaw, "A Family Affair," *Let It Rock*, December 1973, 47.

45. Allman, *My Cross to Bear*, 153.

46. Paul, *One Way Out*, 175.

47. Bangs, "When in Doubt, Kick Ass," 26.

48. Hickey, "Why the Allman Brothers Died Young," 13.

49. Allman, *My Cross to Bear*, 196–197.

50. Ibid., 197.

51. Cameron Crowe, "The Allman Brothers Story," *Rolling Stone*, 6 December 1973, 52.

52. Geoff Brown, "Allman Brothers: Agony and the Ecstasy," *Melody Maker*, 29 September 1973, 41.

53. Ibid.

54. Ibid.

55. Butler, "Luther King Was a Good Ole Boy," 55.

56. James D. Dilts, "Caught in the Act: B.B. King/The Allman Brothers," *Down Beat*, 8 June 1972, 30; Renee Dudley, author's southern rock questionnaire, 10 March 2009.

57. Freeman, *Midnight Riders*, 69.

58. Kershaw, "Family Affair," 47–48.

59. Ibid., 47.

60. Betsy Harris, "Music Is the Focus at the Big House," *Macon News*, 9 June 1970, 1B.

61. See, for example, Ruth Rosen, *The World Split Open: How the Modern Women's Movement Changed America*, rev. ed. (New York: Penguin, 2006), 126; Gretchen Lemke-Santangelo, *Daughters of Aquarius: Women of the Sixties Counterculture* (Lawrence: University Press of Kansas, 2009), 72–73.

62. Hodgdon, *Manhood in the Age of Aquarius*.

63. Robert Christgau, "Lynyrd Skynyrd: Not Even a Boogie Band Is as Simple as It Seems," *Creem*, August 1975, 26. The article was originally published in the *Village Voice*.

64. Ibid., 73.

65. Ibid., 26.

66. Artimus Pyle replaced Bob Burns in 1974. Steve Gaines joined the band in 1976, several months after Ed King's 1975 departure.

67. Brant, *Southern Rockers*, 114.

68. Scott B. Bomar, *Southbound: An Illustrated History of Southern Rock* (Milwaukee: Backbeat Books, 2014), 101.

69. Quoted in ibid., 102.

70. Lynyrd Skynyrd disbanded after the accident and reformed in 1987 with a mixture of original and replacement members. My discussion pertains only to the original version of the band.

71. Ron O'Brien, liner notes, *Street Survivors*, Lynyrd Skynyrd, MCA Records 088 112 750-2, 2001, CD reissue.

72. W. J. Cash, *The Mind of the South* (New York: Knopf, 1941).

73. Ed King, interview by author, 23 July 2009.

74. Philip Elwood, "Rough, Rowdy Ribald Rock," *San Francisco Examiner*, 6 March 1976, 8.

75. Quoted in Doreen Dube, "Local Band's Star Rising on Rock Horizon," *Jacksonville (Fla.) Journal*, 28 December 1973, A-6.

76. Al Kooper, Ronnie Van Zant, and Robert Burns, "Mississippi Kid," *Pronounced 'Lĕh-'nérd 'Skin-'nérd*, Lynyrd Skynyrd, Sounds of the South, MCA Records MCA-363, 1973.

77. See Allen Collins, Gary Rossington, and Ronnie Van Zant, "Tuesday's Gone," *Pronounced 'Lĕh-'nérd 'Skin-'nérd*, Lynyrd Skynyrd, Sounds of the South, MCA Records MCA-363, 1973; Ed King, Gary Rossington, and Ronnie Van Zant, "I Need You," *Second Helping*, Lynyrd Skynyrd, Sounds of the South, MCA Records MCA-413, 1974; Steve Gaines and Ronnie Van Zant, "I Never Dreamed," *Street Survivors*, Lynyrd Skynyrd, MCA Records MCA-3029, 1977.

78. Allen Collins and Ronnie Van Zant, "On the Hunt," *Nuthin' Fancy*, Lynyrd Skynyrd, MCA Records MCA-2137, 1975.

79. Allen Collins, Gary Rossington, and Ronnie Van Zant, "Trust," *Gimme Back My Bullets*, Lynyrd Skynyrd, MCA Records MCA-3022, 1976.

80. Ronnie Van Zant, Gary Rossington, and Al Kooper, "Cheatin' Woman," *Nuthin' Fancy*, Lynyrd Skynyrd, MCA Records MCA-2137, 1975.

81. Parsons, "Skynyrds," 7.

82. Lester Bangs, "Heavy Metal: Brontosaurus M.O.R.," *Creem*, May 1976, 57.

83. Jaan Uhelszki, "Lynyrd Skynyrd: Fifths and Fists for the Common Man," *Creem*, March 1976, 48–50, 69–70; Mitch Glazer, "Live Lynyrd Skynyrd: One Mo' Brawl from the Road," *Crawdaddy*, November 1976, 18, 20.

84. Parsons, "Skynyrds," 7.

85. Quoted in Jeff Giles, "How Lynyrd Skynyrd Built Momentum on 'Second Helping,'" *Ultimate Classic Rock*, 15 April 2014, http://ultimateclassicrock.com/lynyrd-skynyrd-second-helping/ (accessed 8 April 2017).

86. Allen Collins and Ronnie Van Zant, "I'm a Country Boy," *Nuthin' Fancy*, Lynyrd Skynyrd, MCA Records MCA-2137, 1975.

87. Allen Collins and Ronnie Van Zant, "All I Can Do Is Write about It," *Gimme Back My Bullets*, Lynyrd Skynyrd, MCA Records MCA-3022, 1976.

88. Parsons, "Skynyrds," 7.

89. Joanne Jeri Russo, "Lynyrd Skynyrd: Hospitable, Not Hostile, Rock and Rollers," 'Teen, April 1977, 69.

90. Michael Buffalo Smith, email communication to author, 19 April 2009.

91. Anonymous 2, author's southern rock questionnaire, 23 May 2009.

92. Kemp, *Dixie Lullaby*, 157.

93. Uhelszki, "Lynyrd Skynyrd," 49.

94. Mitchell Glazer, "Lynyrd Skynyrd Fight Rock 'n Roll Civil Wars with 'Nuthin' Fancy,'" *Circus*, June 1975, 70.

95. See, for example, Tom Dupree, "Lynyrd Skynyrd in Sweet Home Atlanta," *Rolling Stone*, 24 October 1974, 14.

96. Rich Wiseman, "Lynyrd Skynyrd Turns the Tables," *Rolling Stone*, 22 April 1976, 20.

97. Dupree, "Lynyrd Skynyrd in Sweet Home Atlanta," 14.

98. Ed King, interview by author.

99. Bomar, *Southbound*, 118–119.

100. Peggy Mulloy Glad, "Sound of South Lacks Spark," *Milwaukee Journal*, 21 May 1975; Wiseman, "Lynyrd Skynyrd Turns the Tables," 20; Marley Brant, *Freebirds: The Lynyrd Skynyrd Story* (New York: Billboard, 2002), 122.

101. James Kelton, "Rebel Band Wows 40,000," *San Francisco Sunday Examiner & Chronicle*, 3 July 1977, A3. See one of the photographs that accompanies the article.

102. Nat Freedland, "Lynyrd Skynyrd: 3 Gold LPs in a Row," *Billboard*, 11 October 1975, 42.

103. Keith Coulbourn, "Should Georgia Change Its State Flag?," *Atlanta Journal-Constitution Magazine*, 4 May 1969, 20, quoted in John M. Coski, *The Confederate Battle Flag: America's Most Embattled Emblem* (Cambridge, Mass.: Harvard University Press, 2005), 173.

104. Schulman, *Seventies*, 117.

105. David R. Goldfield, *Still Fighting the Civil War: The American South and Southern History* (Baton Rouge: Louisiana State University Press, 2002), 311.

106. John M. Coski, "The Confederate Battle Flag in American History and Culture," *Southern Cultures* 2, no. 2 (Winter 1996): 205, quoted in ibid., 311.

107. Rick Whitney, author's southern rock questionnaire, 2 June 2009.

108. Patricia Goddard, email communication to author, 9 April 2009.

109. Lawrence Zeitz, author's southern rock questionnaire, 11 March 2009.

110. Neil Young, "Alabama," *Harvest*, Reprise Records MS 2032, 1972.

111. Ronnie Van Zant, Gary Rossington, and Ed King, "Sweet Home Alabama," *Second Helping*, Lynyrd Skynyrd, Sounds of the South, MCA Records MCA-413, 1974.

112. Dupree, "Lynyrd Skynyrd in Sweet Home Atlanta," 14.

113. Richard Riegel, "Lynyrd Skynyrd: Does Their Conscience Bother Them?," *Creem*, December 1976, 62.

114. Jim Cullen, "Reconstructing Dixie: Confederate Mythology in Rock 'n' Roll," in *The Civil War in Popular Culture: A Reusable Past* (Washington, D.C.: Smithsonian, 1995), 126.

115. Randy Stephens, author's southern rock questionnaire, 26 May 2009.

116. Zeitz, author's southern rock questionnaire.

117. Van Zant, Rossington, and King, "Sweet Home Alabama."

118. Christgau, "Lynyrd Skynyrd," 73.

119. Ibid.

120. Ed King, "Second Helping," in "The Music" section of the *Ed King Forum*, http://edking.proboards.com/index.cgi?board=music&action=display&thread=87 (accessed 10 March 2017).

121. Alan Paul, "Lynyrd Skynyrd: Gimme Back My Bullets," *Guitar World*, 10 February 2010, http://www.guitarworld.com/lynyrd-skynyrd-gimme-back-my-bullets?page=4 (accessed 10 March 2017). The interview was originally published in the Winter 2009 issue.

122. King, interview by author.

123. Wiseman, "Lynyrd Skynyrd Turns the Tables," 20.

124. Christgau, "Lynyrd Skynyrd," 73.

125. Lisa Robinson, "Ronnie Van Zant Talks about Skynyrd's Music and Politics . . . ," *Hit Parader*, January 1976, 29.

126. Nagle, email communication to author.

127. Anonymous 3, email communication to the author, 30 March 2009.

128. David Stricklin, "Singing Songs about the Southland: Reaching across Lines Meant to Keep People Apart," in *The American South in the Twentieth Century*, ed. Craig S. Pascoe, Karen Trahan Leathem, and Andy Ambrose (Athens: University of Georgia Press, 2005), 183.

129. Henry Paul relates this anecdote in Michael Buffalo Smith, *Rebel Yell: An Oral History of Southern Rock* (Macon, Ga.: Mercer University Press, 2014), 108.

Chapter 5. "I Respect a Good Southern White Man"

1. Memo, Kaye Pullen to Michael Raoul-Duval, "Carter and the Solid South," n.d., folder: Jimmy Carter, box 14, Michael Raoul-Duval Papers, Gerald R. Ford Library, Ann Arbor, Mich. (hereinafter GRFL).

2. Ibid.

3. Reg Murphy, "Jimmy Carter's Running for WHAT?," *Atlanta Constitution*, 10 July 1974, 4A.

4. Charles Reagan Wilson, "The Myth of the Biracial South," in *The Southern State of Mind*, ed. Jan Nordby Gretlund (Columbia: University of South Carolina Press, 1999), 3–22.

5. "The Spirit of the South," *Time*, 26 September 1976, 30–31, quoted in ibid., 12.

6. Ibid.

7. David Farber and Beth Bailey, "Introduction," in *America in the Seventies*, ed. Beth Bailey and David Farber (Lawrence: University Press of Kansas, 2004), 1. For other studies of the society, politics, and culture of the 1970s, see Edward D. Berkowitz, *Something Happened: A Political and Cultural Overview of the Seventies* (New York: Columbia University Press, 2006); Bruce J. Schulman, *The Seventies: The Great Shift in American Culture, Society, and Politics* (New York: Free Press, 2001); David Frum, *How We Got Here: The 70's: The Decade That Brought You Modern Life (For Better or Worse)* (New York: Basic Books, 2000); Andreas Killen, *1973 Nervous Breakdown: Watergate, Warhol, and the Birth of Post-Sixties America* (New York: Bloomsbury, 2006); Philip Jenkins, *Decade of Nightmares: The End of the Sixties and the Making of Eighties*

America (New York: Oxford University Press, 2006); Peter N. Carroll, *It Seemed Like Nothing Happened: America in the 1970s* (New Brunswick, N.J.: Rutgers University Press, 1982; repr., 1990); Thomas Borstelmann, *The 1970s: A New Global History from Civil Rights to Economic Inequality* (Princeton, N.J.: Princeton University Press, 2012); Dominic Sandbrook, *Mad as Hell: The Crisis of the 1970s and the Rise of the Populist Right* (New York: Knopf, 2011); Rick Perlstein, *Nixonland: The Rise of a President and the Fracturing of America* (New York: Scribner, 2008); and Rick Perlstein, *The Invisible Bridge: The Fall of Nixon and the Rise of Reagan* (New York: Simon & Schuster, 2014).

8. "Startling Surge for Carter," *Time*, 10 May 1976, Academic Search Complete (53517592).

9. Neal R. Peirce, "The South and the Presidency," *Washington Post*, 5 April 1976, A19.

10. See, for example, Theo Lippman Jr., "Southern Presidents," *Baltimore Sun*, 3 June 1976, A22.

11. Jimmy Carter, interview by *Washington Star*, 25 January 1976, folder: Carter, Jimmy—"Factbook"—News Clippings, box F15, President Ford Committee Records, 1975–1976, GRFL.

12. Letter, Judy Carter to Rosalynn Carter, n.d., folder: Memorandums—Political Strategy [3], box 40, Carter Family Papers, Jimmy Carter Library, Atlanta (hereinafter JCL).

13. Susan Fraker, "Qualms about Carter," *Newsweek*, 7 June 1976, LexisNexis Academic (accessed 25 March 2017).

14. Ibid.

15. James Helmer, letter to the editor, *Time*, 29 November 1976, Academic Search Complete (53519004).

16. TRB, *New Republic*, 7 February 1976, quoted in Betty Glad, *Jimmy Carter: In Search of the Great White House* (New York: Norton, 1980), 343.

17. George F. Will, "The Democratic Quest for a November Winner," *Washington Post*, 18 April 1976, B7.

18. Alette Hill, "The Carter Campaign in Retrospect: Decoding the Cartoons," *Semiotica* 23, no. 3 (1978): 307–332.

19. Robert Grossman, political cartoon, *Newsweek*, 19 July 1976, cover.

20. Pat Oliphant, political cartoon, *Newsweek*, 21 June 1976, 16.

21. Hill, "Carter Campaign in Retrospect," 314.

22. Mike Keefe, political cartoon, *Denver Post*, 25 July 1976, 15.

23. Robert Pattridge, "Love and Justice in the White House," *Denver Post*, 25 July 1976, 15.

24. Hill, "Carter Campaign in Retrospect," 329n11.

25. Greg Scott, political cartoon, *Rolling Stone*, 3 June 1976, cover; Mike Keefe, political cartoon, *Denver Post*, 18 July 1976, 19; Frank Interlandi, political cartoon, *Los Angeles Times*, 6 May 1976, pt. 2, 7.

26. Glad, *Jimmy Carter*, 343.

27. Memo, Knox to Jimmy Carter and Hamilton Jordan, "Targeting," 7 May 1975, folder: Memorandums [2], box 30, Jody Powell Papers, JCL. The memo does not make clear who Knox was, but it was most likely Patti Knox, the Michigan state coordinator for Carter's 1976 campaign. My thanks to Albert Nason, former archivist at the Jimmy Carter Library, for this insight.

28. Marshall Frady, "Gone with the Wind," *Newsweek*, 28 July 1975, 11.

29. Ibid.; James T. Wooten, "Carter Now Aims to Win Florida," *New York Times*, 1 March 1976, 32.

30. Elizabeth Drew, *American Journal: The Events of 1976* (New York: Random House, 1977), 128.

31. See, for example, Warren Brown, "A Farewell to the Old South," *Washington Post*, 13 June 1976, A8; Peirce, "The South and the Presidency," A19.

32. Reg Murphy, "Not Since Jefferson and Madison . . . ," *Saturday Review*, 4 September 1976, 9, 10.

33. David S. Broder, "Questions about Carter," *Washington Post*, 31 March 1976, A13. See also Robert Shogan, "Carter Again Lauds Civil Rights Laws," *Los Angeles Times*, 18 September 1976, pt. 1, 13.

34. See, for example, "Jimmy Carter on Civil Rights," folder: Civil Rights, box 419, 1976 Campaign Committee to Elect Jimmy Carter, JCL.

35. The "redneck" line is quoted in Sandbrook, *Mad as Hell*, 143. On coverage of race and the Carter campaign in the 1970 gubernatorial election, see Steven Brill, "Jimmy Carter's Pathetic Lies," *Harper's*, March 1976, 77–80, 82, 84, 88; Alexander Cockburn and James Ridgeway, "The Riddle of Jimmy Carter: Can a Dark Horse Change Its Spots?," *Village Voice*, 12 January 1976, 21; Peter Goldman, "Carter on the Rise," *Newsweek*, 8 March 1976, LexisNexis Academic (accessed 25 March 2017); and George Lardner Jr., "Jimmy Carter—Promises . . . Promises," *Washington Post*, 7 March 1976, C3. On coverage of ethnic purity, see Peter Goldman, "Carter's Trip of the Tongue," *Newsweek*, 19 April 1976, LexisNexis Academic (accessed 25 March 2017); Peter Milius, "Housing Integration a Tough '76 Issue," *Washington Post*, 10 April 1976, A5; "The Purity Flap" (editorial), *Washington Post*, 11 April 1976, C6; Jack Clark, "Ethnic Purity Nonsense," *Progressive*, July 1976, 8; "What Price 'Purity'?" (editorial), *Wall Street Journal*, 14 April 1976, 16; David S. Broder and Myra MacPherson, "Carter Accused of 'Racial Division,'" *Washington Post*, 8 April 1976, A1; Thomas Powers, "Covering Carter," *Commonweal*, 30 July 1976, 502; and "Candidate Carter: 'I Apologize,'" *Time*, 19 April 1976, Academic Search Complete (53517437).

36. Both quotations found in folder: Memorandum-Pat Caddell, Questionnaire/Responses, 6/76, box 199, 1976 Campaign Committee to Elect Jimmy Carter, JCL.

37. "Away from Hate," *Time*, 27 September 1976, Academic Search Complete (53518550).

38. Haynes Johnson, "A Harlem View: 'I Respect a Good Southern White Man,'" *Washington Post*, 12 July 1976, A1.

39. "How Groups Voted in 1976," Roper Center for Public Opinion Research, https://ropercenter.cornell.edu/polls/us-elections/how-groups-voted/how-groups-voted-1976/ (accessed 7 April 2017). This information comes from a CBS survey of a "sample of 15,300 voters as they left voting booths on Election Day."

40. Glad, *Jimmy Carter*, 329–330.

41. Patrick Anderson, "Peanut Farmer for President," *New York Times Magazine*, 14 December 1975, 83.

42. Jimmy Carter, "I See an America . . . ," in *The Presidential Campaign 1976: Volume One: Part One: Jimmy Carter* (Washington, D.C.: Government Printing Office, 1978), 195.

43. Ibid., 198.

44. See Goldman, "Carter's Trip of the Tongue."

45. Borstelmann, *1970s*, 5.

46. Ibid., 4–5.

47. *Baltimore Sun*, 23 May 1976, folder: Southerners, box H32, President Ford Committee Records, 1975–1976, GRFL.

48. Glad, *Jimmy Carter*, 345.

49. Bonnie Angela, "No Longer a Way Station," *Time*, 15 November 1976, Academic Search Complete (53518924); Garry Wills, "The Plains Truth," *Atlantic Monthly*, June 1976, 50; Marquis Childs, "For Carter, the Eve of a More Formidable Ordeal," *Washington Post*, 7 September 1976, A19; Thomas Ichniowski, "Just Plain Plains, or 'Born Again?,'" *America*, 23 October 1976, 251; Karen Elliot House, "Peanut One Was Never Like This," *Wall Street Journal*, 15 November 1976, 26; Helen Dewar, "Georgian Cheered in Plains, Goes to Atlanta for Fete," *Washington Post*, 3 November 1976, A10.

50. Douglas Kneeland, "Pride and Nostalgia Glow in Carter's Town," *New York Times*, 28 July 1976, 9.

51. Helen Dudar, "Jimmy Carter Has Good Teeth and Is Always on Time," *Esquire*, April 1976, 68.

52. Norman Mailer, "The Search for Jimmy Carter," *New York Times Magazine*, 26 September 1976, 19.

53. Mike Chopra-Gant, *The Waltons: Nostalgia and Myth in Seventies America* (London: I.B. Tauris, 2013), 24–25.

54. Sandbrook, *Mad as Hell*, 149.

55. Michael Kilian, "A Nightmare about TV Schedules after Jimmy," *Chicago Tribune*, 12 August 1976, A2.

56. Jimmy Carter, *Why Not the Best?* (Nashville: Broadman, 1975), 13.

57. Ibid., 32.

58. Glad, *Jimmy Carter*, 345.

59. Carter, *Why Not the Best?*, 32.

60. For a discussion of these concerns, see Natasha Zaretsky, *No Direction Home: The American Family and the Fear of National Decline, 1968–1980* (Chapel Hill: University of North Carolina Press, 2007).

61. Statement, Jimmy Carter, Manchester, N.H., 3 August 1976, folder: Catholic, box 419, 1976 Campaign Committee to Elect Jimmy Carter, JCL.

62. Glad, *Jimmy Carter*, 346.

63. Kenneth Reich, "Down-Home Image Aids Carter," *Los Angeles Times*, 1 August 1976, part 7, 3.

64. Helen Dewar, "Carter Savors Triumph at Home," *Washington Post*, 10 June 1976, A4.

65. Kenneth Reich, "Carter Returns Home, Vows to Maintain Strong Ties with the People of Plains," *Los Angeles Times*, 17 July 1976, pt. 1, 3.

66. "Fish Fry and Barbecue," *Time*, 12 July 1976, Academic Search Complete (53518076); Stanley Cloud, "Keeping 'Em Down on the Farm," *Time*, 16 August 1976, Academic Search Complete (53518323); Helen Dewar, "Carter Finds a Good Reason to Host a Fish Fry at Home," *Washington Post*, 27 June 1976, A12; and Jeff Prugh, "Carter Takes His Message to Church," *Los Angeles Times*, 19 July 1976, pt. 1, 6.

67. Kandy Stroud, "Jimmy Carter's Remarkable Women," *McCall's*, July 1976, 58.

68. Susan Fraker, "Plains Women," *Newsweek*, 26 July 1976, LexisNexis Academic (accessed 25 March 2017).

69. Dudar, "Jimmy Carter Has Good Teeth," 71.

70. Maureen Orth, "Nights of the Peanut," *Newsweek*, 26 July 1976, LexisNexis Academic (accessed 19 March 2017). The Cronkite and Hayden quotes come from this article.

71. Ibid.

72. See Perlstein, *Invisible Bridge*, 729–730; and Sandbrook, *Mad as Hell*, 135–137.

73. Malcolm D. MacDougall, *We Almost Made It* (New York: Crown, 1977), 3.

74. Larry L. King, "We Ain't Trash No More!," *Esquire*, November 1976, 154.

75. Kandy Stroud, *How Jimmy Won: The Victory Campaign from Plains to the White House* (New York: Morrow, 1977), 42.

76. Roy Blount Jr., *Crackers: This Whole Many-Angled Thing of Jimmy, More Carters, Ominous Little Animals, Sad Singing Women, My Daddy, and Me* (New York: Knopf, 1980), 90.

77. Stroud, *How Jimmy Won*, 42.

78. "Fish Fry and Barbecue."

79. Bonnie Angela, "Those Good Ole Boys," *Time*, 27 September 1976, Academic Search Complete (53518574).

80. Curtis Wilkie, *Dixie: A Personal Odyssey through Events That Shaped the Modern South* (New York: Scribner, 2001), 227.

81. Genelle Jennings, *Into the Jaws of Politics: The Charge of the Peanut Brigade* (Huntsville, Ala.: Strode, 1979), 113–114.

82. Wills, "Plains Truth," 52.

83. Glad, *Jimmy Carter*, 288.

84. Sandbrook, *Mad as Hell*, 150.

85. My discussion of Carter's connection to progressive evangelicalism is derived from Randall Balmer, *Redeemer: The Life of Jimmy Carter* (New York: Basic Books, 2014), xiv, 20, 51–52, 58, 60–61, 65–68.

86. The *New York* quote comes from a synopsis on the magazine's "Contents" page (3) of a Richard Reeves article titled "Carter's Secret: Understanding America's Spiritual Crisis," *New York*, 22 March 1976.

87. See Michael Novak, "The Hidden Religious Majority," *Washington Post*, 4 April 1976, C1; "Let the Church Stand Up," *Time*, 21 June 1976, Academic Search Complete (53517905); John Dart, "'Born Again'—A Whole New Outlook," *Los Angeles Times*, 24 July 1976, pt. 1, 25; "'Born-Again' Experience Not Rare," *Washington Post*, 22 September 1976, A8; and Kenneth L. Woodward, "Born Again!," *Newsweek*, 25 October 1976, LexisNexis Academic (accessed 19 March 2017).

88. Quoted in Woodward, "Born Again!"

89. Memo, Pat Caddell to Governor Carter, Senator Mondale, and the Carter Campaign, 2 September 1976, "Survey Conclusions and Recommendations," folder: Carter Campaign, box 69, 1976 Campaign Committee to Elect Jimmy Carter, JCL.

90. George Gallup, "Carter's Faith Doesn't Affect Attitude of 70%," *Washington Post*, 10 October 1976, A11.

91. Jimmy Carter, "The Standards God Demands," in *The Spiritual Journey of Jimmy Carter: In His Own Words*, ed. Wesley G. Pippert (New York: MacMillan, 1978), 229.

92. "Startling Surge for Carter," *Time*, 10 May 1976, Academic Search Complete (53517592).

93. Hugh Sidey, "Yearning for Morality," *Time*, 17 May 1976, Academic Search Complete (53517614).

94. See, for example, "For Black Americans, President Ford Is Quietly Getting the Job Done," folder: Press Clippings (2), box F16, President Ford Committee Records, 1975–1976, GRFL; "The Carter Record and the Truth," n.d., folder: Carter Campaign—General (1), box D5, President Ford Committee Records, 1975–1976, GRFL; and Leonard Mason, "Why I Cannot Vote for Jimmy Carter," folder: Carter, Jimmy—Record, box F15, President Ford Committee Records, GRFL.

95. Malcolm D. MacDougall, "How Madison Avenue Didn't Put a Ford in Your Future," *New York*, 21 February 1977, 54.

96. MacDougall, *We Almost Made It*, 23.

97. Untitled handwritten meeting notes, 16 July [1976], folder: Cheney, Richard—Meeting Notes, box 14, Michael Raoul-Duval Papers, GRFL.

98. Handwritten meeting notes, "Agenda: Thaxton Meeting," undated [1976], folder: Subject File—Carter (2), box 19, Jerry Jones Files, GRFL.

99. Quoted in Balmer, *Redeemer*, 71.

100. Quoted in ibid., 69, 70.

101. Jimmy Carter, *A Full Life: Reflections at Ninety* (New York: Simon & Schuster, 2015), 117.

102. Bailey/Deardourff, "Criswell," President Ford Committee, 1976, *The Living Room Candidate*, http://www.livingroomcandidate.org/commercials/1976/criswell (accessed 1 March 2016).

103. Memo, Philip Angell to John Deardourff, Tom Angell, Mal MacDougall, et al., "Evangelical Advertising," 17 October 1976, folder: President Ford Committee—Newsletters (2), box F16, President Ford Committee Records, GRFL.

104. See, for example, Gerald Rafshoon, "South," 1976 Democratic Presidential Campaign Committee, Inc., 1976, *The Living Room Candidate*, http://www.livingroomcandidate.org/commercials/1976/south#4065; and Gerald Rafshoon, "Bio," 1976 Democratic Presidential Campaign Committee, Inc., 1976, *The Living Room Candidate*, http://www.livingroomcandidate.org/commercials/1976/bio#4048 (accessed 28 September 2017).

105. Martin Schram, *Running for President, 1976: The Carter Campaign* (New York: Stein and Day, 1977), 332.

106. Quoted in ibid.

107. Memo, David Gergen and Jerry Jones to Gerald Ford, "The Southern Trip," 24 September 1976, folder: Presidential Handwriting, 9/24/1976, box C49, Presidential Handwriting File, GRFL.

108. MacDougall, "How Madison Avenue Didn't Put a Ford in Your Future," 53.

109. "Memorandum to the President," quoted in Schram, *Running for President*, 267.

110. MacDougall, *We Almost Made It*, 178.

111. Bailey/Deardourff, "Strom Thurmond," President Ford Committee, 1976, *The Living Room Candidate*, http://www.livingroomcandidate.org/commercials/1976 (accessed 19 March 2017).

112. Tommy Thompson, letter to the editor, *Time*, 12 July 1976, Academic Search Complete (53518084).

113. Edward Walsh, "Steamboat Foray in Carter Country," *Washington Post*, 26 September 1976, A1.

114. Ibid.

115. Gerald Ford, "Remarks in Mobile, Alabama," 26 September 1976, *The American Presidency Project*, http://www.presidency.ucsb.edu/ws/?pid=6373 (accessed 4 September 2017).

116. "Pool Report—Air Force One—Mobile/Miami—September 26, 1976," folder: 9/25–9/27/76 La., Miss., Fla. (4), box 82, Ron Nessen Papers, GRFL.

117. Schram, *Running for President*, 267.

118. Charles Osgood, *A Funny Thing Happened on the Way to the White House: Humor, Blunders, and Other Oddities from the Presidential Campaign Trail* (New York: Hyperion, 2008), 128.

119. North Carolina State Fair Speech, draft, October 19, 1976, folder: 10/23/76 N.C. State Fair (1), box 76, Robert Orben Files, GRFL.

120. North Carolina State Fair Speech, folder: 10/23/76 N.C. State Fair (2), box 76, Robert Orben Files, GRFL.

121. Gerald Ford, "Remarks of the President at the North Carolina State Fairgrounds," 23 October 1976, *National Archives Catalog*, https://catalog.archives.gov/id /7346411 (accessed 19 January 2017).

122. "Carter Plans Late Trip to Sway Dixie Vote," *Baltimore Sun*, 18 October 1976, A4.

123. Schram, *Running for President*, 274–275.

124. Letter, Charles R. Jonas to James G. Martin, 9 September 1976, folder: PL/Carter, Jimmy 9/15/76–9/30/76, box 6, White House Central Files Subject File, GRFL.

125. Memo, James E. Connor to John O. Marsh Jr., "Paper Dated 9/2/76 Entitled 'The Waltons' Re: Carter," 6 September 1976, folder: Political Affairs: Carter, box 36, Presidential Handwriting File, GRFL.

126. Pete Axthelm, "A Day at the Races," *Newsweek*, 20 September 1976, LexisNexis Academic (accessed 25 March 2017).

127. Schram, *Running for President*, 275.

128. This term, sometimes used in Marxist analysis, although it was never used by Karl Marx, "refers to ideology dominating the consciousness of exploited groups and classes which at the same time justifies and perpetuates their exploitation." "False Consciousness," *Marxists Internet Archive*, https://www.marxists.org/glossary/terms/f/a .htm (accessed 29 September 2017).

129. Theo Lippman Jr., "The South Has Come Far since the Gorilla-Vote Days," *Baltimore Sun*, 9 May 1976, K2.

130. Douglass Cater, "How Different Is the South?," *Washington Post*, 10 October 1976, C3.

131. E. J. Dionne Jr., *Why Americans Hate Politics* (New York: Simon & Schuster, 2004), unpaginated e-book, Google Books (accessed 15 January 2017).

132. Seth Kaplan and James I. Kaplan, "Many Factors Figured in Carter's Win," *Harvard Crimson*, 3 November 1976, http://www.thecrimson.com/article/1976/11/3/many -factors-figured-in-carters-win/?page=1 (accessed 6 September 2017).

133. Public Broadcasting Service, "The Election of 1976," *American Experience: Jimmy Carter*, http://www.pbs.org/wgbh/americanexperience/features/general-article /carter-election1976/ (accessed 27 April 2016).

134. Quoted in Erica J. Seifert, *The Politics of Authenticity in Presidential Campaigns, 1976–2008* (Jefferson, N.C.: McFarland, 2012), 56.

135. Ibid.

Epilogue. Playing That Dead Band's Song

1. Howard Kurtz, interview with Jimmy Carter, *Reliable Sources*, 2010, http://www .cnn.com/videos/politics/2015/04/24/sot-jimmy-carter-rabbit-attack-reliable-sources -2010.cnn (accessed 3 August 2017); Nancy Isenberg, *White Trash: The 400-Year Untold History of Class in America* (New York: Viking, 2016), 284.

2. Isenberg, *White Trash*, 285.

3. Joseph Crespino, "Did David Brooks Tell the Full Story about Reagan's Neshoba County Fair Visit?," *History News Network*, 11 November 2007, http://historynewsnet work.org/article/44535 (accessed 3 August 2017).

4. Quoted in James C. Cobb, *The South and America since World War II* (New York: Oxford University Press, 2011), 177.

5. Waylon Jennings, "Theme from *The Dukes of Hazzard* (Good Ol' Boys)" (TV version). A slightly different version was released on *Music Man*, RCA AHL1-3602, 1980.

6. Ben Jones, *Redneck Boy in the Promised Land: The Confessions of "Crazy Cooter"* (New York: Harmony, 2008), 162.

7. David Hofstede, *The Dukes of Hazzard: The Unofficial Companion* (New York: St. Martin's Griffin, 1998), xii.

8. Burt Reynolds and Jon Winokur, *But Enough about Me: A Memoir* (New York: Putnam, 2015), 187.

9. Gary Arnold, "A Freewheeling 'Smokey and the Bandit': Screwball Comedy on the Open Road," *Washington Post*, 29 July 1977, B1, emphasis added.

10. Cobb, *South and America*, 165.

11. Peter Applebome, "What Dallas Thinks of 'Dallas,'" *New York Times*, 9 January 1980, C1.

12. George Plasketes, *Warren Zevon: Desperado of Los Angeles* (Lanham, Md.: Rowman & Littlefield, 2016), 82.

13. Warren William Zevon, "Play It All Night Long," *Bad Luck Streak in Dancing School*, Asylum Records 5E 509, 1980.

14. Ibid.

INDEX

POLITICS AND CULTURE IN THE TWENTIETH-CENTURY SOUTH

A Common Thread: Labor, Politics, and Capital Mobility in the Textile Industry
by Beth English

"Everybody Was Black Down There": Race and Industrial Change in the Alabama Coalfields
by Robert H. Woodrum

Race, Reason, and Massive Resistance: The Diary of David J. Mays, 1954–1959
edited by James R. Sweeney

The Unemployed People's Movement: Leftists, Liberals, and Labor in Georgia, 1929–1941
by James J. Lorence

Liberalism, Black Power, and the Making of American Politics, 1965–1980
by Devin Fergus

Guten Tag, Y'all: Globalization and the South Carolina Piedmont, 1950–2000
by Marko Maunula

The Culture of Property: Race, Class, and Housing Landscapes in Atlanta, 1880–1950
by LeeAnn Lands

Marching in Step: Masculinity, Citizenship, and The Citadel in Post–World War II America
by Alexander Macaulay

Rabble Rousers: The American Far Right in the Civil Rights Era
by Clive Webb

Who Gets a Childhood: Race and Juvenile Justice in Twentieth-Century Texas
by William S. Bush

Alabama Getaway: The Political Imaginary and the Heart of Dixie
by Allen Tullos

The Problem South: Region, Empire, and the New Liberal State, 1880–1930
by Natalie J. Ring

The Nashville Way: Racial Etiquette and the Struggle for Social Justice in a Southern City
by Benjamin Houston

Cold War Dixie: Militarization and Modernization in the American South
by Kari Frederickson

Faith in Bikinis: Politics and Leisure in the Coastal South since the Civil War
by Anthony J. Stanonis

"We Who Believe in Freedom": Womanpower Unlimited and the Black Freedom Struggle in Mississippi
by Tiyi M. Morris

New Negro Politics in the Jim Crow South
by Claudrena N. Harold

Jim Crow Terminals: The Desegregation of American Airports
by Anke Ortlepp

Remaking the Rural South: Interracialism, Christian Socialism, and Cooperative Farming in Jim Crow Mississippi
by Robert Hunt Ferguson

The South of the Mind: American Imaginings of White Southernness, 1960–1980
by Zachary J. Lechner

The Politics of White Rights: Race, Justice, and Integrating Alabama's Schools
by Joseph Bagley

CPSIA information can be obtained
at www.ICGtesting.com
Printed in the USA
LVHW02s0220100818
586597LV00002B/555/P